MASOCHISM

Current Psychoanalytic Perspectives

D1570345

MASOCHISM

Current Psychoanalytic Perspectives

edited by
Robert A. Glick
Donald I. Meyers

Psychology Press
Taylor & Francis Group

New York London

First published by Lawrence Erlbaum Associates, Inc. Publishers
10 Industrial Avenue
Mahwah, New Jersey 07430

Reprinted 2008 by Psychology Press

Psychology Press
Taylor & Francis Group
27 Church Road
Hove, East Sussex BN3 2FA

Library of Congress Cataloging-in-Publication Data

   Includes bibliographies and index.
   1. Masochism. 2. Psychoanalysis. I. Glick, Robert A., 1941–. II. Meyers, Donald I.,
1926–
[DNLM: 1. Masochism. 2. Psychoanalytic Theory.
3.Sadism. WM 610 M398]
RC553.M36M37   1987   616.85′835   87-18694
ISBN 0-88163-171-X

Masochism: current psychoanalytic perspectives

 First paperback edition   1993

Printed in the United States of America

10   9   8   7   6   5   4   3   2

Contents

Acknowledgments

The idea for this volume grew out of a symposium held in March of 1983 by the Association for Psychoanalytic Medicine in collaboration with the Columbia University Center for Psychoanalytic Training and Research on the treatment of difficult characters, organized under the guidance of the then president of the Association, Dr. Paul Bradlow. The focus of this symposium was on the understanding and treatment of severely masochistic and narcissistic characters. It was at the suggestion of Dr. Helen Meyers, who pointed to the lack in the psychoanalytic literature of a comprehensive volume on contemporary views of masochism, that we decided to undertake this book. Taking a point of departure the symposium presentations on masochistic pathology and its treatment, we expanded and supplemented them with contributions by other authorities in the field.

We wish to thank the committee that organized the symposium: Drs. Arnold Rothstein (Chairman), Paul Bradlow, Arnold Cooper, Gerald Fogel, Otto Kernberg, Roger MacKinnon, Helen Meyers, Robert Michels, and Roy Schafer, as well as those other participants of the symposium whose contributions were not included in this volume: Drs. Frederick Lane, Roger MacKinnon, Robert Michels, Arnold Rothstein, and Daniel Stern.

There are few people in particular whose help with their clinical and theoretical wisdom, ideas, and insights deserves special mention. They are Drs. Gerald Fogel, Roger MacKinnon, Helen Meyers, and Samuel Perry.

We also appreciate very much the encouragement and support for this project provided by the current president of the Association for Psychoanalytic Medicine, Dr. Robert Liebert, and by the publication committee of the Association under the chairmanship of Dr. Stanley Coen.

We are further grateful to Dr. Paul Stepansky for his encouragement in bringing this volume to life, and we are greatly indebted to Eleanor Starke Kobrin for her patience and invaluable editorial help in its creation.

Finally, Terry Montgomery, the administrative secretary of the Association, deserves our most profound appreciation for her tireless dedication and resiliency under fire in the actual completion of this enterprise.

—The Editors

Contributors

STUART S. ASCH, M.D., Professor of Clinical Psychiatry, The New York Hospital-Cornell University Medical College, New York City; Training and Supervising Analyst, Columbia University Center for Psychoanalytic Training and Research.

STANLEY J. COEN, M.D., Associate Clinical Professor of Psychiatry, College of Physicians and Surgeons, Columbia University; Faculty, Columbia University Center for Psychoanalytic Training and Research.

ARNOLD M. COOPER, M.D., Professor of Psychiatry and Associate Chairman for Education, Department of Psychiatry, The New York Hospital-Cornell University Medical College, New York City; Training and Supervising Analyst, Columbia University Center for Psychoanalytic Training and Research.

ELEANOR GALENSON, M.D., Clinical Professor of Psychiatry, Mount Sinai School of Medicine; Past president, World Association for Infant Psychiatry; Lecturer, Columbia University Center for Psychoanalytic Training and Research.

JOHN E. GEDO, M.D., Training and Supervising Analyst, Chicago Institute for Psychoanalysis.

ROBERT A. GLICK, M.D. (editor), Associate Clinical Professor of Psychiatry, College of Physicians and Surgeons, Columbia University; Associate Director and Training and Supervising Analyst, Columbia University Center for Psychoanalytic Training and Research.

OTTO F. KERNBERG, M.D., Associate Chairman and Medical Director, The New York Hospital-Cornell Medical Center, Westchester Division; Professor of Psychiatry, Cornell University Medical College; Training and Supervising Analyst, Columbia University Center for Psychoanalytic Training and Research.

ROBERT S. LIEBERT, M.D., Clinical Professor of Psychiatry, College of Physicians and Surgeons, Columbia University; Training and Supervising Analyst, Columbia University Center for Psychoanalytic Training and Research; Adjunct Professor of Psychiatry, The New York Hospital-Cornell University Medical College, New York City.

DONALD I. MEYERS, M.D. (editor), Clinical Professor of Psychiatry, College of Physicians and Surgeons, Columbia University; Co-chairman, Child and Adolescent Training Program and Training and Supervising Analyst, Columbia University Center for Psychoanalytic Training and Research.

HELEN C. MEYERS, M.D.,Clinical Professor of Psychiatry, College of Physicians and Surgeons, Columbia University; Training and Supervising Analyst and Assistant Director for Curriculum, Columbia University Center for Psychoanalytic Training and Research.

HERBERT A. ROSENFELD, M.D., F.R.C. Psych.; Training and Supervising Analyst, British Psychoanalytical Society.

CHARLES A. SARNOFF, M.D., Lecturer, Columbia University Center for Psychoanalytic Training and Research; Author of *Latency* and *Psychotherapeutic Strategies in Late Latency Through Early Adolescence*.

ROY SCHAFER, Ph.D., Adjunct Professor, Department of Psychiatry, The New York Hospital-Cornell University Medical College, New York City; Training and Supervising Analyst, Columbia University Center for Psychoanalytic Training and Research.

1 / Introduction

Robert A. Glick
Donald I. Meyers

JUST AS PSYCHOANALYTIC INTEREST in masochism dates from the earliest days of psychoanalysis, the various approaches to its understanding have reflected the developmental vicissitudes of psychoanalytic theory as it moved from its early focus on instinct to considerations of psychic structure and oedipal dynamics, object relations, separation-individuation, self-organization, and self-esteem regulation, and as it progressed into more systematic investigation of child development.

This volume offers an updated review of perspectives on masochism influenced by current developments in psychoanalytic research and theory. The newer emphasis on and investigations of early preoedipal events have, as Cooper stresses in this volume, provided a significant scientific and clinical yield. The application of these newer perspectives to the issue of masochism holds considerable promise.

THEORIES OF MASOCHISM: A REVIEW

Masochism may be succinctly described as "pleasure in pain" or "the pursuit of suffering," suffering being the willing submission to forms of enslavement, humiliation, cruelty, and physical and psychological abuse. Masochism, then, confronts psychoanalysis with a profoundly vexing theoretical and clinical challenge. As with other major issues in psychoanalysis, to examine the nature of masochism is to explore much of the structure of psychoanalytic thought and practice. The contributors to this volume examine current psychoanalytic understanding of this existentially perplexing phenomenon from a variety of perspectives.

This introductory chapter provides a review of some of, though certainly not all, the major contributions on this topic. A schema, or "guide of the terrain," useful in exploration, follows; but like all maps and guides, it is selective and therefore incomplete.

Psychoanalytic theory has developed several models of mind,

within each of which are principal concerns. These models share certain premises but not others. The dynamic unconscious, psychic determinism, unconscious motivation—these are shared by all developmental, dynamic, adaptational frames of reference—these and others are shared by many; structure, wish, and defense by most; energy by few.

Pleasure and pain are defined or emphasized in different and important ways in the various mental models. Thought of *instinctually* and *energically*, masochism is a drive. It is an expression of sexual and aggressive instinctual drive derivatives that have been subjected to partial fusions, defusions, repressions, displacements, and phase or zonal regressions and fixations.

Structurally, masochism represents the appeasement of the superego for the gratification of forbidden, primarily oedipal wishes. The wish for punishment and the pleasurable wish are combined.

From an *ego psychological* view, masochism becomes the ego's defensive responses to a range of internal and external threats from different sources. Here the emphasis is on the ego's synthetic, compromising functions to avoid dangers and foster satisfactions.

Within *object relations* theory, masochism reflects the maintenance of crucial object relations. It is an attempt to protect self- and object representations from potentially dangerous drives or wishes, to stabilize and preserve intact complex, often painful internal object relations. Developmentally, masochism may evolve from the earliest, most primitive organization of bodily organismic sensations in the dawning of the differentiation and individuation of self from object, ego from id, and may become crucial in self-definition and self-lineation through the integration of pain. In terms of *self* development as a distinct developmental line and crucible of psychopathology, masochism may reflect aspects of the maintenance of self-cohesion, self-definition and control, or both; the dilemma of narcissistic vulnerability, grandiosity, and omnipotent wishfulness; and self-esteem regulation.

While masochism, both sexual and characterological, has most certainly existed for eons, psychoanalytic interest essentially started with the publication in 1870 of *Venus in Furs* by Leopold Von Sacher-Masoch. It is from Von Sacher-Masoch that Krafft-Ebing (1906) was to coin the word "masochism" (as he also had done with sadism from the writings of the Marquis de Sade). Sacher-Masoch wrote several autobiographical novellas that attracted notoriety in late 19th century Germany and Austria. In *Venus in Furs*, his narrator begins in a dream conversation with the white marble goddess Venus, wrapped in dark sable furs. Venus taunts him with his passionate wish for enslavement and humiliation.

The narrator spends an evening with a friend, Severin, who fascinates him with a story of his own "Venus in Furs" and who explains the fundamental association of sadism and masochism. Among the many remarkable features of this work, Sacher-Masoch has not only detailed the story of overt sexual masochism but provided clues to many of the crucial concepts that would follow in the elucidation of masochism, (and are explored in this volume), namely, the role of the preoedipal mother and her phallic power, her devouring capacity "within her furs," the history of materal loss in the victim, the intimate relationship of sadism and masochism, bisexuality, constitutional instinctual aberration, the narcissism in masochism with its idealization and devaluation, the fear of object loss, the role of early trauma, the role of pain and skin eroticism, feminine identification in men, the establishment of masochistic contracts, the use of the cruel object for self-definition, and the positive and negative oedipal triangle.

Krafft-Ebing (1906), familiar with the novels of Sacher-Masoch, defined masochism as "the wish to suffer pain and be subjected to force, the idea of being completely and unconditionally subject to the will of a person of the opposite sex; of being treated by this person, as by a master, humiliated and abused" (p. 131). Masochism was for Krafft-Ebing a sexual anomaly wherein the male was impotent except when he had an opportunity to experience suffering, subjugation, and abuse. It was a disorder of sexual instincts insufficiently checked by moral and aesthetic countermotives. It was congenital, not acquired, and led to a burdensome life of misery. In women, subjugation was a physiological phenomenon. Paralleling Freud, Krafft-Ebing equated passivity and submission with femininity, true to the culture of his time. He did report a few cases of masochistic perversions in women.

Krafft-Ebing saw the source of masochism as an intensification of normal dependence that progressed through the phenomenon of sexual bondage. (See chapter 3.) Characterological masochism in love relationships would then progress to masochistic perversions: "When the idea of being tyrannized is for a long time closely associated with a lustful thought of the beloved person, the lustful emotion is finally transferred to the tyranny itself, and the transformation to the perversion is completed" (p. 207). The capacity to develop a perversion, to establish that concrete enactment of a painful attachment, is hereditary, the result of so-called psychopathic constitution, "a tendency to sexually hyperaesthetic natures" (p. 208). This would fuse sexual ecstasy and subjugation. (See chapter 3 for a contemporary view of this phenomenon.)

Freud's Theories of Masochism

Freud's major writings on masochism began in 1905, with his "Three Essays on Sexuality," and culminated in 1924, with "The Economic Problem of Masochism." In "Analysis Terminable and Interminable" (1937), he referred to masochism as a powerful source of resistance.

Freud's achievement in the "Three Essays on Sexuality" was the postulation of sexual instinctual life in human beings. From his study of perversions and inversions (homosexuality), he concluded that mental life centered on drives and their regulation. These drives were the psychical representatives of biologically based bodily sexual needs, which developed in a phase-specific and zone-specific sequence in early life. Through the pursuit of satisfaction of these drives, the growing infant, and later the child, was forced to confront reality in the form of satisfiers and frustrators and to experience love and hate. Man, for Freud, became object related and social through instinctual needs and became civilized through the taming of these needs. Observations of masochistic and sadistic perversions in adults led Freud to the concept of masochistic and sadistic component instincts—component because they were partial, not complete, needs, that could act in concert with the sequence of oral, anal, phallic, and genital instinctual drives. Sadism and masochism were paired opposites; sadism, however, was primary, derived from biologically driven aggression and the instinct to survive, and roughly equated with activity and masculinity. Masochism arose through a change in the object of the drive from the external world to the subject, with sexual excitement associated with pain, suffering, submission, and humiliation. Central to his thinking throughout was Freud's observation that intense stimulation was associated with sexual excitement.

Pleasure in pain, the erotogenic effect of pain, in actual experience or in fantasy, was for Freud postulated as the physiological substrate for all later masochism. Perverse masochism in adults represented the pathological fixation or developmental arrest at this early stage, a drive that was not sufficiently repressed or modified by later genital sexual aims. Freud could not specify the causes for this fixation or failure of repression but suggested a complex compromise between constitutional and environmental influences.

Freud (1915) systematized instinct theory, stressing again that sadism was primary, based on the aggressive drive to master, and masochism represented redirecting the aggression onto the self and changing the mode from active to passive. He explained the satisfaction in masochism as vicarious. The masochist achieves gratification by identifying with the sadist in the act.

As his theoretical work advanced, Freud became increasingly convinced of the centrality of the Oedipus complex in mental life and the role of its resolution in the structuralization of the "mental apparatus" through the internalization of the ambivalently loved parents—the superego. The Oedipus complex was at the core of all neuroses, and guilt became man's primary burden in life.

In "A Child is Being Beaten" (1919), Freud again investigated the origins of sexual perversion. Here he stressed the role of unconscious guilt as the major motive for repression of oedipal wishes, leading to masochism. Offering a clinical study of six patients (four women and two men), mostly obsessionals and hysterics, Freud dissected the structure of the fantasy "a child is being beaten" to put forth what now would be more clearly an aspect of the defensive nature of masochism, not simply or exclusively its instinctual nature. Pain would become a condition for, not a simple cause of, sexual pleasure. This was a modification, though not a replacement, of his earlier and persistent view of the physiological substrate of pleasure in pain. People with beating fantasies as features of their adult sexual lives— and there were many, according to Freud—had become derailed or fixated along the path of infantile sexual development, probably because of constitutional predisposition. This sadistic component instinct, prematurely independent, broke loose from the normal modulating and "metabolizing" effect of sexual development and underwent fixation. Burdened by an excess of aggression, these people established complexly layered beating fantasies in childhood, around the age of five or six. In women, the first phase of this fantasy, not masochistic, was of a rival being beaten by the father. The meaning of this part of the fantasy was that "father only loves me," and the rivalrous aggression was usually directed against a boy child. The second masochistic phase remained unconscious and was reconstructed in analysis. In this phase, the fantasy was "I am being beaten by father on the buttocks." The third phase, which was associated with sexual excitement and masturbation, was the part reported by patients in the clinical setting, that is, "a child is being beaten." In this fantasy, repression forced substitution of another authority for the father and other children for the self. This final fantasy, then, represented a regressive substitute satisfaction for incestuous wishes, which converged with an unconscious sense of guilt; this conflict was repressed, and regression to the anal-sadistic phase allowed the compromise resolution. Freud described only two phases in men: first the unconscious, homosexual wish to submit to being beaten by father; and, second, submission to a beating by a powerful woman who replaces father. In line with Freud's adherence to the oedipal source of all neuroses, it was the father who was the love object for both men and women in their beating fantasies, being a source of both sexual satisfaction and punishment.

Summing up, Freud states:

> Masochism is not the manifestation of the primary instinct, but origi-
> nates from sadism which has been turned around upon the self, that is
> to say, by means of regression from an object into the ego. Instincts
> with a passive aim must be taken for granted as existing, especially
> among women. The passivity is not the whole of masochism. The
> characteristic of unpleasure belongs to it as well—a bewildering accom-
> paniment to the satisfaction of an instinct. The transformation of
> sadism into masochism appears to be due to the influence of the sense
> of guilt which takes part in the act of repression. Thus repression is
> operative here in 3 ways. It renders the consequences of the genital
> organization unconscious, it compels that organization itself to regress
> to the early sadistic anal stage, and transforms the sadism of the stage
> to masochism, which is passive and again in a certain sense, narcissistic
> [p. 193–194].

This formulation of masochism reflects the evolving importance of the superego, which provokes a sense of guilt for sexual and aggressive drives. Freud was at this point in his mental model-building, advancing toward the tripartite hypothesis where the superego became both the major instigator of repression and the heir and product of the resolution of the oedipal phase.

"The Economic Problem of Masochism" (1924) was Freud's last major contribution on masochism, written after "Beyond the Pleasure Principle" (1923) and "The Ego and The Id" (1923). In a remarkably concise fashion, so characteristic of some of Freud's short, gemlike papers, he clarified and modified the pleasure principle, the constancy or Nirvana principle, and the reality principle to accommodate his revised dual instinct theory. Pleasure was no longer equated with quantitative reduction of stimulus-induced tension. Tension reduction was now the expression of the "death instinct." Pleasure now arose from qualitative changes in the rhythm and sequences of the expression of libidinal drives.

Elaborating the complex energics of this dual instinct theory, Freud reversed his prior position on the primacy of sadism in masochism, postulating instead the existence of the components of the death instinct that are fused with libido and self-directed. This *primary masochism* accounted for the physiological substrate of pleasure in pain. The association of sexual excitement with increases in psychic tension Freud called *erotogenic masochism.* That part of the death instinct directed outward in the world as the instinct to master, or sadism, could then secondarily be redirected against the self in later life as *secondary masochism.* Through these processes of fusion, defusion, and refusion of sexual and death instincts, the pleasure principle could be preserved as the regulatory principle in masochism.

Turning his attention to the clinical manifestations of masochism, which could now be explained by his instinct theory, Freud again grounded the vicissitudes of the Oedipus complex and the consequent structure of the mental apparatus firmly in the instincts. This allowed him to integrate the beating fantasy in both perverse masochism in males, so-called *feminine masochism,* and characterologic masochism, so-called *moral masochism,* or the unconscious need for punishment. The unconscious beating fantasy, forged both as satisfaction and defense, was the basis of all later masochism. In feminine masochism, men inhibited in normal sexual arousal and release could regress to the expression of the unconscious wish for the father through the fantasy of being a small, helpless, naughty female child; thus pain, humiliation, and subjugation through identification with the female and the wish to have the father would allow sexual satisfaction.

In moral masochism, noted particularly in the negative therapeutic reaction, "the suffering itself is all that matters" (Freud 1924, p. 165). The connection to sexuality had been loosened, and need for punishment held sway. The superego became the object of the regressively resexualized wish of the ego to be beaten by the father. This stood in contrast to and could be reinforced by the ultramorality induced by the aggressive nature of the superego invested with aspects of the death drive, accounting for its sadistic, harsh, and cruel qualities. The moral masochist relentlessly attempted to satisfy his oedipal wishes through the pursuit of pain, subjugation, and humiliation at the hands of all authority or the hands of fate. "The true masochist always turns his cheek when he has a chance of receiving a blow" (p. 165).

Thus Freud's legacy for masochism places the ego in the center of the struggle with the instincts. He viewed masochism as instinctual (oedipal) and defensive. As derived from the establishment of the superego and the wish to submit to the father and as a defense against castration danger, masochism is ultimately passive and feminine.

Although Freud's thinking on masochism was both incisive and ingenious, it was limited and left many important questions unanswered or even unaddressed.

The relationship of overt sexual masochism and characterological masochism is controversial and complex. Clinically the two do not with any consistency necessarily coincide. It was Freud's theoretical presumption of the ubiquity of unconscious sexualized beating fantasies as the source of masochism that would lead to the therapeutic focus on uncovering these fantasies in the curative process of psychoanalysis. This was to be a challenge taken up by his followers.

Freud's relative neglect of the preoedipal period would ultimately lead to questions of the role of early ego development, separation-individuation processes, narcissism and self-development, the role of pain, and the increasing importance of the defensive, conflict resolving, and "self-protective" functions of masochism.

Post-Freudian Contributions

The assumption of the death instinct as the crucial metapsychological basis for masochism drew much criticism. The notion that man was drawn to suffering and pain as a vicissitude of his instincts has been either attacked or ignored by later writers.

Reich (1933) departed vigorously from certain aspects of Freud's theories while passionately embracing others. Reich was an "arch-libidinalist" whose entire work, including his extreme final orgonomics, placed the sexual drive at the center of mental (and ultimately cosmic) dynamics. Reich was concerned with character as the defensive armoring established to protect against oedipal anxieties. Masochistic characters, for Reich, were victims of aggression who attempted complex compromise formation that became their character armor, with resultant inhibition of sexual pleasure and orgastic release. Suffering was not sought for its own sake but rather as an aspect of defense against the consequences of aggression directed at frustrating and frightening objects. It became galvanized into characterological armoring. Solidly wedded to the oedipal nature of neurosis, Reich saw the future masochist as a person who had been excessively frustrated or hurt in childhood and in whom this interpersonal experience demanded defense against aggression. Endowed with some biological intolerance for psychic tension states, the future masochist suffered deep disappointments and became inordinately demanding of love. This love would be gained or coerced through sufferings at the hand of the love object and through submission to lesser punishments to avoid greater ones.

Reich went on to detail many of the characteristics of masochists in their indirect expression of aggression, their inhibition of exhibitionism, the coercive nature of their suffering, and their attempts to evoke guilt, all the aspects of his formulation that emphasize the regression to the anal-sadistic level.

Further post-Freudian contributions to the theory of masochism depart from Freud in many ways, but not from the idea that masochism is based on pain as a condition for pleasure. It is in the various possibilities, or the various definitions, and range of the wishes and experiences considered pleasurable, that the nature of masochism was to be understood. The central question remained, What is the pleasure in masochism?

Horney was an early critic of some of Freud's views, but from a significantly different perspective from that of Reich. She was disaffected with Freud's notions of femininity and instinct. Her views were much more interpersonal, social, and cultural, veering away from biology and instinctual drives.

According to Horney (1937), the masochist has established the "strategic value of suffering" to defend against the fears associated with feelings of intrinsic weakness or deep feelings of insignificance that leave him with an inordinate need for affection and an inordinate fear of disapproval. Horney was anticipating later concepts of narcissistic vulnerability, injury, and the vicissitudes of infantile omnipotence as crucial factors in masochism. Burdened by the sense of insufficient control, the masochist, in a version of turning passive to active, submerges himself in "an orgy of torment," seeking an ecstasy of pain. Horney suggested a "Dionysian" loss of self in ecstatic states as the crucial underlying motivation in masochism.

> The operating principle in this process is a dialectic one, containing a philosophic truth that at certain point quantity is converted to quality. Concretely it means that though suffering is painful, abandoning oneself to excessive suffering may serve as an opiate against pain [p. 265].

Horney eschewed the Freudian emphasis on the vicissitudes of guilt and aggression and emphasized that guilt is not primary. The masochist repairs his injured omnipotence through striving for the loss of self in the "greater oblivion."

Reik (1941) brought the emphasis back to sadistic aggression while avoiding Freud's metapsychological reliance on "the death instinct";

the pleasurable sadistic fantasy would find expression in fantasy or in action against others, often under a "reversed sign" and often highly "demonstrative" in the masochist's life—"victory through defeat."

The importance of sadistic aggression was stressed also by Brenman (1952). Staying close to clinical observation, Brenman highlighted the role of *projective* mechanisms in masochism, working in concert with denial, and reaction formation as major defensive operations of the ego.

> We see first the projection of insatiable demands in the masochist's assumption that all people are as imperiously needing as he, and he must therefore be inexhaustably "giving." In short, when he is functioning well he gives his objects what he would like to get from them. As the hostile component in his ambivalence mounts his "giving" becomes an aggressive, smothering attempt to control experienced by the object not as a gift but as an enslavement. We see also, however, his *projection* of hostile impulses and accordingly, the provocative gingerly testing approach to all human relations with the pervasive feeling that his chronic misfortunes and disappointments are the other person's fault" [p. 273].

The ubiquity of masochism was an essential postulate in Edmond Bergler's colorful and voluminous contribution to the theory of masochism, culminating in *Curable and Incurable Neurosis—Problems of Neurotic vs. Malignant Masochism*, (1961): "I believe that there exists only one basic neurosis, acquired in the first 18 months of life: psychic masochism. All later neurotic manifestations of libidinous, pseudoaggressive nature are only rescue stations to hide from the basic conflict" (p. 18). Bergler saw psychic masochism as "a desperate attempt to maintain infantile megalomania" (p. 18). The infant is subject to "a septet of baby fears" (p. 19): 1) the fear of starvation; 2) the fear of being devoured; 3) the fear of being poisoned; 4) the fear of being choked; 5) the fear of being chopped to pieces; 6) the fear of being drained; and 7) the fear of castration. The infant, at the mercy of his mother for his satisfaction, can respond to these fears only with fury—his reaction to the assault on his omnipotent sense of control. This fury, however, cannot be expressed against the source of satisfaction, his mother. Following Freud's instinctual energics, Bergler saw the infant as turning passive to active and directing his aggression against himself, thereby regaining his lost sense of omnipotent control. Bergler's views on the early developmental intertwining of masochism and narcissism form an important basis from which Cooper, in this volume, elaborates his concept of the narcissistic-masochistic character.

Bergler emphasized the restitution of infantile narcissism. The superego, all-important in later systematic and characterological ela-borations of masochism in neurotic and malignant forms, becomes the repository or agency for all the accumulated self-aggression. This self-aggression, called "daimonion," while not based on a death instinct, is called "each man's worst enemy. An unconscious force that is adverse to happiness, success, enjoyment of life and whose aim is unhappiness, misery and even self-destruction" (p. 34). The persistence of this narcissistic rage and grandiosity is expressed in the "superego's *principles of self damage.*" Self-torture must follow an elaborate set of rules, which apply along the progression of the phase-specific stages of psychosexual development. The struggle against passivity engendered by the baby's fears and the attendant narcissistic mortification and rage find expression in varying degrees of neurotic symptoms, somatic reactions, and characterological orga-nizations. Bergler's two types of psychic masochism, neurotic and malignant, differed profoundly in their manifestations and signifi-cance. Neurotic masochism was to be found in normals as well as neurotics; malignant masochism, in schizophrenics and borderlines (schizoids).

Whereas Bergler and others suggested that masochism was an intrinsic, inevitable product of childhood, that the root cause lay in the fate of infantile narcissism, Berliner placed emphasis on the child's attempt to cope with traumatic parental cruelty and sadism.

Berliner presented masochism as an attempt to preserve the pre-oedipal oral level object attachment in the face of the reality of the unloving or cruel objects. In a series of papers culminating in 1958, he proposed that

> masochism is neither a pure instinctual phenomena (death instinct), nor the expression of component sexual drive, nor is it the subject's own sadism turned upon himself. It is in the sexual as well as moral form a disturbance of object relations, a *pathological way of loving.* Masochism means loving a person who gives hate and ill treatment [p. 40].

Masochism was the growing child's attempt to meet his needs to be loved and to feel the skin contact of the object, despite the lack of love or the fact of pain coming from that object. Oedipal guilt became a secondary, reenforcing motive colored by the preoedipal experi-ence. Anticipating Kohut and others, Berliner postulated that this abuse experienced by the preoedipal child could be a failure of empathic responsiveness to a growing selfhood, or excessive ambiva-lence, or the projection of hostility. Berliner saw masochism as defensive. The denial and libidinization of suffering, with a repres-sion of the experience of the hatred and ill treatment, encouraged an identification with the aggressor. It was an attempt to deny the sadism through repression and turn unloving ill treatment into love. The introjection of the object's sadism into the superego, not the projection of sadism and aggression, was crucial for Berliner. The ego sought punishment as a form of love from the superego.

In a psychoanalytic treatment of masochism, Berliner (anticipating Kohut's therapeutic approaches) stated:

> The masochist appears in a double light. He is the victim of a traumatic childhood and is a troublemaker who entangles himself in actual conflict by which he constantly makes himself victim again. He is sinned against, and sinning, to paraphrase Shakespeare. We give the analysis of the victim priority over the analysis of the troublemaker [p. 53].

Thus, Berliner's views differed from Freud in several ways. Masochism was oral, not oedipal, in origin; it was not simply retroflexed aggression or self-directed sadism, and, crucially, it was not based on the innate capacity to fuse pleasure and pain or to libidinize a self-directed aggression. It was an adaptive response to a cruel or harsh external reality, the result of a traumatic environment. Libidinization of suffering was an attempt to maintain the love of the object who caused the suffering.

Loewenstein (1957), reviewing the psychoanalytic theory of masochism, described the masochism "of the seduction of the aggressor," a universal tendency in children and a form of protomasochism that defends against both the parental aggression and the child's projected aggression. "Masochism seems to be the weapon of the weak, i.e. in every child faced with the dangers of human aggression" (p. 230). This aggression threatens the child's safety and survival and sexual satisfaction. By inviting punishment, by being the slave or playing out games of punishment and being naughty, the masochist protects himself from the dangers of castration and object loss and turns the dangerously unloving parent, or superego, into a loving one. While preoedipal experiences are influential, the Oedipus complex in both the positive and negative forms is crucial in the development of this protomasochism and later adult masochism. Lowenstein described the many characteristics of masochism that can be traced back to the seduction of the aggressor: passive feminine attitudes in men, passive aggression and the mentality of the slave.

> Underlying the self-destructive tendencies involved in moral masochism, one can see at work in it the desperate attempt to seduce the aggressor, the harsh conscience, to appease the gods of fate by suffer-

ing; i.e., to revert to childhood, to the state when threats and dangers could actually be averted or minimized by using the method which was effective then [p. 230].

Menaker (1953) examined gratification in masochism from the side of the ego. Like Berliner and Lowenstein, she saw the ego's need to control and avoid anxiety, to maintain the love of the object. She extended the defensive definition of masochism further back to the awareness of self and the maintenance of self-worth and to issues of separation and individuation. Anticipating Kohut's later views on the mother's role in self- and narcissistic development, Menaker saw the mother's earliest loving responses to the infant as crucial to its ego development (see also Mahler, Pine, and Bergman, 1975.) and not simply or solely as a basis for instinctual satisfaction. Autonomous ego functions (Hartmann, 1958) can be secondarily drawn into conflict through maternal empathic failure. Mother determines the balance in the ego's experience of self-loving or hating.

The hatred of the self, originating at the earliest level of ego differentiation, and the accompanying feeling of powerlessness become the prototype for later feelings of worthlessness, which characterize the moral masochist. These very feelings are used in the service of ego to protect it from the fear of being abandoned, and to gain for it a fantasy gratification of love. This is the essence of moral masochism, in the defense of the ego [Menaker, 1953, p. 209].

This early self-devaluation distorts and modifies the ego as it matures and serves the drives, the superego, and reality. The crippled ego responds to anal and genital level conflicts with self-deprecation and attempts to preserve an idealization of the maternal introject in fantasied symbiosis. Again foreshadowing Kohut's disintegration anxiety and the absence of the selfobject, Menaker's masochist fears fusion and loss of ego identity.

Valenstein (1973), examining severe negative therapeutic reactions in "difficult" patients, proposes that the attachment to pain derives from preverbal painful experiences in the early tie to the object. The integration of affects evolves within the developing self- and object representations. The affect and the object are equivalent. Painful affects are inextricable elements of the object representations vital to the maintenance of the emerging self. "Giving up such affects, . . . would be equivalent to relinquishing a part of the self and/or self object at the level which those affects represent" (p. 375).

An important implication of this view is that certain aspects of masochism may be inaccessible to interpretation, or may be interpretable to only a limited degree through reconstruction of early painful states. This view of early masochistic development anticipates the perspective emphasized by Gedo in this volume.

Brenner (1959), in his often cited cogent review of the masochistic character, disagreed with this emphasis on the predominantly pre-oedipal roots of masochism. For him

> the essence of masochism appears to consist in an intimate relationship between pleasure and pain or more generally between pleasure and unpleasure, and may perhaps best be defined as a seeking of unplea-sure by which is meant physical or mental pain, discomfort or wretch-edness for the sake of sexual pleasure, with a qualification that either the seeking or the pleasure or both may often be unconscious or conscious [p. 197].

Masochism defined in this fashion becomes a universal characteris-tic of mental life in the relationship of the ego to the superego, and it becomes pathologic only in degree. Masochistic fantasies serve the principle of multiple function in the ego's attempt to find adaptive compromise formation to intrapsychic conflict.

Finally, advancing a *self psychological* frame of reference, Stolorow (1975) focused on the narcissistic function of masochism. With the task of restoring and maintaining "the structural cohesiveness, tem-poral stability and positive affective coloring of a precarious or crum-bling self-representation" (p. 441) placed at the center of psychic life, masochism (and sadism) can be conceptualized as efforts to accom-plish this task through omnipotent control over or identification with an idealized parental imago or through the reparative activation of the grandiose self. By departing from the ego psychological frames of reference (within which it implicitly shares important concerns, e.g. central executive functions, intactness, and defensive adaptation to internal and external threats to structural organization), Stolorow offers a therapeutic, introspective, and interpretative approach to those difficult patients whose psychopathology can be broadly de-scribed as masochistic, narcissistic, and borderline in organization.

CURRENT PERSPECTIVES ON MASOCHISM: AN OVERVIEW

How is masochism currently viewed? Authors continue to differ about what is included under the term. Some reserve it for phenom-ena that conform closely to the original prototype Freud used for his consideration of masochism—the masochistic perversion where the dependence of sexual excitement on pain is required in action, in the perversion, or in conscious or unconscious fantasy, in the masochistic character.

Schafer (chapter 5), for instance, along with other authors (e.g., Brenner, 1959; Grossman, 1986) advises us

> to remain close to Freud (1919) . . . and to reserve the term 'masochistic' for those patterns of action in which suffering seems to be not only self-induced and repetitive but conspicuously, even if unconsciously, sexualized as well. . . . [That is] connected with fantasies of being beaten . . . and [that] is used as a means of promoting sexual excitement and climax [p. 88].

He describes others who are wrecked by success but who, although they represent a frequently observed diagnostic group, do not necessarily qualify for the masochistic label. He points out that "every disorder we work with clinically has its share of unhappiness and unfulfillment, and every one is characterized by repetitiousness, unconsciously designed and executed self-injuriousness," so that broad usage of the term results in loss of its utility for him. However, he points out that in clinical practice we usually encounter mixed cases and various degrees, so that it is usually appropriate to include some kind of qualified statement about masochistic components of being wrecked by success.

Others explicitly or implicitly deemphasize the sexual, genital aspect (as well as the etiologic primacy of oedipal dynamics, see Cooper, chapter 7) and see specifically sexual pleasure less directly involved or more difficult to demonstrate. The term "moral masochism," as contrasted with "sexual or erotogenic masochism," indeed implies a deemphasis of the erotic element in the former. These authors include under the rubric "masochism" a number of self-motivated, self-destructive behaviors and related dynamic constellations that are repetitive and involve pain, failure, subjugation, and humiliation, which are sought after in obligatory connection with a variety of pleasurable goals or gratifications arising at all levels of psychic development: for example, maintenance of self-boundaries, self-cohesion, self-esteem, object attachment, instinctual gratification and neurotic resolution of id, ego and superego conflicts, as well as direct genital sexual discharge, but not necessarily related to sexual excitement.

Kernberg (chapter 4), stressing the universality of masochistic behaviors and the unclear boundary between such behaviors and psychopathology, includes a category of "normal masochism" in his classification of masochistic phenomena resulting from the guilt arising from the integration of normal superego functions and the predisposition to experience a condensation of psychological pleasure and pain emanating from the early integration of sexual excitement and pain. He states, however, that at the extremes of the spectrum the concept of masochism dissolves into such other diagnostic and psychodynamic considerations as the normal tolerance of pain in sublimatory efforts in work and the erotic excitement in the teasing aspect of sexual interaction. He points out that these phenomena contain so many functions and developmental features that the term "masochism" loses its specificity if applied to them. At the pathological end of the spectrum, where we are dealing with extreme self-destructive behavior with little erotization of aggression, he suggests that the equation of self-destruction with masochism dilutes the specific meaning of masochism.

Coen (chapter 3) addresses the element of excitement, sexual and nonsexual, in relation to painful experience and Sarnoff (chapter 12) defines masochism simply as "the passive experience of aggression accompanied by painful and excited affects" (p. 204).

All the authors in this volume agree that there exists a variety of pathological entities that involve an obligatory connection between pain and pleasure and are of great clinical and theoretical significance as self-motivated, self-destructive behaviors. These entities are, therefore, of interest to those struggling with the meaning of masochistic or masochisticlike behavior. Whether they are called "masochistic" or simply "pain dependent," as Rado (1956) has suggested, these phenomena must be accounted for.

Implicit in the broader, more inclusive approach to these phenomena is an effort to arrive at a framework within which to explore the interrelationships that may exist between them and to see how the principle of multidetermination may operate within each entity.

As in the exploration of other syndromes, certain questions arise, many of which have already been indicated in our review of the development of the concept of masochism: At what developmental level and in connection with what developmental task do things go awry? Is the primary traumatic experience operative at one or more levels? How do early traumata influence later developmental phases? What kind of condensations take place between dynamic constellations from earlier and later phases? Do earlier constellations get additional or even their primary force and intensity from experiences at a later developmental phase? An epigenetic view is central in all considerations of masochism. Just as terms like narcissism and masochism have not retained their pristine and specific meanings during the development and elaboration of these psychoanalytic concepts, there are many transformations and changes of function involved in the genesis of a masochistic character.

Schafer (chapter 5), discussing some patients who are wrecked by success, underlines some of the issues of preoedipal–oedipal etiological interrelationships, condensations, and relative contributions of intensity. He points to the role of early narcissistic factors where success presents the danger that unconsciously maintained grandiose ideas of self will be experienced consciously with a loss of reality, so that the patient retreats from self-enhancing recognitions. He believes, however, that such narcissistic crises are not resolvable in terms of Kohut's self psychology alone but that such crises also imply an oedipal crisis and, possibly, a disruption of a preoedipal symbiotic tie or a disturbing sense of merging with grandiose parental imagos, again pointing to transformations and the resulting mix of factors from different developmental levels. Fantasies of irremediable defect referring to a lack of empathic mothering viewed from the self psychological perspective, may well involve later fantasies or fixations and defenses against them, which are revealed if the analysis is not confined to self psychological issues. Schafer notes that "the unempathic mother often proves to be the retaliatory oedipal rival or the rejecting oedipal object, so that, unconsciously, it is the oedipal threat and defeat that give to the ideas of defect and deficit much of their apparent force" (p. 87). The perception or fantasy of self-defect may therefore be used by the superego to enforce oedipally determined self-punishment.

Gedo (chapter 8), reversing the perspective, points out that an earlier determined need to seek unpleasure, based on pathological self-core formation, is easily confused with self-punishment: people tend to be humiliated by their masochistic propensities and may just as readily defend against their primitive self-organizing nature by conceiving of these propensities as expressions of guilt arising from oedipal, superego conflicts.

THE PLAN OF THIS BOOK

The early and continuing division of masochistic phenomena into those referrable to neurotic character formation on the one hand and to the perversion on the other have made it appropriate to begin this volume with a chapter dealing with the psychoanalytic understanding of character. Hence, in chapter 2, Robert Liebert traces the major elements in the development of the concept of character, starting with Freud's views of character—its instinctual origins through later elaboration of defense, object relational, ego psychological, and self psychological theories of the nature of character. Stanley Coen follows with an exploration of the role of excitement in the development of both characterological and perverse masochism and discusses the determinants and functions of perversion as compared to those of characterological or moral masochism.

In the fourth chapter, Otto Kernberg, employing an ego psychological-object relational perspective, presents us with a classification of masochistic phenomena organized according to levels of characterological structural pathology. His comprehensive, well-organized, and detailed classification serves as a good initial orientation to the many levels of masochistic organization. He stresses the need for simultaneous analysis of: (1) the vicissitudes of libidinal and aggressive strivings, their relative balance and integration, with libido predominating in higher forms of masochism and aggression predominating the more severe forms; (2) the role of superego development and the impact of failures of superego integration in the formation of masochism; (3) the level of ego integration—neurotic, borderline or psychotic—that influences the quality of internalized object relations; (4) the pathology of internalized object relations; and (5) the extent to which normal or pathological narcissistic functions predominate.

In chapter 5, Roy Schafer explores the unconscious infantile meanings of failure and success that commonly emerge in the psychoanalysis of "those wrecked by success," particularly analytic success, that is, therapeutic stalemates and negative therapeutic reactions. Viewing them "from the inside," not simply the objective, contemporaneous "outside," Schafer discusses the reasons for "wrecking actions, in analysis and in life. These may involve crucial conflictual identifications and the 'ideal self' as a central and highly conflictual reference point." Using the clinical situation, Schafer examines important manifestations of being wrecked by success in the transference and resistance and in the countertransference. He differentiates masochism from "wrecking action."

In the sixth chapter, Stuart Asch discusses sexual and moral masochism and related masochistic phenomena that are neither clearly sexual perversions nor consistent aspects of a masochistic character structure; the overlapping of masochism with depression and the frequency of negative therapeutic reactions in patients with masochism and depression; and the genesis of masochism as related to problematic, sadistic early object relations and early internalizations. Finally, he addresses technical problems in the treatment of masochism with special attention to countertransference problems.

In his discussion of therapy Asch focuses particularly on "malignant" masochism, where the function of the masochism is to perpetuate a powerful, primitive attachment to an internalized preoedipal object as a residual of an incomplete "separation-individuation" from an early mothering object. He is careful to point out that it is not a true symbiotic mechanism in the Mahlerian sense, with lack of self–object differentiation. The internalized object is more of a separate, enslaving, critical one from whom the child is not able to free himself. The technical approach involves a demonstration of this persisting, primitive, internalized relationship in the transference and of the patient's aim to not succeed in treatment but rather to appease this internal object so as to remain attached to it. Here the patient splits off the bad aspects of the maternal object onto the transference object, where he finds revenge and defends against his passive wishes by defeating the therapist's efforts to help him.

Asch extensively discusses the many countertransference problems encountered in the treatment of masochism. Among them are the need of the masochistic patient to defend against his own anger and to incite anger in the therapist, often through stubborn passivity, denigration, and negative therapeutic reaction. The frequently encountered "need to cure" on the part of the therapist evolves from the need to repair the narcissistic hurts from his own childhood attempts to deal with impaired significant early figures. This leads the therapist to regressively reexperience the felt need to provide ego sustenance for such needy significant objects. Guilt reactions paralyze the analyst's appropriate responsiveness and intensify the masochistic provocations of the patient or lead the analyst to be "giving" rather than interpretive.

In the seventh chapter, Arnold Cooper, arguing for the diagnostic entity of the narcissistic-masochistic character, points to the current relevance of Bergler's early emphasis on narcissistic issues in the development of masochism. He explores the intimate developmental relationship of narcissism and masochism, stressing the ubiquity of masochistic defenses in preoedipal narcissistic development. Pointing to the early role of pain in self-definition, he states that

> a full appreciation of the roles of narcissism and masochism in development and in pathology requires that we relinquish whatever remains of what Freud referred to as the "shibboleth" of the centrality of the Oedipus complex in neurosogenesis. . . . that masochism and narcissism are so entwined both in development and clinical presentation that we clarify our clinical work by considering that there is a narcissistic-masochistic character and that neither appears alone [p. 117].

Cooper, in relating narcissism and masochism, particularly empha-sizes the painful deflation of omnipotence during the rapprochement subphase of separation-individuation. This important narcissistic mortification threatens intolerable passivity and helplessness. Defen-sive restorations of control and self-esteem by making suffering ego syntonic make the pain of the object relation *an actively sought after* experience, not a passively endured one. Where there is excessive early narcissistic humiliation, a narcissistic-masochistic character dis-order develops. Although basically preoedipally determined, this masochistic propensity is later integrated into the oedipal constella-tion, exerting a distorting effect at that developmental level.

In the eighth chapter, John Gedo points to earlier preverbal "sym-biotic" pathology with aberrant patterns of sensations and affect, conditioned before self–object differentiation is complete. This is propelled by the repetition compulsion, with self-sacrificing behavior being related to this pathological self-core formation. Gedo points to the technical modifications necessary in such cases, including clarifi-cation of these preverbal pathological patterns of affectivity in the context of a "holding environment," which enables the patient to reexperience the pathogenic early childhood transactions with the mother in the form of archaic transferences.

A major focus of these authors (for instance Kernberg, Asch, and Sarnoff) is on the quality and vicissitudes of internalized representa-tions of self and objects or rather *selves* and objects. This is especially critical in Herbert Rosenfeld's (chapter 9) exposition, from a Kleinian perspective, of the struggles between various dramatically personi-fied primitive good and bad introjects attempting to achieve a balance of libido and aggression. Like other authors (see Cooper, chapter 7), Rosenfeld stresses the intimate relationship of early narcissism and masochism, particularly the seduction of the libidinal self by the omnipotent and destructive, but hypnotically seductive, narcissistic organization. He stresses, as do Kernberg and others, the role of early intense aggression. He describes the vicissitudes of the battling but variously libidinized part objects of the early paranoid-schizoid posi-tion (Klein 1946) and the attempts at reconciliation and synthesis of these elements into more whole representations in the later depres-sive position. Rosenfeld then offers a complex analysis of the many identifications and primitive psychic operations, particularly splitting denial, omnipotence, introjection, projection, and projective identifi-cation involved in these early processes.

These internalized self–object relationships include states of fu-sion, which may be pleasant but paralyzing and imprisoning. Rosen-feld relates these object relational vicissitudes, as do other authors, to such early mother–child interactions as feeding, which may be experienced as invasive and destructive, and other aspects of extreme ambivalence in the early relationship to the mother. He points to a severe, destructive narcissism, which in the psychotic state completely dominates and overwhelms the patients' sane parts of self and tries to imprison them. This paralyzed, imprisoned state then appears clinically as masochism. He differentiates between benign and destructive mergers—those with the good aspects of mother versus those with the bad, sadistic mother, into whom intense aggression has been projected. He relates masochistic perversions as addictive solutions to or defensive ways of covering up "painful blockage" and seems to be suggesting a certain concrete usage of sexual activity and fantasy to bring the self alive. (See Coen, chapter 2.) This sexuality substitutes for the emptiness due to the blockage by autistic defensive withdrawal from threatening objects. Rosenfeld considers oedipal factors in connection with these early object relational issues and points to the increased destructive omnipotence that can take place at the height of the Oedipus complex. Some of Rosenfeld's descriptions echo the importance of the sudden deflation of the patient's omnipotence in the development of the narcissistic-masochistic character, as referred to by Cooper.

Several of our authors assign a significant role to projective identification in the development of masochism. This is particularly so in Rosenfeld's exposition. As an aid to those readers who may not be familiar with his view of this process, we quote the following description of projective identification, containing quotes from Melanie Klein (1946) that Dr. Rosenfeld presents in another of his writings (1971):[1]

> Projective identification relates first of all to a splitting process of the early ego, where either good or bad parts of the self are split off from the ego and are as a further step projected in love or hatred into external objects which leads to fusion and identification of the projected parts of the self with the external objects. There are important paranoid anxieties related to these processes as the objects filled with aggressive parts of the self become persecuting and are experienced by the patient as threatening to retaliate by forcing themselves and the bad parts of the self which they contain back again into the ego.

---

[1]Dr. Rosenfeld had planned to add an explanatory note regarding the Kleinian perspective on early introjective and projective process for the benefit of those readers not familiar with these concepts. After his tragic death, the editors elected to publish his chapter in its original form and style. We offer the above extensive discussion of these processes taken from a bibliographic reference Dr. Rosenfeld included with his chapter.

In her paper on schizoid mechanisms, Melanie Klein (1946) considers first of all the importance of the processes of splitting and denial and omnipotence which during the early phase of development play a role similar to that of repression at a later stage of ego development. She then discusses the early infantile instinctual impulses and suggests that while the "oral libido still has the lead, libidinal and aggressive impulses and phantasies from other sources come to the fore and lead to a confluence of oral, urethral and anal desires, both libidinal and aggressive" (p. 300). After discussing the oral libidinal and aggressive impulses directed against the breast and the mother's body, she suggests that "the other line of attack derives from the anal and urethral impulses and implies expelling dangerous substances (excrements) out of the self and into the mother. Together with these harmful excrements, expelled in hatred, split off parts of the ego are also projected into the mother. These excrements and bad parts of the self are meant not only to injure but also to control and to take possession of the object. Insofar as the mother comes to contain the bad parts of the self, she is not felt to be a separate individual but is felt to be the bad self. Much of the hatred against parts of the self is now directed towards the mother. This leads to a particular form of identification which establishes the prototype of an aggressive object relation. I suggest for these processes the term projective identification" (p. 300).

Later on in the same paper Melanie Klein describes that not only bad, but also good parts of the ego are expelled and projected onto external objects, who become identified with the projected good parts of the self. She regards this identification as vital because it is essential for the infant's ability to develop good object relations. If this process is, however, excessive, good parts of the personality are felt to be lost to the self which results in weakening and impoverishment of the ego. Melanie Klein also emphasises the aspect of the projected processes which relates to the forceful entry into the object and the persecutory anxieties related to this process which I mentioned before. She also describes how paranoid anxieties related to projective identification disturb introjective processes. Introjection is interfered with, as it may be felt as a forceful entry from the outside into the inside in retribution for violent projections. It will be clear that Melanie Klein gives the name "projective identification" both to the processes of ego splitting and the 'narcissistic' object relations created by the projection of parts of the self into objects [Rosenfeld, 1971, pp. 115–116].

In the tenth chapter, Helen Meyers gives a differential classification of the theory of technique in the treatment of masochism according to the level of origin and function of the masochism. She states that masochism is likely to be multidetermined in all patients and that technique varies according to the developmental level (or levels) from which the masochism under scrutiny during different phases of an analysis derives and the function it serves at that point in the treatment.

The final two chapters view aspects of masochism from the psychoanalytically informed child developmental perspective. Eleanor Galenson, in her discussion of protomasochism, first defined by Lowenstein (1957), uses the data from mother–child observation to augment the data of intrapsychic exploration, focusing particularly on the vicissitudes of aggression in these relationships and their impact on the child; Charles Sarnoff draws on his experience in the psychoanalytic treatment of children and adolescents to discuss the development of masochism and adolescent masochistic phenomena.

Relating her observations of mother–child interactions where there is exaggerated aggression to Loewenstein's ideas of protomasochism resulting from an early imbalance between libidinal and aggressive components in the infant's early ties with the mother (see p. 12), Galenson reviews perspectives on the development of aggression that emerged from the observation of very young children by Spitz and McDevitt, its intensification by traumatic interaction, and other of its vicissitudes in relation to the quality of the mother–child relationship. Finally, she presents observational data demonstrating clinical syndromes related to various disturbances in the handling of aggression in the mother–child relationship and leading to protomasochism.

Sarnoff, in chapter 12, traces the developmental phases of masochism through childhood into adolescence, with particular attention to the influences of cognitive development on its phasic manifestations. He describes the progression of masochism from primary or preobjectal masochism through the development of protosymbolic somatic representations of affects and self–parent amalgams (protosymbols), where the child's aggression is first experienced as directed toward the self. Then, with the development of self–object differentiation, memory, and object constancy, aggressive energies can be experienced by the child as object directed. The introjected parental representation becomes a vehicle for the object relational integration of libido and aggression. With the development of the capacity for symbolization and the related capacity for repression at 26 months, there is an increasing use of purer fantasy to "drain off" aggression and a lessening of the use of actual parental aggression as the source of pain that is a necessary part of the fantasy. He then discusses the modifying effects of phallic-oedipal concerns and the neutralizing effects on aggression of further cognitive development, such as the acquisition of verbal conceptual memory organizations. The further development of restraining ego mechanisms, particularly the in-

creased capacity for fantasies, allows discharge and mastery of conflict on a symbolic level with sadomasochistic play and fantasy in
normal development, and playground teasing, night fears, and paranoid accusation of peers when these ego structures fail. In adolescence there is intensification of anal sadistic drive organizations and a
movement to the world of reality as an arena in which masochistic
fantasies can be lived out. Using clinical examples, Sarnoff discusses
masochistic derivations of adolescence, including masochistic braggadocio (regarding suffering), in which there is a failure in development
in the communicating level in symbol formation. The usage of symbols is limited in purpose to attracting sympathy and evoking prior
painful affect and ego states as a form of repetition compulsion in
service of overcoming narcissistic injury. Sarnoff later relates adolescent misuse of association to this phenomenon. He relates masochistic perversion to a fixation in cognitive development and refers to an
arrest of symbol function in the "march of symbols" used as the
protagonists in persecutory fantasies and their derivatives in latency
and adolescence, for example, parts of the body used as symbols to
express masochistic fantasy at the end of latency and enlistment of
real people as symbols to express masochistic fantasy. He includes
adolescent shyness and prepubescent schizophrenia as forms of
adolescent masochism and elaborates the vicissitudes of introjects
and projective identifications in adolescent masochism. He describes
adolescents with incipient masochistic character traits as those who
involve real objects in the masochistic experiences and therefore can
develop a transference neurosis and an effective therapeutic experience.

REFERENCES

Bergler, E. (1961), *Curable and Incurable Neurosis—Problems of Neurotic vs. Malignant
    Masochism*. New York: Liveright.
Berliner, B. (1958), The role of object relations in moral masochism. *Psychoanal. Q.*,
    27:38–56.
Brenman, M. (1952), On teasing and being teased and the problem of moral maso-
    chism. *The Psychoanalytic Study of the Child*, 8: 264–285. New York: International
    Universities Press.
Brenner, C. (1959), The masochistic character: Genesis and treatment. *J. Amer. Psy-
    choanal. Assn.*, 7:197–226.
Freud, S. (1905), Three essays in sexuality. *Standard Edition*, 7:135–243. London:
    Hogarth Press, 1956.
——— (1915), Instincts and their vicissitudes. *Standard Edition*, 14:117–140. London:
    Hogarth Press, 1957.
——— (1919), A child is being beaten. *Standard Edition*, 17:179–204. London: Hogarth
    Press, 1955.

——— (1920), Beyond the pleasure principle. *Standard Edition*, 18:7–64. London: Hogarth Press, 1957.

——— (1923), The ego and the id. *Standard Edition*, 19:12–59. London: Hogarth Press, 1961.

——— (1924), The economic problem of masochism. *Standard Edition*, 19:159–170. London: Hogarth Press, 1961.

——— (1937), Analysis terminable and interminable. *Standard Edition*, 23:216–253. London: Hogarth Press, 1964.

Grossman, W.I. (1986), Notes on masochism: A discussion of the history and development of a psychoanalytic concept. *Psychoanal. Q.*, 55:379–413.

Hartmann, H. (1958), *Ego Psychology and the Problem of Adaptation*. New York: International Universities Press.

Horney, K. (1937), *The Neurotic Personality of Our Time*. New York: W. W. Norton.

Klein, M. (1946), Notes on some schizoid mechanisms. In: *Developments in Psychoanalysis*, ed. E. Jones. London: Hogarth Press, pp. 292–320.

Krafft-von Ebing, R.F. [1906], *Psychopathia Sexualis*. New York: Physicians & Surgeons Book Co., 1931.

Loewenstein, R. (1957), A contribution to the psychoanalytic theory of masochism. *J. Amer. Psychoanal. Assn.*, 5:197–234.

Mahler, M.S., Pine, F., & Bergman, A. (1975), *The Psychological Birth of the Human Infant*. New York: Basic Books.

Menaker, E. (1953), Masochism—A defense reaction of the ego. *Psychoanal. Q.*, 22:205–225.

Rado, S. (1956), *Psychoanalysis of Behavior*. New York: Grune & Stratton.

Reich, W. (1933), *Character Analysis*. New York: Orgone Institute Press.

Reik, T. (1941), *Masochism and Modern Man*. New York: Farrar & Rinehart.

Rosenfeld, H. (1971), Contributions to the psychopathology of psychotic states. In: *Problems of Psychosis. Volume I*, ed. P. Doucet & C. Launin. Amsterdam: Excerpta Medica.

Sacher-Masoch, L. von [1870], *Venus in Furs*. New York: Wm. Faro, 1932.

Stolorow, R.D. (1975), The narcissistic function of masochism (and sadism). *Internat. J. Psycho-Anal.*, 56:441–448.

Valenstein, A. (1973), On attachment to painful feelings and the negative therapeutic reaction. *The Psychoanalytic Study of the Child*, 28:305–392. New Haven: Yale University Press.

2 / The Concept of Character:

A Historical Review

Robert S. Liebert

IT IS BOTH DIFFICULT AND LIMITING to separate inquiry into the nature of masochism as a controlling adaptive organization for certain individuals from broader consideration of the psychoanalytic concept of character. Indeed, the different metapsychological assumptions and means of effective therapeutic engagement with the problem of masochism expressed by the contributors to this volume achieve coherence, and perhaps validity, only insofar as they are integrated into and consistent with the larger, more complex fabric of character. It is my purpose, therefore, to examine the concept of character, principally by means of presenting its history in psychoanalytic thought.

It has become customary that any paper on character begin by emphasizing the confused conceptual status of the term—a term that comes down to us from ancient Greece. Its etymological roots, significantly, refer to that which is carved or engraved. Character has been a subject of concern for Aristotle, the Stoics, and every theologian, dramatist, gossip, Boy Scout leader, and psychoanalyst ever since. Our exploration of character is further complicated by the fact that the term has technical meaning in our discipline and also has varied connotations that are established in common parlance.

Within psychoanalytic usage certain distinctions have usually been maintained with respect to *character traits, character types*, and *character*. Traditionally, in speaking of "character traits" our referent is clearly delineated, typical, and stable behavior that is readily observable and, importantly, is selected for attention because of its implications for the broader fabric of psychic organization and social adaptation. But even here with the seemingly simple notion of "traits" the problem is complicated by issues involving: (1) the context in which the behavior appears; (2) the values of the observer; (3) the adaptive function for the individual; and (4) distinctions that must be made from *symptoms* with respect to a continuum into which the trait fits— one end of the continuum being that the particular behavior is conflicted, a source of subjective distress, and has little adaptive value, namely, a symptom; the other end being that it is a trait and is ego syntonic. But even with ego syntonicity, which has commonly been regarded as a hallmark of character and character traits, we must be aware, as Schafer (1983) has argued, "What is consciously self-syntonic may, unconsciously, be exceedingly dystonic" (p. 144). Despite these problems, when we speak of character traits, we are usually in the realm of common sense observations about which there would be general agreement and which then lend themselves to interpretive inference.

Character types simply refers to the grouping of individuals who have enough shared and overlapping specific behavioral patterns, such as the "masochistic character" or the "narcissistic character," to enable us to generalize about their common developmental situation, psychic structure, object relationships, self-imagery, and controlling fantasies.

In contrast with character traits, the term *character* is generally regarded as an ill-defined structure, an organization that must be communicated through the language of metapsychological abstractions. Thus, character is frequently spoken of as a supraordinate entity that integrates dark impulses with external reality, id with superego, conflicted pregenital fantasies, largely unconscious, with a smoothly regulating set of defenses. Moreover, its origins are in the flux of a particular stage of development, and it expresses identification with certain internalized imagos. This tendency, exemplified by the definition given for "character" in The American Psychoanalytic Association's *Glossary of Psychoanalytic Terms and Concepts* (Moore and Fine, 1968), has led us to confuse character as observable behavior with character as a set of abstractions. These abstractions are then tied to and vary with the theoretical orientation to which one is partial in explaining behavior. It is as if character determines behavior rather than that it is the codification of a constellation of related behaviors.

There is more to say about the problems that beset us in the study of character. But progress toward clarification and definition may emerge in the course of what follows—a historical review of the concept. Much of what I present will be familiar, but it is my hope that this overview will provide a more articulated template for receiving and ordering the ideas that are proposed in the various discussions of the masochistic character.

HISTORY OF THE CONCEPT

I will begin my survey quite naturally with Freud's treatment of the topic. He explicitly addressed the subject of character in only three, widely spaced papers (1908b, 1916, 1931), and of these, the first alone commands our attention—*Character and Anal Erotism* (1908b).[1] In addition, the foundation stones for the theory of character were set in place in crucial papers at each stage of his thinking in papers that did not, however, deal directly with character.

Freud's formulation of anal character is the crystallization of a remarkable mixture of clinical observation and theoretical abstraction. It grew directly out of his analysis of the Rat Man, begun the year before. Before we examine this paper, it is significant to note that earlier, in reporting the first month of treatment of the Rat Man to his small following in the Psychological Wednesday Society, Freud had said: "In general a human being cannot bear opposite extremes in juxtaposition, be they in his personality or in his reactions. It is this endeavor for unification that we call character" (quoted in Jones, 1955, p. 263).

Freud never offered a definition of "character," but here, at the outset, he clearly asserted his view of the conflictual basis of character, or, to be more accurate, the *function* of character as a means of resolving conflict. This primacy given to resolution of conflict remained an unchallenged proposition for decades, until modified by Hartmann (1939) and now largely contested by Kohut's followers. We recall that at this early period, Freud conceived of the instinctual drives as the energic basis and moving force of the otherwise inert psychological organism. The person evolved through a series of invariable psychobiological stages in which successful adaptation and progress to the next was governed by the reality principle, with repression serving as the major means of transforming the person from primary process beast to civilized being. At this point, aggression had not yet been accorded a companion role to libido as the instinctual driving force.

In this seminal work on character, Freud chose the anal zone and the transformation of the intense erogenicity of this tissue at a specific phase of development into a constellation of related character traits. These traits—orderliness, parsimony, and obstinacy—formed a pattern of observable behavior that was functionally adaptive and en-

---

[1]Baudry (1983) has offered a comprehensive review of the evolution of the concept of character in Freud's writings.

dured over time as the person moved through progressive stages of psychosexual development. The characterological outcome of this particular stage was variable, depending on the interaction of constitutional factors and the predominance of the defensive process employed—sublimation or reaction formation (an issue which he treated in "Three Essays," 1905). At the conclusion of the paper, Freud summarized his conceptual model, stating that he had provided:

> A formula for the way in which character in its final shape is formed out of the constituent instincts: the permanent character-traits are either unchanged promulgations of the original instincts, or sublimations of those instincts, or reaction formations against them [p. 175].

I will not belabor the extent to which Freud's biological orientation informed this early conception of character, but we note that totally absent is the role of the mother or caretaker, and the imprint of the distinctive behavioral interaction between child and mother over the bodily zone and its taming into the use of the toilet. Absent, too, is a consideration of the process of identification with the parents—all hallmarks of later thinking about character.

The revolutionary model presented in "Character and Anal Erotism" (1908a) became the paradigm for the other stages of the natural sequence of psychosexuality—oral, phallic, and genital—with each stage holding the potential for generating a specific set of related character traits. Adult character emerged as a fabric woven with threads consisting of traits derived from each epoch of development. It was a progression marked by fixations and regressions, as well as advances. Once firmly based at the level of genitality, the person became relatively insulated from a regressive reintegration.

Freud's model of a progression in stages of psychosexual development to the final ideal of the genital character has been criticized (most notably by Reiff, 1959) as being a conflation of moral attitude and scientific observation. The criticism is that inherent in this model is that the genital heterosexual character is the only normal adaptation. Thus, other pathways and endpoints of psychosexual development, such as homosexuality, are failures in development, regardless of whether the particular individual meets the other criteria usually applied to measure subjective satisfaction, external functioning, and fulfilling object relations.

As has often been noted, at this 1908 mark, Freud's view of character was hardly comparable in its depth, detail, and complexity to the theory of symptom formation he spelled out in "Hysterical Phantasies and Their Relation to Bisexuality" (1908a), which is as close to the fulcrum of our thought on symptoms today as it was then.

In the years between the introduction of the concept of anal character and the great leap forward in establishing the tripartite structural theory in 1923 in "The Ego and the Id," Freud enunciated several more integral elements in theory of character. In "Remembering, Repeating and Working Through" (1914), the concept of the *repetition compulsion* emerged in relation to both the choice of love objects and the form in which love is expressed, which are shaped by the nature of repressed and unfulfilled libidinal instincts. The repetition compulsion was to receive its full due later in "Beyond the Pleasure Principle" (1920). The other factor relevant to character theory was Freud's formulation of *acting out*, which referred to a pattern of substituting actions of particular symbolic meaning for repressed conflicted memories. Thus, with the introduction of the repetition compulsion and acting out, Freud clarified two attributes of character—its consistency and regularity and its modality of expression.

The third element I wish to underscore is the role of unconscious and conscious *fantasy* in dictating the behavior that becomes each individual's uniquely characteristic adaptive mode. These issues were raised in the paper "A Child Is Being Beaten" (1919), although limited to the dynamic explanation of a specific fantasy. Yet this small model held large import for the subsequent thinking about moral masochism and represented a significant stepping stone from the formula, "Anatomy is destiny" to "Fantasy is destiny."

"The Ego and the Id," which appeared in 1923, ushered in the modern era of psychoanalytic thinking with the introduction of structural theory. Its implications for character formation were profound. In brief, the view of the ego as the heir to abandoned object cathexis, but now assuming the form of structured *identifications* with these lost objects, anticipated the central concern of contemporary object relations theory and heralded our present interest in the complex processes of internalization. Thus, Freud executed a sweeping shift in emphasis—from character as derivative of libidinal drives to character as derivative of identifications with the parents in the form of structured ego representations. The final major step in Freud's thinking was his introduction of superego and ego ideal (1923). With these concepts, the process of identification became more refined with respect to what aspects of the parents were internalized in the ego and what later aspects of them in the superego and ego ideal, and then how distinctive patterns of adaptation grow out of the tension between these two agencies.

Thus, there was a consistent direction to Freud's construction of a theory of character. He began by postulating the force of constitution and libidinal drive. Then he emphasized the function of character in resolving conflict. These concepts were followed by the introduction of the nature of the mechanisms of defense, the role of fantasy, the structures of ego and superego, and the process of identification.

The next analytic thinker to command our attention is Wilhelm Reich. Inasmuch as his contributions to technique were so new and radical with respect to the confrontation of resistance in order to reveal in workable form the negative transference, we might examine some of the theoretical underpinnings to his *Character Analysis* (1933). For Reich, character was the adversary. His very use of the term "armor" underscores its defensive nature. His conception was rooted in Freud's recently elaborated structural theory. He regarded the purpose of character as "primarily and essentially a narcissisic protection mechanism" (1929, p. 125), which developed in response to the dual threats of dangers in the external world and the claims of the id. Psychic energy played a major role in Reich's formulations. He spoke of character as a means of avoiding pain through its capacity to absorb that quantity of instinctual energy which has undergone or escaped repression. From the economic point of view, the main functions of character were "the binding of free-floating anxiety, or . . . the release of damned-up psychical energy" (1930, p. 147).

Like symptoms, character was the conservator of the infantile past, alive in the present. Through its analytic dissection the central infantile conflicts became accessible and subject to resolution. In this pursuit, the adaptive, creative, and non-conflictual aspects of character are relatively disregarded.

Anna Freud's *Ego and the Mechanism of Defense* (1936) may be viewed in part as a reaction to Reich, with whom she taught side-by-side in Vienna until his expulsion from the movement shortly before her book went to press. The contrast between the two was captured by Jenny Waelder-Hall who, reflecting on the climate in Vienna at the time, informally stated at a meeting, "For Wilhelm, resistance [that is, character] was the enemy who was to be smashed in battle; for Anna it was the enemy who was to be treated with respect and won over as an ally."

The contribution of Anna Freud to the theory of character was not simply in the more differentiated description of the defenses and their coordination with specific sources of psychic danger. She also greatly refined the ordering of the mechanisms of defense in a developmental sequence. For example, in addressing *sublimation*, she wrote (1936):

Sublimation, i.e., the displacement of the instinctual aim in conformity with higher social values, presupposes the acceptance or at least the knowledge of such values, that is to say, presupposes the existence of the super-ego. Accordingly . . . repression and sublimation could not be employed until relatively late in the process of development [p. 56].

Refinement of the concept of defense in relation to development was taking place concurrently in the mid-1930s in the work of Melanie Klein. Beginning in 1934 she deviated from Freud's tripartite model with her own structural concept of *positions* (Klein, 1935). In so doing, she took the revolutionary step of changing the emphasis in psychoanalytic from father-dominated oedipal theory to the role of mother in preoedipal development. She also asserted that from the very beginnings of infancy an inner world of fantasy existed that was object relational. For Klein the concept of "position" defined the structure of the ego and superego and the dynamics of their relationship in terms of the *paranoid-schizoid* and *depressive* positions (cf. Klein, 1946; Segal, 1974). That is to say that the form of the resolution of these two fundamental psychic positions in relation to mother characterize all of one's personal relationships thereafter. Position, therefore, connoted much more than a stage in development. It implied a specific configuration of object relations, anxieties, and defenses that persist throughout life and substantially define the character of the individual.

Klein, in contrast with all of the later Object Relations theorists, conceived of the infant as perceiving in the mother and outer world what he has projected onto them, and then internalizing it anew. What is projected and reinternalized is a raging instinctual drama of sex and aggression. Thus, character for Klein is ultimately more a psychobiological entity than an interpersonal or culturally determined one.

Before the post-World War II modifications of Freud's thought had significantly progressed, Otto Fenichel, in 1945, integrated the structural and dynamic aspects of analytic theory into a conceptual model of character. He defined character as "the habitual mode of bringing into harmony the tasks presented by internal demands and by the external world, which is necessarily a function of the constant, organized, and integrating part of the personality which is the ego" (1945, p. 467). In the final outcome of character, Fenichel attributed crucial significance to the strength and nature of the superego, while also acknowledging the importance of cultural variations. The form of the resolution of the structural intrapsychic conflict became the basis for a general classification of character. Fenichel's two broad categories were the *sublimation type* and the *reactive type*. In the former, the ego succeeds in replacing an original instinctual impulse with one that is compatible with the ego, one that is organized and inhibited as to aim. In the reactive type, countercathectic forces block the instinctual discharge and the result is character formation in one of two main directions: *avoidance* and *inhibition* on the one hand, or *opposition*, on the other, distinguished by processes of reaction formation. Within this schema, Fenichel was able to develop a relatively elaborate classification of pathological character types, depending on the dominance of instinctual forces, *superego* (as in the masochistic character), or *external objects* (as observed in extremes of social anxieties and pseudointimate sexuality).

The refinements of classical theory and contributions to the understanding of character of Heinz Hartmann (1939), and then Hartmann, Kris, and Loewenstein (1964), do not lend themselves readily to summary. In contrast to the path taken at the same time by Object Relations theorists, who emphasized the personal identificatory processes and content of the ego, Hartmann wrote impersonally of the *ego* as an integrating organization of apparatuses and automatisms that served the function of internal control and external adaptation. Hartmann introduced the concept of *ego apparatuses*—products of endowment and maturation that were part of our basic adaptive equipment and formed the nucleus of adaptive psychological functioning, which operated relatively free of intrapsychic conflict. Perception and memory are examples. The relative strengths and balance of these apparatuses are manifest in the patterns of conflict resolution, which is identifiable as character.[2]

Another concept of importance to character is Hartmann's discussion of the change in function of a behavioral form, leading to its *secondary autonomy*. Thereby, characterologic patterns that originated in one period of development, primarily serving a defensive function, later become relatively independent structures that operate in a highly adaptive way and also become an integrating feature of personality. An example of this principle is the manner in which intellectualization functions defensively during adolescence and then continues as a newly flexible and creative autonomous character pattern after the instinctual forces that resurged during adolescence have become successfully integrated.

A natural laboratory for testing psychoanalytic postulates regarding character was the study of non-western cultures. Early studies by

[2]Greenacre (1957) has persuasively applied Hartmann's line of thought to the study of individuals with extraordinary creativity.

Roheim (1919) and others confirmed that there did indeed appear to be certain universal patterns, such as incest taboos and oedipal dynamics. Before long, however, psychoanalytic anthropology was pursuing a closed circle. This state of affairs changed dramatically with the investigations of Abram Kardiner in the late 1930s (e.g., 1939). He simply turned the question around from what is the *same* to what is *different* and *why?* Kardiner was faithful to the structural model of the mind, but he also demonstrated, in a way that no one had before, that cultural changes are registered by describable alterations that take place unconsciously in the agencies of the mind (cf. Marcus, 1982). Thus, Kardiner and his associates (1945) introduced the concept of a *basic personality type*, which had characterologic specificity and was shared by the members of any given culture. It reflected the cultural needs and institutional patterns of that society and, in turn, served to sustain the culture. Kardiner emphasized the form and content of the superego as the variable psychic agency that served this individual and collective function. Kardiner and Ovesey (1951) applied this approach in their pioneering study of the characterologic consequences of the racial oppression of blacks in America.

After World War II, as Hartmann and his co-workers embarked on systematically refining and developing psychoanalytic theory largely according to the model of a biological science, it seemed almost inevitable that an additional conception of mind would have to emerge—one that devoted long due attention to the consequences of the dynamic interplay between particular flesh-and-blood mothers and children on the one hand, and the force of social and historical factors, on the other, in the shaping of character. Thus, with the publication of *Childhood and Society* in 1950, and for the following two decades, Erik Erikson was destined to fulfill this role complementary to Hartmann, Kris and Loewenstein.

Whereas Harry Stack Sullivan (1953) as far back as 1925 had with considerable perceptiveness addressed individual mother–child interactions through sequential stages of development and spelled out some of the consequences for character formation, his lack of an overall theory of mind limited any broader impact. Sullivan's relatively isolated position stood in marked contrast to the appeal of Erikson, both within psychoanalysis and in the social sciences.

Erikson offered a psychosocial theory of ego development, in which the individual's social development was traced through the unfolding of his *social character* in the course of his encounters with the environment at each phase of his epigenesis (cf. Rapaport, 1958). Erikson explored the social context of each phase with respect to the radius of significant relations, first with mother, then the basic family, followed by a progression of extrafamilial social institutions. Erikson focused on the process by which society influences the manner in which each individual solves phase-specific developmental tasks in a sequence of phases. These parallel stages of libidinal development that continue throughout the whole life cycle. This ego epigenesis culminates at the end of adolescence in an individual *identity*. Erikson prefers the term "identity" or "ego identity" to character and defines identity as expressing "both a persistent sameness within onself and a persistent sharing of some kind of essential character with others" (1959, p. 102). He elaborates:

> At one time . . . it will appear to refer to a conscious sense of *individual identity*, at another to an unconscious striving for a *continuity of personal character*; at a third, as a criterion for the silent doings of *ego synthesis*; and, finally, as a maintenance of an inner *solidarity* with a group's ideals and identity [p. 102].

Erikson's graphic schemata of psychosocial crises, with their polarities in resolution, have become firmly integrated as part of our collective view of character. The grand scale of his work is captured in his own words:

> From a genetic point of view . . . the process of identity formation emerges as an *evolving configuration*—a configuration which is gradually established by successive ego syntheses and resyntheses throughout childhood; it is a configuration gradually integrating *constitutional givens, idiosyncratic libidinal needs, favored capacities, significant identifications, effective defenses, successful sublimations* and *consistent roles* [p. 116].

In the end, however, it must be said, as Schafer has said (1968, pp. 39–41), that Erikson's use of the term "identity" communicates more the spirit of his overall approach than a clearly definable concept.

The importance of the period of adolescence in character formation was elaborated by Peter Blos (1968), who, along with Erikson, emphasized that the extent to which the developmental challenges of adolescence have been met and successfully negotiated will determine how autonomously character will function thereafter, stabilizing the experience of the self and protecting psychic structure from internal and external stresses.

It is surprising to realize that the current attention to the interaction between infants and young children and their mothers as the crucial matrix for the later development of character and psychic structure is entirely a post-Freudian phenomenon. The emphasis on this as the appropriate field of observation has been the unifying bond among the somewhat varied thinkers grouped together as the Object Relations School. The more prominent names associated with this school are Balint, Fairbairn, Guntrip,[3] Kernberg, and Winnicott. Kernberg, among this group, has endeavored also to maintain a strong link with ego psychology.

Sutherland (1980) has delineated what is common to the group in pointing to their belief that there exists an innate developmental potential, which, if activated by the input of loving, empathic care, will become the psychological matrix for the later capacity to love and enjoy. These theorists view later character formation and patterns of motivation primarily as a function of the adequacy or inadequacy of the fit between the needs of the infant and young child and the responses of the mother. Traditional notions of drive are suspended, though not categorically rejected, thereby distinguishing them from the mainstream of Ego Psychology.

While mindful that clear differences exist between each of the major figures, to illustrate the general approach of this group I will briefly summarize an aspect of a model of character formation offered by Balint. In 1968, Balint wrote a book entitled *The Basic Fault*. This "fault" refers to a subjective sense of something lacking or missing within oneself and is the result of the impaired harmony in the early dyad. Out of this basic fault the individual will develop in one of two typical directions in subsequent object relations. In one, objects are clung to with a primitive intensity, lacking in mutuality and characterized by a pathological hostile dependency. The other line of development involves a reliance on an inner world of fantasy for sustenance, counterposed against precarious and tenuous relations with "real" people. Thus, in this schema, character is largely defined by the nature of the person's later relations with objects and, in the examples given, are directly based on the failure of adequate early mothering. Winnicott's (1960) schema of the *True Self* and the *False Self* has much in common with Balint's concept of the Basic Fault.

The richness of the experiential aspects of the British School has left its imprint on all of us in our thinking about character. At the same time, the relative looseness of their metapsychological formulations has catalyzed the work of such theorists as Kernberg (1976), Meissner (1979), and Schafer (1968, 1976, 1983) in the direction of creating a fuller psychology, particularly with respect to exploring the concept of structure—that is, what is structured, by what process is it

---

[3]Guntrip (1971) has, incidentally, written a survey of central ideas of a number of major psychoanalytic theorists, which is valuable for the comparative study of the concept of character.

structured, and, finally, what are the forms and fates of these structures.

In the 1970s in America, a new approach to character—self psychology—found enthusiastic receptivity. Self psychology is the virtually singular creation of Heinz Kohut (1971, 1977). Its clinical base is
almost entirely derived from the treatment of patients that we now
classify as narcissistic character disorders. For Kohut, the "self" was
conceived of as a separate and organized entity in development and
mature behavior and as the locus of disturbance in most forms of
character pathology. As his work has evolved, self has increasingly
become the superordinate concept in the structure of mind. The
traditional elements of psychoanalytic metapsychology—drives and
the complexities of ego and superego—are subsumed and treated as
constituents of the self. Thus, Kohut and Wolf (1978) spoke of the self
as an "independent center of initiative." As an amalgam of inherited
and environmental factors, the self "aims toward the realization of its
own specific program of action—the program that is determined by
the specific, intrinsic pattern of its constituent ambitions, goals, skills
and talents, and by the tensions that arise between these constituents" (p. 414).

Whereas classical theory has conceptualized all neurotic behavior
as the outgrowth of *intrapsychic conflict*—that is, the resolution of the
dialectic between drives and defenses—Kohut shifted the emphasis
to *deficit*, by which he meant the arrest in the healthy maturation of
the self due to failures of the nurturing environment to provide
sufficient empathic care. The narcissistic pathology we observe clinically is the consequence of this early failure in *empathy*. In his focus on
the crucial importance of the role of the mother's empathic attune-
ment to the infant and young child for the healthy formation of
character, Kohut bore close kinship with the Object Relations School.

Before Kohut, narcissism had been viewed as a way station along
single axis of development, beginning with autoerotism and ending
in object love. According to this model, primary narcissism yielded to
the formation of the ego ideal, which then became the object of the
libidinal cathexis originally directed toward the self. In contrast,
Kohut proposed a dual axis model in which narcissism itself followed
an epigenetic sequence and evolved into mature narcissism, along
with a parallel development of object love. This healthy progression
along both axes takes place unless arrested by inadequate early care.

A crucial issue in the study of the narcissistic pathologies is the fate
of what Kohut termed the "bipolar self." Through the observation of
two predominant forms of transference in his clinical work—the
"mirror" transference and the "idealizing" transference—Kohut re-

constructed the normal development of narcissism. At an intermediate stage, objects who are needed to supply the functions that the immature self cannot autonomously execute are viewed as parts of, or extensions of the self and are referred to as "selfobjects." These selfobjects are experienced in two fundamental ways: (1) as "mirroring," that is, as affirming the fragile self; and (2) as "idealized," that is, as omnipotent and protective. In healthy development of narcissism, the mirroring aspect of selfobjects yields to a characterologic self-assertiveness and realistic ambition; and the idealizing aspect of selfobjects yields to a flexible set of internalized ideals and values. In contrast, in pathology, as a result of the arrest in development, the child's early objects are maintained as internalized selfobjects to provide psychic cohesion.

A final point to be stressed in discussing Kohut's contributions to the subject of character is his abolition of the pejorative connotation of narcissism. In its final transformation, narcissism achieves a secondary autonomy and becomes an intrinsic component in such higher human functions as creativity, wisdom, and empathy.

One more approach to character should be noted—that of Jacques Lacan (1966, 1977). It was Lacan who offered the boldest rethinking of Freud of any of the schools represented. Although he has had virtually no impact on American and British clinicians, Lacan has influenced non-English speaking analysts, particularly in France, where his following is widespread. His psychoanalytic concepts are deeply rooted in the complex ideas of the movement in structural linguistics, particularly in the works of Ferdinand de Saussure, Claude Levi-Strauss, and Roman Jakobson.

A fundamental postulate of Lacan's (1977) is that "the unconscious is structured . . . like a language, that a material operates in it according to certain laws, which are the same laws as those discovered in the study of actual languages . . ." (p. 234).

Thus, in his almost singular reliance on language and speech as the means for understanding human behavior, Lacan moved far from traditional neurobiological concepts of instinctual drive and need, and psychic energy. His orientation, as Leavy (1978) has pointed out, brought Lacan close to Sullivan and Erikson insofar as a person'a identity or character is completely enmeshed in the symbolic structures that hold currency in the particular culture as layed down in his or her unconscious. Finally, American psychoanalysts tend to be bewildered by Lacan's taking issue with Ego Psychology in his view that ego is merely a system of defenses that serves as a barrier to the individual's access to his unconscious, the understanding of which is ultimately essential if one is to achieve true selfhood.

CONCLUSIONS

It is apparent as I conclude my summary of close to a century of
analytic though about character that there is not an agreed upon
definition, not even agreement about the locus of description. As one
path toward some resolution, I will suggest not more definitions, but
rather that we look at the paradigm of dreams. We recognize that the
dreamer is playing many, perhaps all the roles in a dream. Regardless
how large the cast of characters, it is basically a one-person show—
the dreamer's. In a similar way, we are none of us simply one
character type; we are all, rather, a number of coordinated subcharac-
ters. Or, to put it slightly differently, we have many characters, each
the manifest behavioral representation of a unified constellation of
our conscious and unconscious life of fantasy. Character is observable, and fantasy is obtainable, particularly in the clinical situation.
And I cannot overstress the crucial role in my own thought to which I
assign fantasy as the meaningful and workable substratum of character. Now, will this personal repertoire of characters be reasonably
healthy or tainted with pathology in a particular individual? The
answer to that question depends on outcomes along a number of
abstract continua that we find very useful in organizing our thought
on the matter. For example, the outcome depends on the predominant balance of *defenses*—say the higher developmental ones such as
repression and sublimation, rather than more primitive ones such as
projection and splitting. It depends on the nature of such ego capacities as frustration tolerance, thinking, and remembering, rather than
impulsively acting. It depends on the stability or instability, the
constancy or inconstancy of self and inner object representations.
Thus our personal repertoire of characters either will be a harmonious
ensemble of players or will be in conflict with one another, making
contradictory claims, and suffering in palpable ways.

   If we shift our metaphor to the theatre, each character is observable
to the audience, known and defined by a coherent set of actions.
Thus, Hamlet is known to us as a definable character who is repro-
ducible by actors over centuries, because of the way he acts toward
the king, his mother, Ophelia, his deceased father, and others; and
also by the way he talks *of himself* in soliloquies, and by the emotion
he displays when alone. Hamlet makes sense, and we experience
something of ourselves in him and through him. This, then, is the
character of Hamlet. His character is not his tripartite psychic structure, his balance of drives and defenses, his ego appartuses, nor the
stage of psychosexual development he has achieved. These latter
concepts are metapsychological narratives that explain the character

or, more accurately, the many different dimensions of character that comprise Hamlet. Our ability to make sense of his character by employing these explanatory devices is what distinguishes us as psychoanalysts from others in the audience, who employ their respective explanatory devices. What is so exciting about psychoanalysis is that, as rich as our theoretical concepts are for understanding, they are, as we have seen, ever-changing, ever-growing to enable us to better graps what has been indomitable in man since our prehistory—character.

REFERENCES

Balint, M. (1968), *The Basic Fault*. London: Tavistock.

Baudry, F. (1983), The evolution of the concept of character in Freud's writings. *J. Amer. Psychoanl. Assn.*, 31:3–32.

Blos, P. (1968), Character formation in adolescence. *The Psychoanalytic Study of the Child*, 23:245–63. New Haven: Yale University Press.

Erikson, E. H. (1950), *Childhood and Society*. New York: W. W. Norton.

——— (1959), Identity and the life cycle. *Psychological Issues*, Monogr. 1. New York: International Universities Press.

Fenichel, O. (1945), *The Psychoanalytic Theory of Neurosis*. New York: W. W. Norton.

Freud, A. (1936), *The Ego and The Mechanisms of Defense*. New York: International Universities Press, 1946.

Freud, S. (1905), Three essays on the theory of sexuality. *Standard Edition*, 7:123–243. London: Hogarth Preess, 1953.

——— (1908a), Hysterical phantasies and their relation to bisexuality. *Standard Edition*, 9:155–66. London: Hogarth Press, 1959.

——— (1908b), Character and anal erotism. *Standard Edition*, 9:167–76. London: Hogarth Press, 1959.

——— (1914), Remembering, repeating and working through. *Standard Edition*, 12:145–56. London: Hogarth Press, 1958.

——— (1916), Some character-types met with in psychoanalytic work. *Standard Edition*, 14:309–36. London: Hogarth.

——— (1919), A child is being beaten. *Standard Edition*, 17:175–204. London: Hogarth Press, 1955.

——— (1920), Beyond the pleasure principle. *Standard Edition*, 18:1–64. London: Hogarth Press, 1961.

——— (1923), The ego and the id. *Standard Edition*, 19:1–59. London: Hogarth Press, 1959.

——— (1931), Libidinal types. *Standard Edition*, 21:215–20. London: Hogarth Press, 1961.

Greenacre, P. (1957), The childhood of the artist. *The Psychoanalytic Study of the Child*, 12:47–72. New York: International Universities Press.

Guntrip, H. (1971), *Psychoanalytic Theory, Therapy, and the Self*. New York: Basic Books.

Hartmann, H. (1939), *Ego Psychology and The Problem of Adaptation*. New York: International Universities Press, 1958.

———, Kris, E., & Loewenstein, R. (1964), Papers on psychoanalytic psychology. *Psycholog. Issues*, Monogr. 4. New York: International Universities Press.

Jones, E. (1955), *The Life and Works of Sigmund Freud*, Vol. 2. New York: Basic Books.

Kardiner, A. (1939), *The Individual and His Society*. New York: Columbia University Press.

——, Linton, R., du Bois, C., & West, J. (1945), *The Psychological Frontiers of Society*. New York: Columbia University Press.

—— & Ovesey, L. (1951), *The Mark of Oppression*. New York: World.

Kernberg, O. (1976), *Object Relations Theory and Clinical Psychoanalysis*. New York: Aronson.

Klein, M. (1935), A contribution to the psychogenesis of manic-depressive states. *Internat. J. Psycho-Anal.*, 16:145–74.

—— (1946), Notes on some schizoid mechanisms. In: *Developments in Psycho-Analysis*, ed. J. Riviere. London: Hogarth Press, 1952.

Kohut, H. (1971), *The Analysis of The Self*. New York: International Universities Press.

—— (1977), *The Restoration of The Self*. New York: International Universities Press.

—— & Wolf, E. S. (1978), The disorders of the self and their treatment: An outline. *Internat. J. Psycho-Anal.*, 59:413–26.

Lacan, J. (1966), *Écrits*. Paris: Seuil.

—— (1977), *Écrits: A Selection*. trans. A. Sheridan. New York: W. W. Norton.

Leavy, S. (1978), The significance of Jacques Lacan. In: *Psychoanalysis and Language*, vol. 3 of *Psychiatry and the Humanities*, ed. J. H. Smith. New Haven: Yale University Press.

Marcus, S. (1982), Psychoanalytic theory and culture. *Partisan Rev.*, 49:224–37.

Meissner, W. W. (1979), Internalization in the psychoanalytic process. *Psychological Issues*, Monogr. 50. New York: International Universities Press.

Moore, B., & Fine, B. (1968), *A Glossary of Psychoanalytic Terms and Concepts*. New York: American Psychoanaly. Assn.

Rapaport, D. (1958), A historical survey of psychoanalytic ego psychology. *Bull. Phila. Assn. Psychoanal.*, 8:105–20.

Reich, W. (1929), The genital character and the neurotic character. In: *The Psychoanalytic Reader*, ed. R. Fleiss. New York: International Universities Press, 1948.

—— (1930), Character formation and the phobias of childhood. In: *The Psychoanalytic Reader*, ed. R. Fleiss. New York: International Universities Press, 1948.

—— (1933), *Character Analysis*. New York: Noonday Press, 1949.

Reiff, P. (1959), *The Mind of The Moralist*. New York: Viking.

Roheim, G. (1919), *Spiegelzauber*. Leipzig: Internationaler Psychoanalytischer.

Schafer, R. (1968), *Aspects of Internalization*. New York: International Universities Press.

—— (1976), *A New Language For Psychoanalysis*. New Haven: Yale University Press.

—— (1983), *The Analytic Attitude*. New York: Basic Books.

Segal, H. (1974), *Introduction to The Work of Melanie Klein*. New York: Basic Books.

Sullivan, H. S. (1953), *The Interpersonal Theory of Psychiatry*. New York: W. W. Norton.

Sutherland, J. D. (1980), The British object relations theorists: Balint, Winnicott, Fairbairn, Guntrip. *J. Amer. Psychoanal. Assn.*, 28:829–60.

Winnicott, D. W. (1960), *The Maturational Processes and The Facilitating Environment*. New York: International Universities Press, 1965.

3 / Sadomasochistic Excitement:
Character Disorder and Perversion

Stanley J. Coen

THE PSYCHOANALYTIC LITERATURE by and large regards the etiologic differences between masochistic character disorder and masochistic perversion as unknown. The interrelations between masochistic character disorder and masochistic sexual excitement are complex. More generally, there have been few psychoanalytic studies of excitement, sexual or otherwise. It is not sufficiently appreciated that sadomasochistic enactments, both sexual and not explicitly sexual, are exciting, often intensely so. Our task here is to examine the excitement, sexual and nonsexual, of the masochist. We define perversion rigorously, following Bak (1974), as an adult psychopathological formation, consolidated through adolescent development, which is obligatory for adult sexual functioning (see Coen, 1985).

Stoller (1976) proposed that sexual and nonsexual excitement involves rapid oscillation among fantasied danger, repetition of prior trauma, and fantasied triumph and revenge. He especially emphasized excitement as defense against anxiety. Shapiro (1981) suggested that what is exciting for the sexual sadomasochist is playing at giving in to fantasies of dominance and submission. However, this in no way distinguishes the moral masochist from the masochistic pervert. It leaves us wondering why all moral masochists are not perverts inasmuch as they all share conflicts about dominance and submission.

It is helpful to consider Freud's (1905) early proposal that sadism and masochism are erotic expressions of aggression. That is, a focus on the erotic in sadomasochism will keep us close to the excitement. Sadomasochistic object relations is a way of loving (and hating) others and oneself. It is especially concerned with intense ways of engaging another so as to mitigate dangers of separateness, loss, loneliness, hurt, destruction, and guilt. Aggression and sexuality are adapted to this end of intense connectedness with another person. Multiple defensive and adaptive functions are subserved. Sadomasochistic object relations can be viewed schematically as a complex defensive system against destruction and loss, within which relationships are continually pushed to the brink, with the reassurance that the relationship (at least some imaginary parent–child relationship) will never end.

Usually, layers of anxiety, defense, and guilt cover the excitement of sadomasochism. In my experience, patients with sadomasochistic character disorder have sadomasochistically distorted sexuality, usually not, however, with a structured perversion. Like excitement more generally, this distortion is not readily apparent; it is uncovered only by analysis.

Certain similarities in defense and adaptation are described between sadomasochistic object relations and sadomasochistic perversion. The content of the excitement and the dynamic uses made of it are similar in both. Sadomasochistic excitement involves entering into what is ordinarily dangerous and forbidden: incestuous, exploitative, inappropriate, hurtful, infantile, regressive. Excited, intense feelings and experiences substitute for genuine love and caring; they defend against negative feelings in oneself and in the other. This is the background for erotized repetition. Genetic and dynamic links, especially in relation to defense against hostile aggression, are described among sexual seductiveness, sexualization, and sadomasochism. Similarities are noted in the object relations (perverse misuse of others) of certain patients with sadomasochistic character disorder and sadomasochistic perverts.

Patients with masochistic character disorder are *relatively* able to express conflict in fantasy, to handle it within their own mind. Masochistic perverts differ in being impelled to enact unconscious fantasies into concrete reality so as to render them valid and credible. They cannot accomplish this intrapsychically; their ability to symbolize and to resolve conflict in fantasy is impaired.

EROTIZED REPETITION

Contemporary psychoanalysts have tended to overly desexualize masochism. (See Maleson, 1984, and Grossman, 1986, for discussions of this.) It certainly has been helpful to differentiate moral masochism from masochistic perversion and to trace Freud's views of sadism and masochism as component instincts. Further, a multiple-function approach to masochism must certainly emphasize the variety of nonsexual meanings encompassed in clinical descriptions. Nevertheless, this tack has tended to minimize the motivational pressure, the driven excitement, in sadomasochism. Defensively sexualized repetition remains a useful perspective from which to view clinical samples of sadomasochism. Sexualization of hostile aggression is an important contributor to sadomasochism. Sexualization as defense is usually considered in relation to painful affects, hostile aggression, and narcissistic needs. To be sure, not all samples of sadomasochistic behavior can be demonstrated to involve defensively sexualized repetition. But I am impressed with the confluence of moral masochism with defensively sexualized repetition. Similar genetic and dynamic issues tend to occur where sexualization is used as a predominant form of defense and in sadomasochistic character pathology. Separateness, loss, helplessness, and destruction are central dangers to be defended against by sexualization and by moral masochism. Sexualization and sadomasochism are both especially useful ways to manage intensely frightening destructiveness.

What is exciting is the ability to induce intense affective responses in another person, to overcome the other's barriers; to feel in control and dominant, able to make the other feel bad, guilty, weak, inferior, defective. It is exciting to hold another person in the palm of one's hand, to push another to the point of losing control, attacking, leaving, and then to be reassured that this will not occur. Underneath the layer of game playing is a more serious destructiveness—destroying another's autonomy and free choice. Others can be simultaneously gotten rid of and held onto. It is exciting to repeat what a parent (mother) did with one. Indeed, the excited, erotized repetition serves to ward off the horrors of destructiveness, mother's and one's own. Erotization tames destructiveness; one can pretend that it is a kind of loving relatedness, an exciting game sought by both participants. This is very different from acknowledging that one person hates, envies, and begrudges another his own life, his own separateness and autonomy, and wants to destroy this (cf. the contract between Wanda and Severin in Sacher-Masoch, 1870). Dangers of fusion through passive masochistic surrender are defended against by the illusion of sadistic omnipotent control, the ability to render another helpless.

GENETIC BACKGROUND: EROTIZED SADOMASOCHISM

One common genetic background for both sexualization (when extensively used) and sadomasochism is a relationship with a relatively unavailable, depressed mother, who is sometimes inappropriately and overly seductive but much of the time is unresponsive and unempathic. Extractiveness in the service of mother's pressing needs combines with her sexualized defense against her own destructiveness and rejection of the child. This is commonly expressed in a sadomasochistic relationship between mother and child. Terrors of loss and destruction must be countered by the illusion that mother and child will remain tightly bound together forever. Such mothers resent the burdens of child care. They wish to be the one who is cared for. They envy the child its new chance in life, its autonomy, capacities, strength, youth, attractiveness, phallus. Out of envy and hatred, the mother unconsciously wishes to destroy these attributes of the child. She cripples the child, bonding the child forever to her, with a reversal of roles. Idealization of pretended loving (reaction formation) and seductive overstimulation emphasize that the mother–child relationship is good and loving rather than exploitative and destructive. The child identifies with mother's predominant defensive positions and relates to her in a complementary way. This encourages both sexualization and sadomasochism as defensive and adaptive phenomena to contain and soothe intolerable affects.

Sadomasochistic provocation of a child can lead to overstimulation of sexuality and aggression, overwhelming the child with affects of arousal, rage, hurt, and humiliation. Being the object of such intense attention from a parent in sexually seductive or sadomasochistic ways stirs feelings of specialness and exception. These alternate with feelings of neglect and loneliness, guilt at one's transgressions (sexual or sadomasochistic), overstimulation, rage, and helplessness at one's exploitation and neglect. Defensive identification and erotic or sadomasochistic repetition aim to master the overwhelming affects, as well as to repeat the idealized pleasures. Being the child of sadomasochistic parents can be a chronic strain trauma, with the child especially flooded with anger and sexual arousal without adequate parental protection for modulating these affects. As with Case C, to follow, there may be a lack of clear boundaries between family members. Autonomy is not to be respected but destroyed in the service of intense neediness. Family members are not to be separate and different, each responsible for tolerating and resolving his or her own difficulties. Bear in mind that masochism need not have this particular genetic background; there need not have been sadomasochistic parents. What is emphasized here are consequences of having had sadomasochistic parents.

PSYCHODYNAMICS OF EROTIZED SADOMASOCHISM

The child attempts to get and maintain some mothering in an otherwise very difficult situation. Rage, hurt, humiliation, exploitation, neglect, and betrayal require powerful regressive defenses. Both sexualization and sadomasochism are especially useful for the illusion that destructiveness is caring. Excited, intense feelings and experiences are idealized and defensively focused on. Here are important dynamic similarities between sadomasochistic character, sexualization, and perversion. The excitement from mixing together intense, hostile aggression and sexuality allows such patients, like perverts, temporarily to master rage and other negative affects. During imaginary as well as enacted seductive and provocative encounters, there occurs a temporary defensive transformation of negatively toned, aggressively infiltrated images of self and other(s) into positive, pleasurably regarded ones. I have described elsewhere (1981, 1985; Bradlow and Coen, 1984) how sexual arousal, masturbation, and enactment of seductive fantasy all help one temporarily to disown negative aspects of the self and to appropriate dangerous aspects of the object. Sexual responsivenes, in fantasy or in actual enactments, reassures against fear of loss or destruction of the object or oneself. We could also discuss "aggressivization" of object relations in sadomasochism; abundantly available aggressive drive derivatives infiltrate libidinal object relations in the service of intense attachment, relatedness, and domination.

Sadomasochistic object relations are similar to sexual seductiveness in that the object cannot be left alone outside of one's own orbit. The pair can neither be comfortably together nor apart. Hatred drives the couple apart; fear of separateness and loneliness forces them together. Control, domination, submission, and arousal of intense affects by omnipotent manipulation keep the couple engaged. Denial and projective identification aim to put into the other what cannot be tolerated within oneself. The other is made the "bad one," who then must seek absolution and loving forgiveness from oneself. Badness is then repeatedly made not to count. It is magically turned into goodness. Fixed, clear moral standards have little force. What matters is to be accepted by the other, however this is accomplished. During phases of *sexualized* reunion, each partner feels accepted, forgiven, and no longer bad. The badness in each has been magically repudiated. Both partners are now good; it is others who are bad.

SOME CLINICAL VIGNETTES

Case A

A. complained of feeling depressed and hopeless that she would ever have a satisfactory love relationship. She had again broken up with X., although this was, she thought, the best relationship she had yet had. X. had told her repeatedly that he would not tolerate her provocative fighting. They had just resumed their relationship after another "ending." On Christmas day, A. gave X. a number of gifts. The previous day she had complained on the phone that X. had not gotten her any gifts. He arrived with a lovely bouquet of flowers. As X. unwrapped the gifts A. had gotten him, A. became more and more incensed that he had not gotten her anything besides the flowers. She tried to ignore her feelings but found herself instead boiling up, wanting to go at X. Finally, she could not resist. She attacked X. for his lack of generosity, working herself and him into a frenzy. He tried to calm her down and briefly got her interested in sex, but there was no stopping A. X. left, again announcing that the relationship was over. A. called his home repeatedly, then took a long cab ride to his home. She left him a note and multiple messages on his answering machine, apologizing, saying that she wanted to see him again. This was a repetitive pattern. When she felt ignored, neglected, or abandoned, she would attack the other person; she would try to provoke him into fighting with her and make him feel guilty and responsible for her. She was now well aware how exciting this was and how difficult it was for her to resist the temptation to engage others in such fights. The multiple other factors that led A. to spoil a love relationship will not be considered here.

Case B

B. had felt anxious and uncomfortable on an initial date with V., an attractive, capable woman. That she had been "all over him" physically had especially made him anxious. He thought there was an inconsistency between her apparent strength and her so quickly coming on to him. B.'s anxiety was related, in part, to his own wishes to have sexual control over V. He was very uncomfortable with his wishes that V. would become so aroused sexually that he could do anything he wanted with her. She would go helplessly out of her mind with desire, so that B. could, in effect, lead her around by her genitals. He relished V.'s feeling humiliated and debased as she abjectly desired that he satisfy her. He would be cool, indifferent, powerful, strong. Then B. would not have to fear that V. could humiliate or hurt him.

B.'s mother was an infantile, alcoholic, martinet, who tyrannized the family with verbal putdowns and taunts of deficiency, weakness, and vulnerability and physical attacks. B. was born with celiac disease, which was not diagnosed until age six; the ailment made him feel more vulnerable and defective. At times, mother would be especially indulgent of him while sadistically torturing the rest of the family, for instance by serving the entire family only foods the patient could eat.

To the wish to sexually dominate V., B. associated an adolescent memory he had recently recalled. When he was 16, mother had had one of her usual fights with the entire family, especially taunting father for not being a man, for being a fairy. Removing her blouse and bra, mother had stood, bare breasted, in front of their home, defying father and patient to stop her, inviting sexual attack from "anyone man enough to handle her." B. recalled, and now could allow himself to feel with hatred and lust (and tears), how much he wanted to go at his mother. He wanted to teach her a lesson, to make her behave herself; she should act like a normal mother, who would not humiliate and attack his father and him. He also wanted to possess this wild sexual animal that was his mother. B. could now connect his masturbatory fantasies of strangling women by squeezing their necks with his hands with wanting to shut his mother up. This would stop her from saying all those horrible things. He wanted to destroy mother (women) while also enjoying her body as he pleased. The intensity of his sexual sadism frightened him. He quickly resumed his defensive posture, feeling anxious, insecure, vulnerable; his aggression was again projected onto others.

Case C

C., a toddler, was watching her parents in another intense sadomasochistic fight. Mother was screaming obscenities at father, trying to claw at him; she seemed to be out of control. Father, angry and helpless, grabbed her hands, yelling at her to stop fighting in front of C. C. became excited, overstimulated, overwhelmed. She too began to scream, "Shut up, you fuckin' bitch!" grabbing at her mother. Father was horrified, thinking that C. looked just like his wife—she was becoming a toddler sadomasochist! C. had been overindulged, the parents making conscious attempts to keep her from feeling frustrated. C. had been allowed unlimited access to the parental bed and to the mother's body; the mother had overidentified and confused herself with the frustrated child. C. had not been provided with reasonable limits to her need satisfaction and reasonable experiences of frustration. These would have been necessary for her to develop tolerance and patience while learning to soothe and comfort herself. She was encouraged to identify with her parents' urgent demandingness and wish that there be no frustration or (reasonable) separateness. Parents and child repeatedly recreated an exciting and entitled primal scene from which no one was to be excluded. C. too could go after whatever bodily gratifications she wanted. In these fighting scenes, this young child had to deal with her parents' being out of control, enraged, and destructive. There was a temporary loss of a protective parent to help modulate her affects.

A BRIEF SAMPLE FROM L. VON SACHER-MASOCH [1870]
VENUS IN FURS

Severin: "I want your power over me to become law; then my life will rest in your hands and I shall have no protection against you. Ah, what delight to depend entirely on your whims, to be constantly at your beck and call! And then—what bliss!—when the goddess shows clemency, the slave will have permission to kiss the lips on which his life and death depend" (p. 163).

Wanda to Severin: ". . . you are no longer my lover, and therefore, I am relieved of all duties and obligations towards you; you must regard my favors as pure benevolence. You can no longer lay claim to any rights, and there are no limits to my power over you. Consider that you are little better now than a dog or an object; you are my thing, the toy that I can break if it gives me a moment of pleasure. You are nothing, I am everything; do you understand?" (p. 164).

The *contract* between them: "Mrs. von Dunajew may not only chastise her slave for the slightest negligence or misdemeanor as and when she wishes but she will also have the right to maltreat him according to her humor or even simply to amuse herself; she is also entitled to kill him if she so wishes; in short, he becomes her absolute property." (fragment, p. 184).

ON THE WAY TO PERVERSE ENACTMENT

Intensity of arousal and connectedness are similar in sexual seductiveness and in sadomasochistic object relations. Intensity substitutes for genuine love and caring. The more that negative feelings in oneself and in the other must be denied, the more need there is for repetitive arousal of the other and of oneself. Erotized repetition not only expresses the pleasure of infantile love, but also attempts active mastery of hostility, loss, narcissistic injury, and homosexuality (Blum, 1973).

Both sexual seductiveness and sadomasochism between parent and child lead to attempts to idealize the intensely exciting encounters. What becomes special for the parent–child couple is their intense, exciting bond. They do what others dare not. The psychology of the exception not only is used as protection against guilt about such transgression but is elaborated more generally to protect against hostile aggression (Coen, in press). Superego corruption is fostered between parent and child by denial of complicity in such seductive and sadomasochistic transgressions (cf. Blum, 1973). Specialness, entitlement, the ability to seduce and arouse others are all used to defend against superego criticism for one's destructiveness. Such patients have, by and large, not completed the task of superego integration; they remain with harsh, personified, poorly integrated superego forerunners. During childhood, the ordinary rules and expectations did not apply. At times, a parent could do as she or he wanted regardless of the consequences for the child. Reality was not reasonably assessed and clarified for the child by the parent. Reality could be what such a needy parent deemed it to be. Such children had to struggle between times of great indulgence and attention, with sexual and sadomasochistic arousal and times of feeling ignored, neglected, abandoned by the parent, who could not remain appropriately emotionally involved with the child. Of course, such children will seek to re-engage the parent in whatever ways work (sexual seductiveness or sadomasochistic provocation). They will have little reason to assess themselves according to ordinary reality. They will seek to share in the parent's narcissistic specialness as expressed in special indulgence, stimulation, excitement, and even special shared guilt. Here they can again feel grandiose rather than worthless. Erotized or sadomasochistic repetition seeks to recapture such specialness.

One aspect of what is exciting is the sense of what is ordinarily forbidden, what should not be, which is transgressed: incestuous, exploitative, inappropriate, hurtful, infantile, regressive. The excitement itself, and excited repetition, serve to ward off guilt at awareness of what one should not do. Immersion in the excitement and idealization of the forbidden and wrongful behavior are focused to distract from more realistic, guilty self-assessment. Sadomasochistic excitement, like sexual seductiveness, involves similarly entering into dangerous and forbidden territory. The masochistic patient gives in to regressive wishes to escape from autonomy by becoming embroiled with another in hostile aggressive and erotic contact. This stirs up, and mixes up, who is who in an exciting and consuming surrender. The knowledge that this behavior is wrong, destructive to oneself and to the other, and infantile and regressive adds to the excitement. The patient disclaims responsibility for his behavior. He plays the sadomasochistic game with the analyst, who is to try to stop him—or become so frustrated, angry, hopeless, defeated that he is unable to help the patient. What is dissociated here is the patient's difficulty with autonomy and self-regulation and acknowledgment of the serious destructiveness embedded within such sadomasochistic game playing. The excitement of the game denies the seriousness of the intended destructiveness.

Sexual seductiveness and sadomasochism tend to come together in nonperverse masochistic patients once defenses against such awareness have been interpreted. What then becomes exciting is making another person vulnerable, or becoming vulnerable oneself, to control, domination, exploitation, and humiliation through sexual arousal. To arouse and control another through his or her own intense sexual arousal makes the patient feel powerful, an irresistible seducer. Negative qualities in the object and in oneself are warded off by emphasis on one's own magical ability to bring the other to life sexually. For the moment it is as if nothing else matters. This too may repeat childhood patterns of seductiveness in a sadomasochistic relationship with a parent. Exploitation, misuse, and humiliation of the vulnerable one, with associated rage, hurt, and betrayal, are defended against by excited sexualized repetition. Even in such reversal from passive to active, in the initiation of such scenes, the patient clings to the regressive and destructive parent–child relationship. Excited repetition puts off until another day such relinquishment of the parent–child relationship and responsibility for one's own affects.

Sadomasochism, in this sense, is a complex regressive defense against varied dangers of autonomy. It is a kind of running home to what is safe and familiar. One person is to beat and punish another repetitively in order to contain and atone for what is "bad" within oneself. The patient runs away from what frightens him within himself and runs toward his craving for protection against such dangers. To the degree that autonomy (and responsibility for one's own wishes and affects) is frightening, regressive defensive solutions will be sought.

We have not discussed sexuality other than as an excited sadomasochistic capturing or surrender to another. However, we are still not in the area of perversion. Patients may indeed feel driven to arouse, seduce, and conquer in the service of sadomasochistic exploitation, bondage, and domination. Unless this is obligatory for adult sexual functioning, unless there is no other way, this is not structured perversion. The need to enact seductive fantasy with another, who is made to fit one's own fantasies, does move toward perversion.

SADOMASOCHISTIC PERVERSION

The (sadomasochistic) pervert, in contrast to the neurotic, tends to have a sexual fantasy life that is rigid and impoverished. He has only one way to become sexually aroused. Unlike the neurotic, the pervert is relatively unable to resolve conflict solely within fantasy. Hence, the patient's obligatory fantasy must be repetitively enacted so as to validate his needed illusions. We can make a schematic, heuristic division of perverts into higher level and lower level types (see Coen, 1985). The higher level sadomasochistic pervert uses perverse behavior *primarily* to permit sexual functioning and orgasm, as a defense against castration anxiety and oedipal guilt. He attempts by his act to validate his unconscious fantasy (of the phallic woman: signifying that castration does not occur) in order to defend against intense castration anxiety, so as to be able to function sexually. At a lower level, the primary goal of sadomasochistic perversion is not to allow sexual functioning, but to adapt sex to other, earlier, more pressing needs. Here we have sexualization in the service of narcissism, closeness, need satisfaction, defense, repair, adaptation, and the preservation of psychic equilibrium and structure. Of course, the lower level pervert is also enabled to function sexually through his perversion.

The object relations of the higher level sadomasochistic pervert can resemble those of neurotics, except for the focal sector of the concretely perverse defense against castration anxiety and oedipal guilt. The object relations of the lower level pervert are grossly impaired. Typically, there is incomplete self–object differentiation, with extensive use of *projective identification*. The external object is used primarily to satisfy the lower level pervert's needs, with little acknowledgement of the other as a separate person entitled to the satisfaction of his own needs.

Sadomasochistic perversion involves some humiliation or suffering, usually not intense physical pain. For example, the man may be insulted or humiliated by the woman, tied or blindfolded, urinated on, or symbolically dominated. At the highest level, the humiliation or suffering represents a punishment, symbolic of castration but precluding castration, for incestuous wishes and actual sexual functioning. By participating with him, the woman reassures him against castration and is a willing accomplice to his incestuous wishes. She undoes the danger that she will actually castrate him by participating with him and administering a token "punishment" under the patient's absolute control and staging of the performance. Seduction of the castrator, a variant of Loewenstein's (1957) term, "seduction of the aggressor," is an apt way to describe this attempt to change the woman's image from aggressive and threatening into accepting and participating. The woman usually is dressed in "phallic" clothing to further counter castration anxiety. Dangerous qualities in another and in oneself can be changed, easily and magically, by change of clothing, gesture, or appearance. This is theater. To a degree, perverse enactments are "auto-erotism à deux," in Khan's (1979, p. 24) phrase. Perverse practices can be thought of as a form of staged enactment of masturbatory dramas. Other people are assigned parts so that the pervert can authenticate himself, his fantasies, and his defensive transformations.

The patient's control and staging of the performance must be respected by his actress. If the woman steps out of her assigned role, the game is spoiled; for example, if she hits too hard, enjoys her role too much, or functions too autonomously.

The masochistic pervert, more than the neurotic masochist, exploits and clings to erotization and action. For the pervert, action has a magical defensive quality (action "makes it so") involving repetitive reenactment of seductive childhood experiences. The magical quality of action for the pervert may partly be determined by the fact of childhood seduction or seductionlike experiences. This contributes to the illusion that magically the child's wishes have been actualized. "Magical happenings" may then be used to deal with frustration and painful affects. Confusion between reality and fantasy usually occurs about what has happened and what can happen. This confusion protects against the negative affects and frightening perceptions associated with childhood sexual overstimulation (Shengold, 1963, 1967, 1971, 1974; Blum, 1973). Masturbation and seduction of others become vehicles for demonstrating one's magical powers to affect oneself and others. Such illusions of magical ability protect against the felt helplessness and inadequacy that usually occurs with childhood seduction experiences. This concept of the magic of action complements the view that repetition of the seductive gratifications is desired and attempts to master and repair the associated traumatic affects of overstimulation, rage, and helplessness.

We are emphasizing how childhood seductive experiences are erotized and repeated for defense and repair. Most (not all) psychoanalytic authors agree about the role of maternal seductiveness in the childhood of the future pervert. Typically, a depressed mother attempts to defend against her depression, so that neither mother nor child is consciously aware of mother's depression. Mother and child collude to protect themselves from awareness of mother's pathology. The mother is sexually seductive with the child. The child "libidinizes" the body, including the genitals, in response to the deficiency in maternal care. Since such mothers are usually experienced as intrusive, the child tends to regard his own private bodily and fantasy experiences as sacrosanct. Similarly, during analysis premature pressure from the analyst to reveal and explore perverse fantasy will heighten the pervert's defensiveness and withdrawal. In the future pervert's childhood, masturbatory reveries aim to preserve and idealize the good aspects of the mother–child relationship apart from his rage at her. These reveries may assist preservation of a part of the self separate from the mother and her moods, to which one does not (fully) surrender. This more autonomous self is validated in the masturbatory reveries.

This model for the development of sexualized defense in perversion involves three central factors: (1) intensely available sensual feelings early in life, far in excess of what is ordinarily experienced; (2) the prominence of sexualized defense in the mother–child relationship; and (3) the usefulness of sexualized defense for mastering large quantities of hostile aggression. The genetic model we have considered here (which of course is only one possibility) is the mother's seductive overstimulation of the child when it is associated with her relative neglect of his emotional needs. This situation creates an intrapsychic setting in which sexual drive pressure and the ego's attempts to master it are then available for further use by the ego to express and master other conflicts. The child uses the predominantly available mode of relating with mother in order to compensate for her relative emotional unavailability, in the hope of reviving her flagging interest in him. The child himself may already at a very early age have turned to sexual stimulation to cope with felt trauma and neglect (Greenacre, 1960). Identification with the mother's defense of sexualization combines with the child's needs for defense. The need to master sexual overstimulation by active repetition and recreation leads to a model in which multiple other defensive functions can be simultaneously served. The preponderant drive derivatives, affects, early defensive patterns, and identifications are drawn upon for vital defensive and adaptive needs. Not only sexuality, but also an unusually large quantity of aggression from early frustration, deprivation, and teasing overstimulation must be managed.

Mother and child collude in their mutually shared pleasure in, and defensive focus on, seductive bodily closeness, in contrast to other forms of relating. The typical mother is depressed (or otherwise withdrawn or detached), with substantial impairment of her ability to relate to the child as a unique, autonomous being. The depressed mother comes to life with seductive bodily stimulation, which she seeks from her child. Sexual seductiveness eventually becomes the child's predominant mode for relating to others and for expressing his intense object hunger. During the future pervert's childhood, sexualized defense becomes elaborated in masturbation and masturbation fantasy. In his masturbatory world, he attempts to comfort and soothe himself, separate and apart from the insufficiently available and inappropriately responsive mother. He idealizes his masturbatory pleasures and his self-sufficiency and omnipotence in creating them on his own. Masturbation contributes to the magic of action. Illusions of omnipotence are enhanced by the masturbator's magical manipulation of his own genitals.

We have emphasized here sexualized defense against rage, helplessness, depression, and overstimulation. Imagine that masturbation fantasy is played out on a kind of stage, on which the images of self and object(s) to be enacted are projected. As the masturbator feels and watches his own sexual sensations and increasing arousal, the role of illusion is enhanced by the continual change in body image, sensations, and state of consciousness. The fantasied relationship between self and others becomes more vivid, more real (see Nydes, 1950). As the masturbator experiences and observes his drama, he can deny negative, dangerous aspects of himself and of his object, or defensively interchange aspects of self and object. The object's passionate responsiveness assuages his fears of loss or destruction. Superego components are also brought into the masturbatory game, allowing for temporary illusory transformation. At the scene's finale, transformed self- and object images are reintrojected by vision and touch. A make-believe ceremony, a ritualized masturbatory game, has disguised and eased a dangerously aggressive confrontation between self and other. This is the training ground for perverse seductive enactments. The pervert, unable to master his conflicts within his own mind, will need to enact his sexualized fantasy. The patient with masochistic character disorder is relatively better able to handle conflict intrapsychically. This is the meaning of perversion as the enactment of masturbatory fantasy.

The pervert oscillates between viewing his activities as literal, concrete, real, and as make-believe, only a game, play-acting. The make-believe ceremony, the ritualized enacted masturbatory game disguises and eases a dangerously aggressive confrontation between self and other. Ritualized repetition may aim to master specific intense childhood trauma by concrete images and introjection (in visual, tactile, and olfactory ways). The pervert's need for action also involves severe internal psychic deficiency with the need for magical incorporation; defense against sadism and aggression, concretely demonstrating that nothing has been destroyed; definition of bodily boundaries by use of a phallic integrating agent. For the lower level pervert, omnipotent control of the external object is intended to prevent frustration or the evocation of guilt when the pervert is sadistically attacked. The lower level pervert maintains control, induces surrender in the partner, and then identifies vicariously with him. The greater the danger of sadistic destruction or passive surrender, the more ritualization or distance from live human beings may be required. Instead of genuine human connectedness through the sexual experience, excitement and intensity are focused on. The partner is used to actualize one's needed fantasies, making them more real, less illusory. Nevertheless, these games remain illusory because no matter how much the pervert transforms his object into his unconscious images, he is not psychotic; the differentiation between the other and his assigned role is preserved.

THE PERVERSITY OF OBJECT RELATIONS IN SADOMASOCHISM

Note the similarity in the object relations of lower level perverts with patients overtly involved in sadomasochistic object relations. The other person is, to a degree, to be used for the patient's imperative needs; a partial denial of his separate identity allows for his illusory transformation into a needed fantasy object. Dehumanization, degradation to the status of part-object, projective identification, omnipotent manipulation, and exploitation occur in both. The other person is to be controlled within one's own subjective world, denied his separateness and autonomy. Of course, as illustrated throughout this volume, masochism is seen at every level of psychic integration and object relations. Patients for whom sadomasochistic excitement becomes irresistible tend to resemble perverts in what they need from their partners, in the illusory games they play, and in their relatively perverse misuse of others. Sexual, sadomasochistic, and perverse excitement are similar in the promise of what will occur with one's partner. The patient is beckoned by something forbidden, something that should not happen, something dangerous, appealing, leading backwards. He returns to the exciting, special games of yesterday; once again he is embroiled in a dangerous, destructive relationship with an enticing, exploitative parent. If he can keep repeating the excitement that beckons him, then he need not face the horrors to which he has made himself a party. Excited, endless repetition avoids the truth of abuse, neglect, misuse, and exploitation—destructiveness in the parent and destructiveness and complicity in oneself.

SUMMARY

Certain similarities in defense and adaptation are described between sadomasochistic object relations and sadomasochistic perversion. Excitement, common to both, involves the ability to induce intense affective responses in another person against the other person's will; to feel in control, dominant, able to make another feel bad. Sadomasochistic excitement involves entering into what is ordinarily dangerous and forbidden: incestuous, exploitative, inappropriate, hurtful, infantile, regressive. The excitement is enhanced by the knowledge that it is wrong, destructive to oneself and the other, to give into regressive wishes to escape from autonomy by becoming embroiled with another in hostile, erotic contact. Excited, intense feelings and experiences substitute for genuine love and caring and defend against negative feelings in oneself and in the other. This is the background for erotized repetition.

I have suggested that once defenses against such acknowledgement have been interpreted, patients with masochistic character disorder are often found to have a sadomasochistic infiltration of their sexuality. Sexual seductiveness, sexualization, and sadomasochism are commonly linked genetically and dynamically, especially in relation to defense against hostile aggression. Similarities in the object relations of certain patients with sadomasochistic character disorder and sadomasochistic perversion are described. Perverse misuse of others occurs; a partial denial of the separate identity of the other allows for illusory transformation into a needed fantasy object.

REFERENCES

Bak, R. (1974), Distortions of the concept of fetishism. *The Psychoanlytic Study of the Child*, 29:191–214. New Haven: Yale University Press.
Blum, H. (1973), The concept of erotized transference. *J. Amer. Psychoanal. Assn.*, 21:61–76.
Bradlow, P. A., & Coen, S. J. (1984), Mirror masturbation. *Psychoanal. Quart.*, 43:267–285.
Coen, S. J. (1981), Sexualization as a predominant mode of defense. *J. Amer. Psychoanal. Assn.*, 29:893–920.
——— (1985), Perversion as a solution to intrapsychic conflict. *J. Amer. Psychoanal. Assn.*, 33 (Supp.):17–57.

———— (in press), Superego aspects of entitlement (in rigid characters). *J. Amer. Psychoanal. Assn.*

Freud, S. (1905), Three essays on the theory of sexuality. *Standard Edition*, 7:135–243. London: Hogarth Press, 1953.

Greenacre, P. (1960), *Emotional Growth*, Vol. 1. New York: International Universities Press, 1971.

Grossman, W. I. (1986), Notes on masochism: A discussion of the history and development of a psychoanalytic concept. *Psychoanal. Quart.*, 55:379–413.

Khan, M.M.R. (1979), *Alienation in Perversions*. New York: International Universities Press.

Loewenstein, R. M. (1957), A contribution to the psychoanalytic theory of masochism. *J. Amer. Psychoanal. Assn.*, 5:197–234.

Maleson, F. G. (1984), The multiple meanings of masochism in psychoanalytic discourse. *J. Amer. Psychoanal. Assn.*, 32:325–356.

Nydes, J. (1950), The magical experience of the masturbation fantasy. *Amer. J. Psychother.*, 4:303–310.

Sacher-Masoch, L. von [1870], *Sacher-Masoch, An Interpretation by Gilles Deleuze, together with the entire text of "Venus in Furs,"* trans. J. M. McNeil. London: Faber & Faber, 1971.

Shapiro, D. (1981), *Autonomy and Rigid Character*. New York: Basic Books.

Shengold, L. (1963), The parent as sphinx. *J. Amer. Psychoan. Assn.*, 11:725–741.

———— (1967), The effects of overstimulation: Rat people. *Internat. J. Psycho-Anal.*, 48:403–415.

———— (1971), More about rats and rat people. *Internat. J. Psycho-Anal.*, 52:277–288.

———— (1974). The metaphor of the mirror. *J. Amer. Psychoan. Assn.*, 22:97–115.

Stoller, R. J. (1976), Sexual excitement. *Arch. Gen. Psychiat.*, 33:899–909.

4 / Clinical Dimensions of Masochism

Otto F. Kernberg

LAPLANCE AND PONTALIS (1973) PROVIDE the briefest and, in my view, most satisfactory definition of masochism in the psychoanalytic literature.

> . . . sexual perversion in which satisfaction is tied to the suffering or humiliation undergone by the subject.
>
> Freud extends the notion of masochism beyond the perversion as described by sexologists. In the first place, he identifies masochistic elements in numerous types of sexual behaviour and sees rudiments of masochism in infantile sexuality. Secondly, he describes derivative forms, notably 'moral masochism', where the subject, as a result of an unconscious sense of guilt, seeks out the position of victim without any sexual pleasure being directly involved [p. 244].

I agree that masochism cannot be understood without simultaneous analysis of the vicissitudes of both libidinal and aggressive strivings, superego development and pathology, levels of ego organization and pathology of internalized object relations, and the extent to which normal or pathological narcissistic functions predominate (Grossman, 1986). But because of the universality of masochistic behaviors and conflicts, it is not always easy to know when masochism belongs to the field of psychopathology.

In what follows, I propose a general classification of masochistic psychopathology and describe relations between this clinical domain and other types of psychopathology that might be confused with it. My main objective is to provide an outline of masochistic pathology relevant for diagnostic, prognostic, and treatment considerations. The classification I am proposing is based on the severity of the psychopathology.

Modified version of a paper originally published in the *Journal of the American Psychoanalytic Association*, Vol. 36, No. 4, 1987.

MASOCHISTIC CHARACTER PATHOLOGY

"Normal" Masochism

Insofar as the price paid for the integration of normal superego functions is the disposition to develop unconscious guilt feelings when repressed infantile drive derivatives are activated, a proneness to minor self-defeating behaviors—for example, in response to what is unconsciously perceived as oedipal triumph—is fairly universal. Also ubiquitous are obsessive behaviors that unconsciously express magical reassurance against threatened activation of infantile prohibitions and their clinical correlates, such as characterological inhibitions and, in simple terms, restrictions of a full enjoyment of life. The tendency for realistic self-criticism to expand into a generally depressive mood is another manifestation of such self-defeating superego pressures (Jacobson, 1964). In short, minor manifestations of "moral masochism" are an almost unavoidable correlate of normal integration of superego functions. The sublimatory capacity to endure pain as a price (by means of hard work) for future success or achievement also has an underpinning in this generally normal masochistic predisposition.

In the sexual realm, the normal preservation of polymorphous "perverse" infantile sexuality should permit sexual arousal with masochistic and sadomasochistic fantasies and experiences. As I have stressed in earlier work (1985a), the sadomasochistic dimension of infantile sexuality is of particular importance in maintaining the normal equilibrium between libidinal and aggressive strivings because it represents a primitive form of synthesis between love and hatred. Sexual excitement and pain become one, and therefore to give or receive aggression in the form of painful stimuli may also signify to give or receive love in the form of erotic stimulation. It is this condensation of physical pleasure and pain that, by means of transformational processes that are still unexplored, leads to the predisposition to experience a condensation of psychological pleasure and pain when superego-determined accusations and attacks are directed against the self.

The Depressive-Masochistic Personality Disorder

This constellation of pathological character traits constitutes, together with the obsessive-compulsive personality disorder and the hysterical personality disorder, one of the three most frequent personality disorders of "high-level" or "neurotic" character pathology ("neurotic personality organization": Kernberg, 1984). All these personality disorders present with a well-integrated ego identity; they show nonspecific manifestations of ego strength (good anxiety tolerance, impulse control, and sublimatory functioning), and they also present an excessively severe but well-integrated superego. All these patients are also able to establish well-differentiated object relations in depth.

The depressive-masochistic personality disorder proper presents three dominant types of behavior (Kernberg, 1984): (1) traits reflecting excessively severe superego functioning; (2) traits reflecting over-dependency on support, love, and acceptance from others; and (3) traits reflecting difficulties in the expression of aggression.

(1) The "superego" features of the depressive-masochistic personality are reflected in a tendency to be excessively serious, responsible, and concerned about work performance and responsibilities. These patients have a somber quality and are overconscientious. They may lack a sense of humor. They are highly reliable and dependable and tend to judge themselves harshly and to set extremely high standards for themselves. They also may occasionally, in contrast to their usually considerate, tactful, and concerned behavior, be harsh in their judgment of others, a harshness that may take the form of "righteous indignation." When these patients do not live up to their own high standards and expectations, they may become depressed. In more severe cases, excessive demands on themselves are matched by their tendency to unconsciously put themselves into circumstances that will induce suffering or exploitation, thus unconsciously creating or perpetuating an external reality that will justify their sense of being mistreated, demeaned, or humiliated.

(2) The traits that reflect overdependency on support, love, and acceptance from others also reveal, on psychoanalytic exploration, a tendency to excessive guilt feelings toward others because of unconscious ambivalence toward loved and needed objects, and an excessive reaction of frustration when their expectations are not met. These patients show an abnormal vulnerability to being disappointed by others, and they may go out of their way to obtain sympathy and love. In contrast to the narcissistic personality, who is overdependent on external admiration without responding internally with love and gratitude, the depressive-masochistic personality typically is able to respond deeply with love and to be grateful. Their sense of being rejected and mistreated as a reaction to relatively minor slights may lead them to unconscious behaviors geared to making the objects of their love feel guilty. Vicious cycles oof excessive demandingness, feelings of rejection, an unconscious tendency to make others feel guilty, and consequent actual rejection from others may spiral into

severe problems in intimate relations and also trigger depression connected to loss of love.

(3) The "faulty metabolism" of aggression shows in the tendency of these patients to become depressed under conditions that would normally produce anger or rage. In addition, unconscious guilt over anger expressed to others may further complicate their interpersonal relations, adding to the vicious cycles described before: a tendency toward "justified" attacks on those they need and feel rejected by, followed by depression and overly apologetic, submissive, or compliant behavior, only to be followed by a second wave of anger over the way they are treated and their own submissiveness.

All these dominant traits of the depressive-masochistic disorder correspond to the description of "moral masochism" in the psychoanalytic literature (Freud, 1916, 1919, 1924; Fenichel, 1945; Berliner, 1958; Brenner, 1959; Laughlin, 1967; Gross, 1981; Asch, 1985). Typically, the corresponding unconscious dynamics center on excessive superego pressures derived from infantile, particularly oedipal, conflicts and may also express themselves in an unconscious, defensive regression to preoedipal dynamics, and in general masochistic behaviors that are at a considerable distance from their infantile sexual conflicts. In other cases, however, unconscious sexual conflicts are closely related to the masochistic behaviors, so that it is particularly in the sexual realm that they manifest self-punitive behaviors as a reflection of unconscious prohibitions against oedipal impulses. These patients may tolerate a satisfactory sexual experience only when it is carried out under conditions of objective or symbolic suffering, and the depressive-masochistic personality structure may be accompanied by an actual masochistic perversion at a neurotic level. In any event, it is patients with this personality structure who most frequently present masochistic masturbation fantasies and masochistic sexual behaviors without a masochistic perversion per se. The masochistic behaviors that directly express unconscious guilt over oedipal impulses link the depressive-masochistic and the hysterical personality disorders (Kernberg, 1985b).

Sadomasochistic Personality Disorder

These patients typically show alternating masochistic and sadistic behavior toward the same object. I am not referring here to the person who submits to those above him in command and tyrannizes those who are beneath him, a social behavior compatible with various pathological character constellations. Here, the self-demeaning, self-debasing, self-humiliating behaviors alternate with sadistic attacks on the very same objects these patients feel they need and are deeply involved with.

Sadomasochistic personalities usually present borderline personality organization, with severe identity difffusion, nonspecific manifestations of ego weakness (lack of anxiety tolerance, of impulse control, and of sublimatory channeling), predominance of part-object relationships, and prevalence of primitive defensive mechanisms (splitting, projective identification, denial, primitive idealization, omnipotent control, and devaluation). Within the chaos of all their object relations, the intensification of chaotic interactions with those whom they are most intimately involved with stands out. These patients usually experience themselves as the victims of others' aggression, bitterly complain about the mistreatment, and adamantly justify their own aggressions toward those whom they are dependent on. The "help-rejecting complainer" (Frank, Margolin, Nash, Stone, Varon, and Ascher, 1952) is typical of this character; the severity of these patients' interpersonal and social difficulties may lead to chronic failure at work, in social life, and in intimate relations.

In contrast to the impulsive, chaotic, arrogant, and devaluative narcissistic personality functioning on an overt borderline level, the sadomasochistic personality has much more capacity for investment in depth in relations with others; he shows dependency and clinging in contrast to the aloofness of the narcissistic personality.

The dynamic features of these cases include both severe oedipal and preoedipal conflicts, particularly an internal dependency on primitive maternal images experienced as sadistic, dishonest, and controlling; a dangerous primitive mother exacerbates oedipal fears and condenses unconscious oedipal and preoedipal issues in these patients' behaviors much more than occurs with preoedipal regression of patients with depressive-masochistic personality and essentially oedipal dynamics.

One male patient experienced severe feelings of insecurity and inferiority toward his analyst while berating him continuously, insulting him while yet feeling depreciated and insulted by the analyst. In his relations with girlfriends, he was both extremely fearful that they might drop him for more attractive men and extremely demanding of them for their time and attention; his separations from girlfriends were followed by pathological mourning, with intense paranoid reactions alternating with a depressive sense of having been abandoned.

The lack of integration of superego functions, the reprojection of primitive superego precursors in the form of paranoid traits, and the tolerance of contradictory behaviors—in fact, the rationalization of their aggressive behaviors—all illustrate the corruption of superego functions in these patients, in marked contrast to the rigid superego integration of the depressive-masochistic personality disorder.

Primitive Self-Destructiveness and Self-Mutilation

In earlier work (1975) I described a group of patients who tend to discharge aggression indiscriminately toward the outside or toward their own body. These are patients with manifest self-destructive behavior and, as uncovered in psychoanalytic exploration, with severe lack of superego integration, a remarkable absence of the capacity for experiencing guilt, and the general characteristics of borderline personality organization. The most typical examples are patients who obtain nonspecific relief of anxiety by cutting themselves or some other form of self-mutilation, or by impulsive suicidal gestures carried out with great rage and almost no depression.

These patients fall into three groups (Kernberg, 1984):

(a) The first type includes patients with predominantly histrionic or infantile personality disorder, the type that also corresponds quite closely to the descriptive disorder of borderline personality disorder in DSM-III (APA, 1980). Here self-mutilating behavior, and/or suicide gestures emerge at times of intense rage attacks or rage mixed with temporary flare-ups of depression. The function of this behavior is frequently an unconscious effort to reestablish control over the environment by evoking guilt feeling in others—when, for example, a relationship with a sexual partner breaks up or when parents strongly oppose the patient's wishes.

(b) A severer type of chronic self-mutilating behavior and/or chronic suicidal tendencies can be seen in patients with "malignant narcissism" (Kernberg, 1984). These are patients with borderline personality organization and a narcissistic personality disorder functioning on an overt borderline level—that is, with a general lack of impulse control, anxiety tolerance, or sublimatory channeling. In contrast to the group mentioned earlier, these patients do not show intense dependency or clinging behavior and are rather aloof from and uninvolved with others. Their attacks of rage and related self-destructive or self-mutilating behavior occurs when their pathological grandiosity is challenged and they experience a traumatic sense of humiliation or defeat. In these cases, the self-destructive behavior often occurs along with overtly sadistic behavior. Their grandiosity is fulfilled by their feeling of triumph over the fear of pain and death and their "superiority" over all those who are shocked and chagrined by their behavior.

(c) A third type of chronic self-mutilating and related suicidal behavior is found in certain atypical, chronically psychotic conditions that mimic borderline pathology. These patients' history of bizarre suicide attempts marked by unusual degrees of cruelty or highly idiosyncratic features may alert the clinician to the possibility of an underlying psychotic syndrome.

Jointly all these patients illustrate a most primitive type of self-destructiveness, with conscious or unconscious pleasure connected with the pain they inflict on themselves; they display a severity of aggression directed against themselves that is neither centered in their superego pathology (an unconscious sense of guilt) nor directly linked with erotic strivings (or, at least, such erotic strivings occupy a very secondary role to that of aggressive impulses). These patients may be considered to illustrate clinically a basic level of self-destructiveness that is dependent on the intensity of primitive aggression, primitivization of all intrapsychic structures, lack of superego development, and a recruitment of libidinal and erotic strivings in the service of aggression. All these self-destructive and self-mutilating patients derive a sense of power from their diffuse destructiveness, a triumphant sense of autonomy, of lack of need of others; they show what are clinically the most blatant efforts to destroy love and relatedness, gratitude and compassion, in themselves and in others. It is questionable whether this group of patients still may be considered as part of masochistic psychopathology in a strict sense: unconscious guilt as well as erotization of pain are usually absent.

In more general terms, looking at this entire group of masochistic character pathology, we might say that as we move toward the severer pole of this spectrum, we find a gradual decrease of the integration of the superego and of the participation of the superego in the consolidation of masochistic pathology and an increase of primitive and severe aggression, together with primitivization of object relationships and defensive operations. Erotism also fades out at this polarity of the masochistic spectrum.

THE SYNDROMES OF PATHOLOGICAL INFATUATION

Chasseguet-Smirgel (1985), in disagreeing with Freud (1921, pp. 111–16) that in the act of falling in love the ego is depleted of libidinal cathexes (which are invested in the love object as a replacement of the ego ideal), points to the enrichment of libidinal investment of the self of the person in love. Particularly under normal circumstances, either a love object is abandoned in a process of mourning when it does not reciprocate the subject's love, or, when love is consolidated in a reciprocal relationship, this very reciprocity enhances the self-esteem of the lovers. The difference between normal falling in love and a masochistic pattern of falling in love is precisely that masochistic personalities may be irresistibly attracted to an object who does not respond to their love. In fact, the unconscious selection of an object who is clearly unable or unwilling to respond to love characterizes masochistic infatuations and constitutes a "high level" of this kind of pathology.

It is important to differentiate such impossible love affairs from a masochistic sexual perversion, in which a love object provides sexual gratification in the context of physical pain, debasement, and/or humiliation. Although both patterns may coincide, more often they do not. The description of sexual masochism by Sacher-Masoch (1881) in *Venus in Furs* corresponds to the writer's relation with his first wife and, later, with his second wife, typically perverse practices in the context of a stable relationship with a loved object.

To sacrifice oneself and all interests in life for someone who does not reciprocate, dramatically illustrated in Heinrich Mann's novel *The Blue Angel* of 1932, may constitute a major, singular aspect of a personality structure that in other respects does not fulfill the characteristics of the depresssive-masochistic personality disorder. To the contrary, the dramatic self-sacrifice, the abandonment of all previous commitments and engagements, the ease with which an entire life pattern seems to be brushed aside in the pursuit of the idealized, unavailable love object may impress the clinician as presenting almost narcissistic features—the neglect and sacrifice of all others except the love object, the total self involvement of the afflicted individual, the apparent lack of commitment to preestablished values and engagements. In fact, the patient presenting such pathological infatuations manifests a sense of narcissistic gratification and fulfillment in the enslavement to an unavailable object. There is an unmistakable pride in the image of oneself as the greatest sufferer on earth, dynamically related to the narcissistic gratification of being "the *greatest* sinner" or "the *worst* victim."

At this level of pathological infatuation, the love of the unavailable object indeed represents submission to the ego-ideal aspects of the superego that were projected onto the object, and the painful and unsatisfactory love fills the individual with pride and emotional intensity. This constellation may also be present in patients with hysterical personality structure, whose masochistic involvement with unavailable love objects is the price paid for the unconscious oedipal meanings of all sexual interests, as, for example, the woman who can fall in love only with men who mistreat her. In other cases, it is not an unavailable love object but a clearly sadistic one who has to be chosen.

The arrogant rejection of all those who would interpose themselves between the patient and his or her self-sacrificing love affair may impress the observer as narcissistic, but, in my view, it reflects normal infantile and not pathological narcissism. The masochistic patient's sense of superiority ("I am the greatest sufferer of the world") refers to the specific area of suffering, but not to all other areas of the patients' life.

One female patient, for example, maintained an unsatisfactory relationship with a sadistic, largely unavailable man and at the same time was able to maintain stable relations in depth with other friends and social acquaintances, as well as commitments to her work and family and cultural interests. In the transference, her critical and belittling behavior toward any analytic effort to point to the self-demeaning aspects of the relation with this man corresponded, at a deeper level, to her effort to maintain the psychoanalytic relationship as unsatisfactory because of unconscious guilt feelings over oedipal longings for the analyst.

At a second, severer level of pathological infatuation, the opposite development takes place, namely, the severely masochistic pursuit of an impossible love relation while all the patient's other object relations are narcissistic. For example, one patient, a young lady of considerable charm and beauty, mercilessly denigrated and devaluated men and was interested only in pursuing a man who was physically attractive, socially prestigious, wealthy, or powerful, attributes she hoped to acquire for herself through the man. Rejection from such a man would trigger deep depression in her, suicidal attempts, and denial that he had rejected her. She even went so far as to deny his lack of interest by erroneously interpreting, over a period of many months, any conventional friendliness from him as a sign that their relationship had a future.

Not surprisingly, when any man did reciprocate the patient's love, within weeks she was devaluating him as she had devaluated all the other men in her life. In fact, the growing awareness of this pattern led her to search for even more unavailable men and to set up, unconsciously, a situation in which she would be rejected, so that her investment in the "ideal man" would continue unchallenged. In all her other object relations she presented typical features of a narcissistic personality disorder.

Here we find the projection not of a normal ego ideal onto the unavailable love object but of a pathological grandiose self, with an effort to consolidate a relationship that unconsciously would confirm the stability of the patient's own grandiosity. On analytic exploration, the masochistic love affairs of narcissistic personalities may represent an unconscious effort to consolidate a symbolic integration within the grandiose self of the characteristics of both sexes by means of establishing a symbiotic unit with the idealized object.

In these latter cases the relation to the idealized love object typically reflects a condensation of oedipal and preoedipal issues, the idealized positive oedipal love object, and the superimposed sadistic yet needed preoedipal love object as well. Cooper (this volume) has drawn our attention to the combination in clinical practice of narcissistic and masochistic character features. Although I disagree with his proposal that these two character constellations correspond to basically one type of character pathology and I think he underestimates the differences between normal infantile and pathological narcissism in these patients, I do believe the syndrome of pathological infatuation requires a careful evaluation of both its masochistic and narcissistic features.

MASOCHISTIC SEXUAL BEHAVIOR AND PERVERSION

Masochism as a sexual perversion is characterized by the restrictive, obligatory enactment of masochistic behavior to achieve sexual excitement and orgasm (Freud, 1905; Laplanche and Pontalis, 1973). Masochistic behavior may include the need for experiencing physical pain, emotional suffering, self-debasement, and/or humiliation. There are levels of severity of the sexual perversion that parallel the levels of severity of masochistic character pathology already referred to.

MASOCHISTIC PERVERSION AT A NEUROTIC LEVEL OF PERSONALITY ORGANIZATION

Sexual masochism at this level typically takes the form of a "scenario" enacted in the context of an object relation that is experienced as safe. Typical unconscious dynamics centering on oedipal conflicts include the need to deny castration anxiety and to assuage a cruel superego in order to obtain sexual gratification that has incestuous meanings. These patients' unconscious scenarios also include the enactment of conflictual identifications with the other sex and the identification with a punishing, sadistic incestuous object. The "as if" quality of the sexual scenario, its play-acting qualities, are common to all perversions at the level of neurotic personality organization (Kernberg, 1985a). The sexual perversion may include symbolic enactment of primal scene experiences, such as the oedipal triangle in the form of a *ménage a trois*, in which the masochistic subject is forced to witness sexual relations between his love object and a rival as a precondition for sexual intercourse and gratification.

Masochistic perversion usually but not necessarily involves a partner. There are masochistic forms of masturbation in which the individual ties himself up and watches himself in a mirror while experiencing pain as a precondition for orgasm, and masturbation fantasies may have an obligatory masochistic quality. At a deeper level, of course, the presence or absence of an object is less important than the fact that, in my view, all sexual behavior implies an object relation; the manifest characteristics are less important than the conscious and unconscious fantasies that reflect the obligatory structure of the perversion. Usually the perverse scenario is spelled out in great detail by the individual himself, and the repetitive and strict enactment of that scenario is a source of powerful reassurance against unconscious anxieties as well as a precondition for sexual pleasure and the capacity to achieve orgasm.

SEXUAL MASOCHISM WITH SEVERELY SELF-DESTRUCTIVE AND/OR OTHER REGRESSIVE FEATURES

In contrast to the typically circumscribed masochistic scenario that is part of a containing or protective object relation, has a play-acting quality, and corresponds to a neurotic personality organization, are situations that seem devoid of such safety features and have an open-ended quality of danger that may lead to mutilation, self-mutilation, and even accidental death. These masochistic situations are found in patients with borderline personality organization.

One patient with a masochistic homosexual perversion demanded being tied up by men he met casually in bars frequented by sadomasochists. He provoked these men into serious fights in which he was physically hurt. On several occasions he had been threatened at gunpoint and robbed while engaging in such casual sexual encounters. This patient presented a narcissistic personality with overtly borderline features.

Another patient, a woman in her early twenties, was able to experience sexual excitement only when prostituting herself to much older men or to black men in dangerous neighborhoods (the patient was white and upper middle class). This woman was aware that the potential danger to her life was one source of excitement in such encounters. She also suffered from a narcissistic personality with infantile and masochistic features.

A third patient was able to achieve orgasm only if her arms were seriously twisted during intercourse so that she suffered exquisite pain and fear of a dislocation or fracture; she also prostituted herself at the request of her sadistic (and antisocial) boyfriend. This patient presented masochistic and infantile features and a borderline personality organization.

In these and similar cases the sexual perversion breaks out of the "as if," or play-acting, frame and may bring about an authentic threat to the patient's survival; these cases reflect a severe pathology of object relations. In other cases there is no self-mutilating behavior proper, but a bizarre quality of sexual activity in which undisguised anal, urethral, or oral contents color the masochistic pattern, giving it a primitive, pregenital quality. One patient had the following preferred mode of sexual relations with his wife: In order to be able to achieve orgasm through masturbation, he had her sit on a specially constructed toilet that permitted her to defecate on his face while he was watching her. This patient had severely paranoid personality features in addition to a sadomasochistic personality structure.

Another patient's preferred mode of masturbatory gratification was to wade in a local brook in an area so muddy that he sank knee deep in the mud while masturbating in the water. He did this at night in order to avoid being observed by neighbors. This patient also presented borderline personality organization, with paranoid, schizoid, and hypochondriacal personality features and extreme social isolation.

All these cases have in common (1) strong, primitive aggressive impulses; (2) severe pathology of object relations; (3) a predominance of preoedipal conflicts and aims in the sexually masochistic scenario; and (4) lack of integration of superego functions. These patients also revealed confusion of sexual identity, so that both homosexual and heterosexual interactions were part of their sexual life, with the masochistic scenario representing its primary organizing feature. In my view, these cases illustrate, at the level of severely regressive sexual masochistic perversion, a general deterioration of superego structure and object relations and a predominance of primitive aggression, together with the dynamic regression to anal conflicts in which the differentiation of sexes and object relations deteriorate jointly (Chasseguet-Smirgel, 1984; Kernberg, 1986).

Extreme Forms of Self-Mutilation and Self-Sacrifice

The severest level of masochistic sexual perversion can be illustrated by patients who are intent on self-castration as part of a religious ritual or a submission to an idealized, extremely sadistic primitive object. I have not personally seen any of these cases, except patients whose self-mutilating wishes and behavior were part of clearly psychotic pathology. At this level I would also place some borderline patients with self-mutilating behavior that has an erotic quality; for example, patients who bite and swallow their buccal mucosa or their fingernails, or who are engaged in chronic self-mutilation of fingers and toes, or whose masturbatory behavior is linked to self-mutilating damage inflicted on their genitals. The patients I have seen with these characteristics presented the syndrome of malignant narcissism, that is, a narcissistic personality with severely paranoid, antisocial, and ego-syntonic sadistic features (Kernberg, 1984). This group pretty much overlaps the characterologically self-destructive, impulsively suicidal, and/or self-mutilating group mentioned earlier. The major difference resides in the chronic, repetitive, erotized, self-mutilating behavior that impresses one as more insidious and bizarre than the explosive self destructive crises of the group mentioned earlier. The erotization of pain and self-mutilation usually has acquired the meaning of a triumph over life and death, over pain and fear, and, unconsciously, over the entire world of object relations. These patients usually have poor prognosis for psychotherapeutic treatment.

SOME IMPLICATIONS OF THE PROPOSED CLINICAL GROUPING OF MASOCHISTIC SYNDROMES

The description of clinical constellations related to masochism points to the broad spectrum of pathology that may rightly be classified under this heading and to the various structural and psychodynamic preconditions that codetermine the clinical features and the severity of each of these syndromes.

One major and obvious dimension is the universality of sexual masochistic features as part of the sexual life at all levels of normality and pathology, a point I have stressed in earlier work (Kernberg, 1985a, 1986). The relation between erotic masochism and aggression, both in their intimate connection in sadomasochistic fantasies and behavior and in the crucial function of the severity of aggression in codetermining the clinical form of masochism, points to a basic dynamic of instinctual conflicts at all levels of psychopathology: the mutual interplay and recruitment of libidinal and aggressive features.

At milder levels of masochism, aggression is recruited in the service of erotism; at severer levels of masochism, erotism is recruited in the service of aggression; at the severest level of masochism, erotism fades out altogether and leaves the field to what seems to be an almost pure culture of aggression.

The quality and degree of superego integration appears as an additional central organizing aspect of masochism, not only in the gradual transformation of erotic masochism into moral masochism, but in providing a frame for both erotic and moral masochism that clearly differentiates higher level masochistic pathology with good superego integration from lower level syndromes with severe superego pathology.

The general level of ego organization, whether borderline or neurotic, colors both the quality of object relations that constitute the matrix for masochistic fantasies and behavior and the extent to which sexual masochism may be contained within an integrated love relation.

Finally, the consolidation of a pathological grandiose self as part of a narcissistic personality structure determines idealization processes completely different from those of normal narcissistic functioning in the context of an integrated tripartite intrapsychic structure. Erotic idealization that reflects the projection of the ego ideal produces results very different from erotic idealization that reflects the projection of a pathological grandiose self.

In short, ego organization, object relations, superego development, narcissistic organization, and the extent of integration of polymorphous perverse infantile sexuality codetermine the level and clinical features of masochistic pathology. The psychodynamics of the oedipal constellation, including castration anxiety and incestual conflicts, are central in moral masochism and masochistic perversion in neurotic personality organization; the condensation of these conflicts with pathologically dominant preoedipal conflicts centering around preoedipal aggression are related to the more regressive conditions of all the codeterminants of masochistic syndromes.

The clinical syndromes I have summarized illustrate how, at the extremes of the spectrum, the concept of masochism dissolves into other diagnostic and psychodynamic considerations. Thus, for example, the normal tolerance of pain (in hard work, postponement of gratification, acknowledgment of one's own aggression) as part of sublimatory efforts is no longer masochism in a strict sense; the erotic excitement with milder forms of pain, playful debasement, and humiliation as part of normal sexual interactions contains so many functions and developmental features that the term masochism no longer says anything specific about such behavior. At the other extreme, the self-destructive and self-defeating effects of borderline and psychotic psychopathology may no longer warrant the term masochism either: in such cases, self-destructive aspects may be present, but there is hardly any erotization of pain and even less moral masochism. It is true that Freud (1920, 1924, 1937) linked masochism with the hypothesis of the death instinct, so that, in his view, primary masochism represents the origin of early forms of self-destructiveness; but the equation of masochism and self-destructiveness at the severest levels of psychopathology dilutes the specific meaning of masochism.

Another dimension that limits the boundaries of the concept of masochism is that of normal and pathological narcissism. Masochistic surrender provides narcissistic gratification; the depressive-masochistic personality obtains narcissistic gratifications from the sense that he or she is being unjustly treated and is implicitly morally superior to the object. The self-punitive price paid for sexual gratification or for success or creativity also provides approval from the superego and, by the same token, an increase in self-esteem. Insofar as the normal and the neurotic superegos regulate self-esteem by self-directed approval or criticism, masochistic behavior patterns have important functions in neurotically maintaining self-esteem and, in metapsychological terms, in assuring the ego's narcissistic supplies. But, then, all neurotic character formations have such a narcissistic function, and there is no unique linkage here between masochism and narcissism. The self-idealization in fantasy linked to masochistic infatuations may be considered a particular example of this narcissistic consequence of an underlying masochistic structure.

In contrast, at the severer level of pathological infatuation described, the projection of the pathological grandiose self creates a narcissistic aspiration that has self-defeating qualities and impresses the observer as profoundly masochistic. Yet here the masochism restricted to one object relation is essentially a reflection of narcissistic psychopathology reflected in all the other object relations of the patient and does not have the deeper, specific functions of moral masochism and pleasure with pain.

In earlier work (1984) I described negative therapeutic reactions typically found in patients with severe masochism. I defined negative therapeutic reaction as a worsening of the patient's condition, particularly as reflected in the transference, at times when he is consciously or unconsciously perceiving the therapist as a good object who is attempting to provide him with significant help. I suggested three levels of negative therapeutic reaction: (1) that derived from an unconscious sense of guilt, typical for depressive-masochistic personalities; (2) that derived from the need to destroy what is received from the therapist because of unconscious envy of him, which is typical of narcissistic personalities; and (3) that derived from the need to destroy the therapist as a good object because of the patient's unconscious identification with a primitive, sadistic object who requires submission and suffering as a minimal condition for maintaining any significant object relation.

In light of the findings presented here, I would now restate that the first and mildest level of negative therapeutic reaction, namely, that derived from an unconscious sense of guilt, is indeed typical of depressive-masochistic personality structures and may also emerge in the course of the psychoanalysis of a masochistic perversion at a neurotic level. In contrast, the second and third levels of negative therapeutic reactions are more complexly related to other types of masochistic pathology.

The second level—the negative therapeutic reaction owing to unconscious envy of the therapist—is indeed typical of patients with narcissistic personality structure but may also develop in patients with sadomasochistic personalities whose unconscious sense of guilt over being helped is reinforced by their resentment of the therapist, who is free from the destructive and self-destructive potential that these patients cannot escape from. I therefore suggest that negative therapeutic reaction resulting from unconscious envy is not as specifically linked to narcissistic pathology as I suggested earlier.

The severest types of negative therapeutic reaction linked to the experience of a primary love object as simultaneously a destructive one—so that love can be expressed only as destruction—seem to me an essential dynamic of the severest cases of masochistic pathology I have described, in terms of both diffuse self-destructive behaviors that have characterological implications and primitive sexual masochistic perversions with dangerous—even life-threatening—primitivization of aggression. In earlier work and based on Jacobson's (1964) description of superego development, I (1984) referred to the following "scenario" as responsible for these patients' pathology of object relations and of superego development:

(1) the experience of external objects as omnipotent and cruel; (2) a sense that any good, loving, mutually gratifying relationship with an object is frail, easily destroyed, and, even worse, contains the seeds for attack by the overpowering and cruel object; (3) a sense that total

submission to that object is the only condition for survival and that, therefore, all ties to a good and weak object have to be severed; (4) once identification with the cruel and omnipotent object is achieved, an exhilarating sense of power and enjoyment, of freedom from fear, pain, and dread, and the feeling that the gratification of aggression is the only significant mode of relating to others; and (5) as an alternative, the discovery of an escape route by the adoption of a completely false, cynical, or hypocritical mode of communication, an erasing of all judgment that implies a comparison between good and bad objects, and negation of the importance of any object relation or successful maneuvering in the chaos of all human relations [p. 299].

I have also found Fairbairn's (1943) idea of the setting up of a "moral defense against bad objects" in the form of an intrapsychic transformation of internalized relations with bad primary objects a helpful alternative formulation of this state of affairs. In fact, Jacobson's (1964) description of early levels of superego development and Fairbairn's description of the vicissitudes of the internalization of bad objects have striking correlations—once one goes beyond semantic barriers and leaves aside their basic metapsychological incompatibilities. Let me quote Fairbairn in some detail:

In becoming bad he is really taking upon himself the burden of badness which appears to reside in his objects. By this means he seeks to purge them of their badness; and, in proportion as he succeeds in doing so, he is rewarded by that sense of security which an environment of good objects so characteristically confers. To say that the child takes upon himself the burden of badness which appears to reside in his objects is, of course, the same thing as to say that he internalizes bad objects. The sense of outer security resulting from this process of internalization is, however, liable to be seriously compromised by the resulting presence within him of internalized bad objects. Outer security is thus purchased at the price of inner insecurity; and his ego is henceforth left at the mercy of the band of internal fifth columnists or persecutors, against which defenses have to be, first hastily erected, and later laboriously consolidated [p. 65]. . . . Insofar as the child leans toward his internalized bad objects, he becomes conditionally (i.e. morally) bad vis-a-vis his internalized good objects (i.e. his superego); and, insofar as he resists the appeal of his internalized bad objects, he becomes conditionally (i.e. morally) good vis-a-vis his superego. It is obviously preferable to be conditionally good than conditionally bad; but, in default of conditional goodness, it is preferable to be conditionally bad than unconditionally bad. . . . It is better to be a sinner in a world ruled by God than to live in a world ruled by the Devil. . . . In a world ruled by the Devil the individual may escape the badness of being a sinner; but he is bad because the world around him is bad.

Further, he can have no sense of security and no hope of redemption. The only prospect is one of death and destruction [p. 66].

I realize that these extracts hardly do justice to the complexity of Fairbairn's ideas, but I trust this quotation illustrates an alternative model that attempts to clarify severe, primitive developments in the transference. In any event, the dominance of early sadistic superego precursors, an essential feature of the severest levels of masochistic pathology, has devastating effects on the internalization of object relations. In these patients' internal world, and therefore in their perceptions of their interpersonal reality, one is either extremely powerful and ruthless or one is threatened with being destroyed or exploited. If good object relations are in constant danger of destruction by such malignant forces, they may be devalued because of their implicit weakness. In this way, primitive superego pathology and pathology of internalized object relations reinforce each other. The activation of these sadistic superego precursors in the transferences of the severer types of masochism within the total spectrum explored is reflected in sadomasochistic relations with the analyst that determine the severest types of negative therapeutic reactions. The patient needs the therapist to be bad as a primitive defense against otherwise diffuse and dangerous aggression; but this very badness of the therapist threatens the patient with the inability to receive anything good from him. The analyst's persevering interpretation of this regressive level of transference is of crucial importance in helping patients to overcome severely regressive masochistic psychopathology.

REFERENCES

American Psychiatric Association (1980), *Diagnostic and Statistical Manual of Mental Disorders*. Washington, DC: American Psychiatric Press.
Asch, S. (1985), The masochistic personality. In: *Psychiatry 1*, ed. R. Michels & J. Cavenar. Philadelphia: Lippincott.
Berliner, B. (1958), The role of object relations in moral masochism. *Psychoanal. Quart.*, 27:38–56.
Brenner, C. (1959), The masochistic character: genesis and treatment. *J. Amer. Psychoan. Assn.*, 7:197–266.
Chasseguet-Smirgel, J. (1984), *Creativity and Perversion*. New York: Norton.
——— (1985), *The Ego Ideal: A Psychoanalytic Essay on the Malady of the Ideal*. New York: Norton.
Fairbairn, W. (1943), *An Object-Relations Theory of the Personality*. New York: Basic Books, 1954.
Fenichel, O. (1945), *The Psychoanalytic Theory of Neurosis*. New York: Norton.

Frank, J. D., Margolin, J. Nash, H. T., Stone, A. R., Varon, E., & Ascher, E. (1952), Two behavior patterns in therapeutic groups and their apparent motivation. *Hum. Rel.,* 5:289–317.

Freud, S. (1905), Three essays on the theory of sexuality. *Standard Edition,* 7:125–245. London: Hogarth Press, 1953.

———— (1916), Some character-types met with in psycho-analytic work. *Standard Edition,* 14:309–333. London: Hogarth Press, 1957.

———— (1919), A child is being beaten. *Standard Edition,* 17:175–204. London: Hogarth Press, 1955.

———— (1920), Beyond the pleasure principle. *Standard Edition,* 18:1–64. London: Hogarth Press, 1955.

———— (1921), Group psychology and the analysis of the ego. *Standard Edition,* 18:69–143. London: Hogarth Press, 1955.

———— (1924), The economic problem of masochism. *Standard Edition,* 19:157–170. London: Hogarth Press, 1961.

———— (1937), Analysis terminable and interminable. *Standard Edition,* 23:209–253. London: Hogarth Press, 1964.

Gross, H. (1981), Depressive and sadomasochistic personalities. In: *Personality Disorders: Diagnosis and Management,* ed. J. R. Lion. Baltimore: Williams & Wilkins.

Grossman, W. (1986), Notes on masochism: A discussion of the history and development of a psychoanalytic concept 1. *Psychoanal. Quart.,* 55:379–413.

Jacobson, E. (1964), *The Self and the Object World.* New York: International Universities Press.

Kernberg, O. (1975), *Borderline Conditions and Pathological Narcissism.* New York: Aronson.

———— (1984), *Severe Personality Disorders: Psychotherapeutic Strategies.* New Haven: Yale University Press.

———— (1985a), The relation of borderline personality organization to the perversions. In: *Psychiatrie-Psychanalyse.* Quebec: Gaetan Morin Editeur.

———— (1985b), Hysterical and histrionic personality disorders. In: *Psychiatry 1,* ed. R. Michels & J. Cavenar. Philadelphia: Lippincott.

———— (1986), A conceptual model for male perversion. In: *The Psychology of Men: New Psychoanalytic Perspectives,* ed. G. I. Fogel, F. M. Lane, & R. S. Liebert. New York: Basic Books.

Laughlin, H. (1967), *The Neuroses.* New York: Appleton-Century-Crofts.

Laplanche, J., & Pontalis, J.-B. (1973), *The Language of Psycho-Analysis.* New York: Norton.

Sacher-Masoch, L. (1881), *La Venus de las pieles.* Madrid: Alianza Editorial, 1973.

5 / Those Wrecked by Success

Roy Schafer

IT IS NO EXAGGERATION to assert that every psychoanalytic undertaking is pervaded by phenomena that may be usefully subsumed under the heading "Those Wrecked by Success." This assertion may be made all the more confidently if one takes into account the wreckage associated with the mere anticipation of success and also if one allows that being wrecked may be a matter of degree, as in the case of neurotic mediocrity. Neurotic mediocrity is at issue when, for neurotic reasons, a person, though able to perform adequately, is obviously unable to function up to his or her potential. The treatment process itself is pervaded by this phenomenon. Freud noted long ago the common, if not universal, fear of "getting well," and "getting well" may be classified as a form of success, that is, success as an analysand. We may also classify the negative therapeutic reaction, which in varying degrees also pervades our clinical work, as a variant of being wrecked by analytic success or the prospect of such success. The negative therapeutic reaction (Freud, 1923) is in question whenever an obvious step forward is regularly followed by an intensification of the disturbed functioning being analyzed. And to all this we may add that certain extremely common analytic phenomena, otherwise classified as variants of masochism, are more fully understandable when they are also viewed from the standpoint of the threats and problems posed by success. Consequently, being wrecked by success is a theme that should be of primary interest to analysts, psychotherapists, and all others who try to help people in distress to function more effectively and with less suffering.

Freud (1916) introduced the heading "Those Wrecked by Success." (The other two types he described were "The Exceptions" and "Criminals from a Sense of Guilt.") With respect to those wrecked by

Portions of this paper, in slightly different form, were first published as one section of "The Pursuit of Failure and the Idealization of Unhappiness," *American Psychologist* 39:398–405, 1984. Reprinted here by permission.

success, Freud emphasized particularly the oedipal triumph signified by some forms of worldly success and the guilty self-punishment for this triumph that is signified by the personal and occupational wreckage subsequent to success. It can be shown, however, that the applicability of Freud's idea is far greater than is suggested by his typically direct focus on oedipal dynamics, even though one can only be impressed by the interpretive success of that focus throughout the history of psychoanalysis.

SUCCESS AND FAILURE IN PSYCHICAL REALITY

Strictly speaking, the characterization of certain people as "those wrecked by success" is not psychoanalytic, it being made mainly "from the outside" rather than "from the inside." Hence, it tends to limit one to the consideration of dramatically overt instances, such as the depression that follows on the heels of a long-desired promotion or on the consummation of a long-desired love relationship. These consequences are common enough, but they are far from exhausting the possibilities. The approach "from the inside" is the approach through psychical reality. Through psychical reality, the analyst seeks to establish in each instance just what constitutes success and just what constitutes being wrecked by it. The individual, subjective, mostly unconsciously maintained conceptions of success and wreckage are not always what common sense would lead one to expect, and they do not often meet the eye. This divergence from common-sense expectation and observation is immediatley apparent once it is taken into account that, as a rule, people are more or less unconsciously conflicted with respect to their aims in life. On account of these conflicting aims, what is success according to one set of aims is failure according to other aims. Freud (1900, p. 604) made this point in connection with pleasure, when he observed that what is pleasurable for one psychical system may be painful for another. To restate this point in the terms of his later structural theory (1923), it may be said that he had in mind particularly those instances in which so-called id gratification conflicts with the defensive and synthesizing aims of the ego and the archaic moral aims of the superego. In this connection, symptom formation is a prime case in point in that it can be understood only as an attempted compromise of conflicting aims.

   Not only success but wreckage must be looked at from the same complex, apparently paradoxical vantage point. From the vantage point of psychical reality rather than conventional reality, wreckage may represent more than painful defeat or punishment. For example, it may also represent the triumph of archaic moral aims over infantile libidinal aims; similarly, it may represent the triumph of the ego aims of reducing psychical pain to a minimum by withdrawing from those situations of worldly success that threaten to bring on intolerable anxiety or depression. Thus, for example, although it may be an administrative error to promote someone to the level of his or her incompetence, in many cases that promotion may be the reason for the incompetence that follows hard upon it. Consequently the analyst must keep on asking the questions, What is the failure in success? and What is the success in failure? It was in this vein that Reik (1941) emphasized the concept of victory through defeat in his analysis of masochism.

The clinical examples that follow are for the most part organized around pathological formation of that essential component of character structure, the ego ideal. There are some invaluable papers by Annie Reich (1953, 1954, 1960) on this topic. It is hardly possible to discuss success psychoanalytically without taking up the ego ideal. It is, however, preferable to speak of the ideal self rather than the ego ideal because one may then more freely take into account the primitive wishful, the defensive, and the adaptive aspects of ideal-formation along with its archaic moral aspects, that is to say, its id and its ego aspects, and its superego aspects. (See Sandler, Holder, and Meers, 1963, and Schafer, 1967). The ideal self, then, emerges as a central and highly conflictual reference point in understanding the character structures of many people who seem to be wrecked by success or the prospect of it and who unconsciously, in their psychical reality, define success and failure in idiosyncratic ways that can be established and modified only through a psychoanalytic approach.

CLINICAL EXAMPLES

Consider, for example, a young man whose ideal it was to be an underachiever. That this was his ideal was established only after some analytic exploration of the psychical reality of his trials and tribulations in school, at work, and in the analysis. To be an underachiever was to conform to the role his family appeared to have assigned him from early in his life. This role warded off his siblings' envy and disparagement, and it earned love in the form of his father's compassionate help when, but only when, he was in trouble. One might want to question calling underachievement an ideal, even though that was his term for it, but I would argue that it is appropriate to call it his ideal in that typical feelings of unworthiness were associated with achievement, whereas feelings of being "a good kid" were associated with lack of achievement and self-disparagement. His self-esteem rode on his being an underachiever. Erikson (1956) has discussed similar phenomena in negative identity formation.

To present this young man's problem in terms of ideal self is not to ignore the castrating oedipal defeat that was entailed by meeting this negative ideal. Nor is it to ignore this young man's experiencing the ideal self in a conflictual manner, for it was obvious in other respects that he had not entirely renounced his positive oedipal strivings. He deviated from this negative ideal, but owing to the painfulness of acting otherwise than self-destructively, he could not sustain his attempt to depart from it. In his analytic sessions, for example, he could hardly finish a sentence in which he said something that was at all positive about himself; although he tried to bring in the positive, he had to interrupt with self-criticism of some sort.

Thus, in this young man's psychical reality, being wrecked was also a success of a kind; being a success was to be a failure. In his transference he worked energetically to invite the analyst's compassionate help by presenting himself as stupid, ineffectual, and desperate. And while consciously he professed to be ashamed of himself for his inadequacies, unconsciously, as it developed over the course of the analysis, he was being "a good kid," feeling like one, and expecting the analyst to be pleased with his failures and his need for help.

In another case, one of the dominant ideas of success was based on identification with an antisocial, gambling father who had had more than his share of worldly success and worldly failure. The son felt most alive and manly when he was working recklessly and unnecessarily at the brink of failure.

In yet another case, a young man's tendency to fail served unconsciously to protect the self-esteem of a weak, unsuccessful father. At the same time, this tendency served other important functions: in one way it amounted to a rebellion against his father's demands on him for a conformist type of dedication to success; in another way it amounted to compliance with his family's general inclination to romanticize emotional distress as the way to be interesting, a tendency that appeared to be based on a powerful sadomasochistic pattern of family interaction. Thus, in this case failure was a way of being sadistically and masochistically lovable as well as defiant; being successful in a neutralized, well-organized way was to invite painful exclusion from the family drama and from the opportunity for oedipal thrills and perhaps ultimate victory.

Another young man had identified himself with a pretentious, egoistic father in a way that could only lead to overt failure in his conventional undertakings. For this paternal identification required him to be a pretentious, self-undermining poseur himself, and it made him intolerant of his own limitations. At the same time, however, in going to extremes he was enacting an angry mockery of his father. Also, he was not challenging his father on psychically real oedipal grounds; the real challenge would have been to be a solid, sincere, esthetically sensitive achiever of the sort that his unhappily married mother responded to romantically.

Thus, for this young man to be manly in character and not castrated psychosexually meant repudiating his identification with his father, and this we know to be a difficult feat for any man. What was here in question, however, was only a partial repudiation of paternal identification; for not only was the father an achiever in his own right, whatever his pretensions, but, as always, there lay in the background of these derogated images of the father the unconsciously maintained imago of the powerful phallic father that had been developed during the analysand's years of very young boyhood. This is the father who, in psychical reality, is never seen in all his complexity, conflictedness, and insecurity. It is important to emphasize this point about the powerful primordial father because, in my experience, analysands insistently represent only the father of later periods of development; they hope thereby to get the analyst to accept these representations as complete. Although these derogated representations have their place in the network of interpretations, the analysis of being wrecked by success, as of so many other problems, depends on getting beyond this limited and later representation to the early father, who is sexually powerful enough to overwhelm, satisfy, and impregnate mother and to castrate the oedipally rivalrous son. In this regard, it is only the analysis of transference and resisting that enables one to get beyond the later, problematic, consciously asserted representations of the father as weak and disappointing.

Early in his analysis, this young man consciously idealized his father. He felt that he could never be as poised, witty, literate, and daring as his father. He promptly idealized the analyst in a similar manner and elaborated an extravagant, superficial identification with him. Consciously, his self-esteem shot up with his analytic pretentiousness. As a result, he was hardly approachable through analytic interventions. This father–son repetition in the analytic relationship was his initial transference neurosis, and it was obviously his initial major mode of resisting. Before the analytic relationship itself could be taken up analytically, however, it was necessary to carry out a close and patient examination of contradictory ideas and feelings concerning his idealized father. This work outside the transference was necessary to show him that he also felt betrayed, enraged, and despondent and that the ideal self he was playing at was flimsy, exhausting, and painful. This phase of the work required the analyst to make some forceful confrontations. Only subsequently could the transference and resisting be taken up analytically and a similar account of his relationship to the analyst be developed. Through this work, the way was opened to an analysis of the primordial father and thereby to alternatives to being wrecked by success.

ENVY, GRANDIOSITY, AND DEFECT

As I mentioned, the preceding examples have been organized mainly around disturbances of ideal-self formation. But now it must be added that, during analysis, being wrecked by success becomes tied in with many other factors as well. For one, there is the previously mentioned obvious problem of warding off envy. Of the many variants of envy that could be mentioned in this connection, it is important to single out the psychically real envy of the child felt by one or another parent: envy felt by the father who views himself as less well-endowed and less attractive to his wife than his son; envy felt by the mother who views herself as less feminine, less competent, less attractive to her husband than the daughter. Consequently, the successful child often faces the threat of experiencing some form of unconsciously desired, envious filicide. In these settings, any strong positive emotional response of the nonenvious parent is threatening, too, in its incestuous implications and, through those implications, in its being conducive to that certain fluidity or "laxity" of repression which Freud (1916/17, p. 376; see also 1915, p. 195) noted was both the gift and the burden of creative people. Thus, it is not only that too much harm seems to be threatened by the envy of one parent, but that too costly gratification seems to be threatened by the positive response of the other parent. In all such instances we are usually dealing with a significant amount of projection of love and hate onto the parents along with a significant kernel of good, though perhaps unacknowledged, reality testing.

In other connections, success presents the danger that the unconsciously maintained grandiose ideas of the self will be experienced consciously. Kohut (1971, 1977) had some significant points to make in this regard. Some analysands experience significant, possibly panicky disorientation of an incipiently manic or paranoiac sort in response to recognizing and asserting their own special achievements or the special talents that are implied in these achievements. During these moments of truth, they indicate a sense of loss of reality and contact with others, even a sense of being crazy. Consequently, these analysands will retreat from these self-enhancing recognitions and assertions, and they will do so repeatedly until their frightening fantasies, expectations, and reactions are identified, interpreted, and worked through.

I believe, however, that this crisis of narcissism is not resolvable through Kohut's self psychology alone. Although those self psychological considerations may help gain access to fears of a latent grandiose self and latent exhibitionism, it seems that, as a rule, this crisis of narcissism also implies the oedipal crisis on which Freud centered his attention. The crisis may also imply a disruption of a preoedipal symbiotic tie or a disturbing sense of merging with the grandiose imagos of the parents of very early childhood. Annie Reich (1953, 1954, 1960) showed a keen attentiveness to the mix of oedipal and preoedipal factors in these narcissistic crises.

In some cases, the path to success seems to be blocked unconsciously by the fantasy of irremediable deficit or defect. Ideas of deficit and defect do often refer to mothering that was not "good enough" or empathic enough, but that this is so does not mean that there is no network of oral, anal, and phallic-exhibitionistic fantasies or fixations, and of defenses against them, which are latent sources of the idea of having been damaged by poor care. Nor does the importance of empathic failure imply that infantile wish fulfillments have no place in the foundations of fixed and pervasive ideas of damagedness. If the analysis is not confined to self psychological issues, the unempathic mother often proves to be the retaliatory oedipal rival or the rejecting oedipal object, so that, unconsciously, it is oedipal threat and defeat that give to the ideas of defect and deficit much of their apparent force. These ideas of crippledness may also be used to cope with problems of bisexuality: psychical castratedness used by the male in this way; repudiation of phallic aspirations, by the female. Further, defect may be used unconsciously as a malignant phallus or a poisonous breast to triumph over the world, and in this way it may represent victory exhibitionistically and omnipotently snatched from the jaws of defeat.

I have argued elsewhere (1983) that unconsciously maintained and elaborated ideas of being imprisoned or empty may be used by some analysands in the same way that others use ideas of being damaged or defective. Whatever the case, conventional or analytic success for these people means giving up quite a lot. For this reason it may be an occasion for painful mourning at least and more likely for painful depression. What is lost is the mother's breast, however bad, the secret penis, the omnipotence, the "secret self," that make up the fantastic assumptions on which character structure is based. As viewed analytically, the issues of success and failure are primarily infantile rather than contemporary. Certainly any contemporary success of a conventional public sort gives rise to many new problems of personal synthesis and interpersonal relationship, but all these new stresses and strains derive their influence from being construed unconsciously in the terms of infantile attachment, loss, seduction, defeat, and other dangers. For those who appear to be wrecked by success, there may therefore by much of value that is hidden among the ruins.

MASOCHISM

So far I have touched only incidentally on the relation between being wrecked by success and masochism and on questions of technique. In my remaining remarks I shall comment on these two topics at greater length, though still only sketchily.

Masochism's relation to being wrecked by success may be approached by stating first that the two should not be confused, as they often are. This confusion results from a careless use of the term masochism. Every disorder we work with clinically has its share of unhappiness and unfulfillment, and every one is characterized by repetitious, unconsciously designed and executed self-injuriousness. Consequently, analysands seem to be bringing on much of their misery and to need to do so. These features alone do not, however, warrant speaking of masochism; otherwise, every significant clinical phenomenon would have to be regarded as masochistic, and the term masochism would lose its utility.

It is advisable to remain close to Freud (1919) in this connection and to reserve the term masochistic for those patterns of action in which suffering seems to be not only self-induced and repetitive but conspicuously, even if unconsciously, sexualized as well. By sexualized I mean that suffering is connected with fantasies of being beaten and is used as a means of promoting sexual excitement and climax; also, it is a means of seducing others to be abusive to this very end, and, thus, is a means of conducting actual or imagined heterosexual or homosexual love-relationships. Earlier, I mentioned one analysand who romanticized suffering and who cultivated sadomasochistic interactions as a way of being lovable and promoting his oedipal chances. In a context of this sort, the term masochistic, or more exactly sadomasochistic, makes sense. But, in other contexts, analysis establishes only that, unconsciously, failure is a punishment for forbidden wish fulfillment or a protection against intolerable demands on the ego, the self, or one's own person; in these contexts, reference to masochism does not make sense. As always, we encounter mixed cases and questions of degree, so that it is usually in order to include some kind of qualified statement about masochistic components of being wrecked by success. In such cases, however, the term masochism is being used in a *discriminating* way. It should go without saying that the term masochism should never be used in an *incriminating* way; however, certain countertransferences to the manifest negativity of these analysands are sometimes expressed in the forms of implicit accusations of masochism.

TECHNICAL CONSIDERATIONS

In conclusion, I turn to the question of technique in relation to the phenomenon of being wrecked by success. It has already been indicated that the most important areas to work in are transference and resisting. At appropriate times, the analyst must point out to the analysand how, when, and why he or she tries to bring about failure or to experience failure, or dwells on failure in the analytic situation, and does so particularly whenever the reality or prospect of some significant advance in the work or in one's daily life is in the air. The analyst will refer to the automatic dismissals or minimizations of good feelings, such as pride, commitment, or sexual pleasure; the analyst will refer also to the concealment of such good feelings until they are betrayed by a slip of the tongue or a dream. Often it is necessary to take up the demoralizing effect on the analyst that is consciously or unconsciously intended by this pattern of action. This must be done when the analyst begins to experience incipient countertransferential feelings of deadness, hopelessness, and tedium, or frustration and anger. In these instances, however, the analyst should not conclude hastily that these feelings are being deliberately, even if unconsciously, induced; for the analyst may have many other reasons to experience these feelings, and these other reasons may have to do with an incorrect understanding of the case as well as with factors peculiar to the analyst. Barring the influence of these extraneous factors, the analyst must, as I said earlier, ask just what is wrong unconsciously or in psychical reality with conventional, manifest success of one or another kind and what is right about the apparent or subtle wreckage. The best approach may be through analysis of the unconsciously grounded ideal self.

On the most general level, the analyst must slowly, patiently, tactfully, and neutrally establish that it is not success that wrecks the analysand; rather, it is the analysand who wrecks conventional success or the prospect of such success. And it must be established that the analysand engages in this wrecking action for reasons that include maintaining a sense of personal coherence, warding off the envy of others, guaranteeing defensive security, inflicting guilty self-punishment, and providing infantile wishfulfillment. This is the model that Freud established in his essay on this topic. It is a model of unconscious activity disguised mainfestly as passivity, and it is a model of unconsciously gaining pleasure or security through manifest unhappiness.

In severe cases, interpretive efforts may be of little or no avail. Nonetheless, this is the model, and these are the interpretive efforts that give success-wreckers their best chance to move beyond therapeutic stalemates and negative therapeutic reactions and all that they imply, and to assimilate their own talents and conventional successes into their lives and to enjoy them, whatever real or imagined burdens they may also entail.

REFERENCES

Erikson, E. (1956), The problem of ego identity. *J. Amer. Psychoanal. Assn.*, 4:56–121.
Freud, S. (1900), The interpretation of dreams. *Standard Edition*, 5:339–625. London: Hogarth Press, 1953.
———— (1915), The unconscious. *Standard Edition*, 14:159–215. London: Hogarth Press, 1957.
———— (1916), Some character-types met with in psycho-analytic work. *Standard Edition*, 14:309–333. London: Hogarth Press, 1957.
———— (1916/17), Introductory lectures on psycho-analysis, Part III. *Standard Edition*, 16. London: Hogarth Press, 1963.
———— (1919), A child is being beaten. *Standard Edition*, 17:175–204. London: Hogarth Press, 1955.
———— (1923), The ego and the id. *Standard Edition*, 19:3–66. London: Hogarth Press, 1961.
Kohut, H. (1971), *The Analysis of the Self*. New York: International Universities Press.
———— (1977), *The Restoration of the Self*. New York: International Universities Press.
Reich, A. (1953), Narcissistic object choice in women. *J. Amer. Psychoanal. Assn.*, 1:22–44.
———— (1954), Early identifications as archaic elements in the superego. *J. Amer. Psychoanal. Assn.*, 2:218–238.
———— (1960), Pathological forms of self-esteem regulation. *The Psychoanalytic Study of the Child*, 15:215–232. New York: International Universities Press.

Reik, T. (1941), *Masochism in Modern Man*. New York: Farrar & Rinehart.

Sandler, J., Holder, A., & Meers, D. (1963), The ego ideal and the ideal self. *The Psychoanalytic Study of the Child*, 18:139–158. New York: International Universities Press.

Schafer, R. (1967), Ideals, the ego ideal, and the ideal self. In *Motives and Thought: Psychoanalytic Essays in Memory of David Rapaport*, ed. R. R. Holt. [*Psychological Issues*, monogr. 18/19.] New York: International Universities Press, pp. 131–174.

——— (1983), *The Analytic Attitude*. New York: Basic Books.

6 / The Analytic Concepts of Masochism:
A Reevaluation

Stuart S. Asch

THE TERM MASOCHISM COVERS a wide territory of phenomenology and dynamic meaning. As a result it has remained a confusing and perplexing category that includes the personality type, a symptom complex, and even part of normal and adaptational psychology.

Masochism takes two main forms: the masochistic perversion (sexual masochism) and the masochistic character ("moral masochism"). They have the common element of an active seeking for, or facilitation of, pain and suffering. Whereas the perversion includes conscious pleasure in the exciting sexual gratification, the masochistic character is unaware of such an aim, nor are sexual derivatives readily apparent in the usual behavior.

My intention is not to provide a summary of the different theories of masochism that followed Freud's original 1924 concept, which was centered on a need to satisfy unconscious guilt. Most of these are well known and readily available in the literature (see, for example, Reik, 1941; Brenman, 1952; Stein, 1956; Loewenstein, 1957; Brenner, 1959; Stolorow, 1975; Lax, 1977, 1978; Grossman, 1986). Rather, I will present some observations on masochism that may be less familiar. To do this I will bring in material from a variety of clinical conditions, dissecting out aspects that can be collated under the rubric "masochism," in the hope that data from divergent arenas will evoke new connections with additional understanding of the term.

SEXUAL MASOCHISM

The masochistic perversions have a much wider incidence than is recognized by most psychiatrists. They encompass a variety of debasing and/or physically painful practices, which include whipping, mutilations, autoerotic asphyxia, to all of which the subject responds with sexual excitement and pleasure. Sexual masochism, its official title in DSM III (APA, 1980) was introduced in 1895 by Krafft-Ebing in his catalogue of these sexual perversions. He derived the name from Leopold von Sacher-Masoch, an author who had written several romances dealing with men whose sexual gratification lay in their being painfully treated by a special kind of woman—e.g., "Venus in Furs," his most famous novel (1870). Krafft-Ebing himself, however, did not insist that actual physical pain be a part of the symptom complex. "The common element in all these cases is the fact that the sexual instinct is directed to ideas of subjugation and abuse by the opposite sex" (1895, p. 146).

While the phenomenology of sexual masochism is familiar enough, the explanation of a willingness to accept pain and suffering, with its enhancement of the sexual pleasure, has remained obscure. There is a plethora of theories, their very multiplicity suggesting how multidetermined the syndrome may be.

The belief is still maintained by many that it is the pain itself that is sexually exciting. Certainly it is observable that orgasm can be achieved during the sexual abuse and that the pain seems to enhance the pleasure. But it remains unclear why pain itself can be sexually exciting, even orgasmic. The human organism has demonstrated that any sensation may become a source of sexual excitement. The conventional explanation has been that a special kind of physical pain was early associated with pleasure; that through various reinforcements, the perversion took on the significance of a gratifying love relationship. In early studies, emphasis was placed on the inherent erotogenicity of the skin libidinized by specific reinforcement of the skin erotogenicity through spanking (Sadger, 1926). These studies presumably associated whipping with sexual gratification. Unfortunately, like many explanations for perversions, this too may be tautological and does not fully explain *why* the whippings are pleasurable.

The classic psychodynamic explanations are more economical and inherently more consistent, although they too leave many questions unanswered. They are essentially based on the concept that certain people unconsciously believe that sexual activity is forbidden. The perversion is thereby used as the price for sexual gratification, a "bribe" to that part of the individual psyche that proscribes normal sexual activity. The perversion of being beaten, for example, is accepted as a much milder substitute for an expected punishment that is anticipated to be much more severe. According to the earlier theorists, the ultimate specific punishment expected (unconsciously) was castration. The masochistic perversion was then understood as the need for painful punishment *after* the fact of the forbidden pleasurable sexual act and its pleasure (or as a payment in advance, in anticipation of the sexual pleasure).

It is true that when masochistic mutilations do occur, they almost always spare the genitals or at least leave them essentially intact. Self-castration does occur, although mainly in psychosis. This is clearly more difficult to explain as a defense against castration. If these instances are examined, however, they often represent an extreme wish to exhibit the individual's relinquishment of forbidden sexual and aggressive tendencies. The act serves to prove his submission to the powerful authority and to arrange for the omnipotent figure to love and protect by merging with him. This is a common religious theme. Thus Father Oregon castrated himself to show God he had given up pleasure of the flesh and had accepted God as the All Powerful One and that he should be loved by God as a fully devoted disciple. Self-castration, fortunately not common, is a magical means of entering into this great protecting union. It is as if the person says, "It's not true that I want to castrate father, and I will prove it by castrating myself or letting him castrate me." The man thereby retains his own power because *he* has *actively* arranged for the mutilating act himself. By stressing passivity, by arranging for mastery by some-body else, the person hopes for a partnership with a powerful, protective figure. As Fenichel (1945) put it, ". . . a stressing of one's own helplessness and littleness may aim at appealing to the mercy of the threatening protective power" (p. 359). Control and the union with a powerful figure have become more important than castration.

The element of control is of supreme importance in both the masochistic perversion and thee personality disorder itself. Both categories of patients need to be in control of the painful or unplea-surable relationship (although this is usually masked in the personal-ity disorder). The basic issue of control in the moral masochist will be discussed later.

In the perversion, the prime significance of control is emphasized in several ways:

a. Perfection and narcissistic control is crucial. It is *by no means* merely a gratuitous enactment of pain.

b. The proceedings must be carried out exactly as in the script without modification, or the gratification is lost. The technique must always be the same.

c. The strict restriction against any change, the requirement of precise repetitiveness, is similar to the more familiar unmodifiable *compulsive* ritual, with which it has many dynamic similarities. In both instances it suggests that a *specific* childhood event (and its distortion) is being re-enacted.

d. By actively setting up a painful or humiliating situation, by arranging for the torture and preparing the necessary paraphernalia for the enactment of his perversion, the masochist believes he is controlling his fate. He hopes he will no longer be vulnerable to the expected torture at a time, or even in a manner, he has not anticipated.

The need of most personalities to play the active role is a familiar mechanism to analysts. As had been described, manifestly passive roles are usually screens for latent devices for mastery and control of the overtly active partner. In the immediate aftermath of the Castro revolution of Cuba some years ago, when hundreds died before firing squads, it was startling to see how many victims, invoking the traditional privilege of a last wish, themselves chose to give the order to fire. It was as though by taking an active role in their own execution they could avoid the passive, powerless role of victims and fleetingly preserve their own self-esteem (Asch, 1980, p. 53).

Early psychoanalytic writers emphasized that perverse activities were deviations of infantile sexuality chosen by persons who believed "adult" sexual activity was forbidden because it unconsciously represented an oedipal triumph. Such incestuous wishes are defended against by regressing to the preoedipal objects or aims, such as the mother with a phallus (or body as phallus), aims of oral, or anal activities, cuddling, touching, sucking, constricting. Frequently a reverse Oedipus was postulated—having someone who symbolized a phallic figure administer beatings or spankings (in an unconscious fantasy of passive anal intercourse). In this way, the wish and the punishment are economically combined. If a woman is selected to administer the beatings, the use of special accoutrements during the perverse acting out is usually essential—furs, high boots, a whip. These usually belong to the man, who is only lending them to the woman (Reik, 1941, p. 204). The accoutrements are fetishistic, that is, they represent a phallus and symbolically transmute the woman into a masculine (albeit female) persona. This phallic woman is a condensation of the infantile mother, who is perceived as having a penis, or of the phallically endowed father (Bak, 1968). If another person is required in the perversion, and this is often not true except in the accompanying fantasy—viz. autoerotic asphyxia (Asch, 1984)—it is probable that this assistant is never an oedipal object in fantasy, that is, never an anatomically correct adult.

Perversion is seldom seen in the analyst's office probably because it is an *effective* technique for dealing with the anxiety that motivates the perverse act. Many masochistic perversions occur in people who function quite well, as long as the perversion is gratified. Gratification usually can be accomplished quite easily and quietly in private. What is visible to the public is often a fairly well-functioning personality. The perverse act is usually not *physically* destructive—and if it is, then the police become involved at that point. It is for this reason that law enforcement agencies are much more familiar with the varieties of sexual perversion than the psychiatrist or analyst is. Cases of autoerotic asphyxia to enhance sexual gratification, for example, come to our attention only when the bondage enthusiast has overdone it and is unable to release himself (Hazelwood, Dietz, and Burgess, 1983). But it is the police rather than the analyst who is called. No complete study of masochistic perversion can be undertaken without consulting the experts—the police and prostitutes.

Every major police department and hospital emergency room is acquainted with regular instances of such phenomena. Psychiatrists come across isolated examples occasionally. The author was recently consulted about a young man of 25 who confessed to ten years of preoccupation with unbearable guilt over his "evil" sexual desires. In frantic attempts to subdue episodes of sexual excitement, he would make deep gashes in his erect penis in order to drain off the "bad blood." During a severe psychotic episode, his attempt to control these sexual feelings were externalized and displaced. Using a meat cleaver he attacked and killed two people who he believed were responsible for his evil and devilish thoughts. Flannery O'Conner's (1962) story "Wise Blood" describes an almost identical situation. A young man, tormented by his sense of evilness, progressively tortured and mutilated himself, even to wearing not merely a hair shirt, but a barbed wire coiled around his chest under his shirt. The story was made into a bizarre and depressing movie by John Huston that was artistically exceptional but an inevitable commercial failure.

The incidence of masochistic perversion as a major activity is not known. Reik (1941) is probably correct to rank sexual masochism as one of the commonest perversions. Like many other perversions, the behavior is so effective in curbing or dispelling anxieties that it infrequently comes to the attention of the medical community, and psychiatry doess not have accurate statistics. The few studies reported in the literature are based on a small number of patients and hence have led to skewed inferences. For example, it has long been claimed that sexual masochism occurs almost exclusively among men, inasmuch as few women masochists have been reported. Reik

and other have claimed that for those few women in whom the
perversion does seem to occur, its main incentive is the need to
maintain a relationship with a sadistic man who requires the act. The
sexual element was not considered to be as prominent an aspect in
women's masochistic perversions as in men's. Reik even claimed,
mistakenly, that women's involvement in masochistic activities is
much more attenuated and lacks the ecstatic and intense lust of
masculine masochistic sexual experiences! As the women's movement has expanded the psychoanalyst's knowledge of women's desires, it has become clear that these earlier, narrow views can justly be
considered to be chauvinistic masculine distortions. Women's sexual
desires and activities, including sexual masochism, are demonstra-
tably as ubiquitous and intense as men's. There is no evidence of any
gender differences in incidence.

RELATED MASOCHISTIC PHENOMENA

There is a group of masochistic phenomena that are neither clearly
sexual perversions nor consistent aspects of a masochistic character
structure. The Jewish custom of circumcision is the oldest and best
known example. In return for dispensing with Akedah, the ancient
sacrifice of the first born as an act of fealty, Abraham and God the
Father accepted circumcision as a substitute. The son would wear this
symbol of submission to the Father and in return would be assured of
His protection as one of the chosen people.

Familiar variants are found in the initiation rites, forms of submission, and minor mutilations that occur in almost all societies. By
accepting the community's requirements for a *pars pro toto* partial
castration—for example through scarification in primitive societies or
through the demeaning, humiliating experiences of fraternity initia-
tions, or even symbolically (viz. the knighting of the young squire by
the King's sword carefully touching *only* the youth's shoulder)—they
obliged the powerful authority to grant the supplicant all the rights of
an adult (including sexuality) while pledging his omnipotent protection and favor. In some cultures these customs extend to young girls
also. It is possible to consider that young adolescent girls in our own
society who pierce their ears are unconsciously also acknowledging a
similar *rite du passage* to adulthood; so too in many Moslem sects
where the girls are subjected to clitoridectomies. A similar meaning
can be discerned in the vows of chastity required by some religious
orders as obedience to God the Father. In these instances the threat of
sexual competition is removed in a nonhumiliating way, although the

symbolism remains the same. That the punishment of breaking this contract is death or actual castration is perhaps best known from the cautionary tale of the mutilations of Heloise and Abelard in the 12th century.

Self-mutilation as a means of atonement for "sins" was an accepted religious practice up to the middle ages. Wearing a hair shirt was carried out literally as a means of constantly reminding oneself of past and future sinning. It was a common device among the ascetic early religious fanatics. Henry II in England, in atonement for his responsibility for the killing of the Archbishop of Canterbury, Thomas à Becket (dramatized in T. S. Elliott's (1964) "Murder in the Cathedral"), had himself publicly flogged on the steps of the Canterbury Cathedral on each anniversary of the murder. Becket himself wore a hair shirt so that the irritation would serve as a constant reminder of the need to be pure.

Apparently it was a common sight on the main roads of medieval Europe to meet penitents flagellating themselves as they travelled in groups to some major cathedral seeking absolution. (Ingmar Bergman's movie "The Seventh Seal" has several such vivid scenes.) But the practice became so widespread in the middle ages that the Church was forced to recognize that the pain of whipping had dissolved the repression of the gratification. The Church finally decided that this form of atonement, which had become a masochistic gratification, be designated as a sin in its own right. "The flagellation which had originally served the purpose of self-castigation with these early Christian monks and ascetics had become transmuted into a means of sexual excitement. The increase of pain produced ecstasies" (Alvarez, 1972, p. 123).

T. E. Lawrence ("Lawrence of Arabia") is a well-known historical figure. Although most students have long recognized his masochistic character (moral masochism), studies (Rattigan, 1960; Mack, 1976) have presented evidence that he also had a masochistic perversion. Recently it was revealed that he indulged in a specific whipping perversion. As an enlisted man in the RAF (it had been characteristic for him to degrade himself by repeatedly eschewing the officer's rank to which he was entitled), he arranged to have himself whipped regularly by a gullible fellow soldier. He had convinced his colleague, through a series of forged letters, that a wealthy uncle had stipulated that he, Lawrence, be beaten weekly for some mysterious crime he had committed in his youth. He was not to receive the uncle's inheritance unless he accepted these punishments. Mack (1976) in his biography of Lawrence suggests that the pattern of flagellation was laid down during the young Lawrence's development by his strict

Scottish Presbyterian mother, who would whip him regularly for minor infractions.

MORAL MASOCHISM

Moral masochism is the form with which analysts are most familiar. It is a character pathology that seems endemic to our culture and is a common motivation for patients to seek analytic treatment. The disorder can perhaps be best defined as a lifelong pattern of unconsciously arranged difficulties or failures in multiple areas of functioning. This is the "loser" in our society, the person who needs to be unnecessarily encumbered or even to fail. He tends to fail at work and love despite what are sometimes the best credentials. He either cannot form a gratifying relationship or, if he does, he inevitably, although unconsciously, arranges for it to founder. He may achieve great preliminary success but somehow snatches defeat from the jaws of victory and fails at the penultimate moment. Endowment with innate or high intelligence can be a counterbalance to some degree, but most success is achieved at great emotional expense and at a level far below what should be expected. It is *pride* in self-abnegation, in taking the "harder" way, in diminishing material gain that is the hallmark of the moral masochist. The underlying sexual gratification, overt in the perversion, is not visible to the observer, nor experienced as such by the patient.

It is intriguing that toward the milder end of the continuum of such a character type, the "wimp" is often liked by his associates. Associates often feel sorry for him but usually add that he is a "nice guy." The less intense moral masochistic is "likable" because he shows little overt hostility and appears passive and unthreatening. The moral masochist allows his hostility to come through mainly by attrition of his objects, seldom by confrontation. One finally becomes exasperated by the self-denial, by the resistance to all suggestions, by the constant exhibiting of disappointments. Some people avoid recognition or ignore the masked hostility of the masochist, at least initially, in order to maintain repression of their own sadism. This may be a problem for those analysts who tend to see some aspect of their own passivity in masochists of this type. It is bound to create serious countertransference problems, an important technical consideration in the analysis of masochism, which I discuss further on.

Overt submission masks the hostile wish to control as well as the desire to engender guilt. Submissiveness seems to be the basis of certain typical but perplexing masochistic object relations. These are the instances in which an obviously destructive relationship persists. The masochist blindly and progressively humiliates himself in submission to the denigrating partner, who is incapable of guilt feelings. This is often persisted in with the hope that his increasingly flagrant and humiliating submission will eventually succeed in provoking guilt. Relationships of this type, leading inexorably to destruction, are a favorite theme of many writers. The movie "The Blue Angel" describes the almost literally fatal fascination that a previously highly self-controlled, respected, and honored man has for a self-indulgent, amoral, manipulating woman. The attraction of this woman lies in her hedonistic, guiltless abandon, which the moral man envies and attempts to bring down. He is unconscious of his desperate need to arouse guilt feelings in her, and his continued failure to achieve this goal leads to ever greater humiliation, until he is destroyed.

It is too easy to believe that moral masochism is both less flamboyant and less damaging to oneself than the perversion. Quite the opposite, the moral masochist can be very self-destructive. He frequently unconsciously creates situations in his relations with people or his environment that may quickly pass from his own control and take on an inexorable self-destructiveness of their own. One end of the moral masochism continuum must be labelled as *malignant* because of the intensity of the moral masochist's self-destructive desires. With these types of moral masochists, the hostility, although still not worn as a chip on the shoulder, is rapidly apparent. Malignant seems an appropriate term, for such patients march unswervingly to their self-arranged doom (unless treatment does succeed). They proceed into a negative therapeutic reaction to treatment, into dangerous life situations, or even to acting out long-threatened suicide.

What follows is a description of a patient who is a prototype of this latter extreme.

Case I: A Patient with Malignant Masochism
Demonstrating a Negative Therapeutic Reaction

A young man in his early 20s sought treatment because of chronic feelings of depression combined with severe indecisiveness. His character problems prevented him from achieving any chosen life goal. He was a brilliant man, capable of achieving excellent grades in any area of schooling that he selected. He came from a prominent family whose members were all highly successful in various careers.

Despite the outward trappings of unusual intelligence, strong and interested family support, and almost unlimited opportunities, he had been unable to make a career choice. He failed similarly in all his attempts to form a relationship with an appropriate woman.

Consciously he believed that his inability to function was in reaction to his highly successful father. The patient felt that his father was overinvolved and was insisting on the patient's working in the same field as he (which was not true). He had near paranoid ideas that father wanted to control him and make him submit. It became clear that the patient was struggling with his own masochistic wish to submit to father. His character defense was to substitute the goal of getting control, becoming the master, for the reality goal of success in his own life. He would render father impotent by disappointing him in each attempt, even though he would thereby have to subvert his own goals. Whenever he succeeded in making father or the analyst fail with him, to a striking degree he exhibited the overt and inappropriate glee that such personality disorders tend to exhibit in the face of some real life defeat.

The origins of this behavior lay in prepuberty experiences with the patient's mother. She was an obese, phobic, withdrawn woman, chronically but mildly depressed. It was her habit to take naps during the day, and from his latency period forward she would urge her pubescent son to lie on the couch with her. This was always sexually exciting for the patient and progressively so as he reached puberty. When he thought his mother had fallen asleep, he would rub his body against her, eventually reaching orgasm without using his hand by rubbing his penis against her. (Until the analysis he had never allowed himself to decide whether she was sufficiently awake to be aware of what he was doing.) At 17 he had his first sexual experience with a girlfriend, rubbing against her to orgasm, just as he was *still* doing with mother. At 19 he began masturbating manually by himself and gave up mother as a partner.

Maintaining the doubt about whether mother was aware of what he was doing was always essential, to protect mother from his rage. The doubting gradually extended until it contaminated almost all of his activities, interfering with their completion. When he finally broke off contact with her, it was without either of them ever acknowledging or discussing their secret activity. His mother's denial of their secret and her obfuscation of reality led to uncertainty about his sense of self and impaired his reality testing. He was left with guilt and an unquenchable rage at her and at his father for not having protected him from mother. The conscious aim of not acquiescing to any goal that he believed father or mother might want for him was a resistance to submitting to any wish of either parent and could be readily traced back to the seduction. It was an activity that had demeaned him. It had made him feel helpless and enslaved by the overwhelming passions mother could arouse in him whenever she chose. At those times he had felt unable to control his lust and felt ashamed and degraded; but at the same time he was unable to control his desires for her. This was clearly the origin of his refusal to "submit," displaced to current life situations.

Initially father was the overt object of his rage and struggles. The patient made himself fail in order to defeat father. It was only after a year of analytic work that he could talk about the sexual activity with mother and then he began to attack her just as he had father before. The negative Oedipus, the identification with mother, remained an important part of his life, however, and the struggles over who was in control remained constant. He could not progress past this level but kept his object choices shifting, moving back and forth from father to mother. He was similar to patients who report a burgeoning eruption of rage when they are forced to passively experience progressive stimulation of any kind. An analogy would be the reaction to being given an enema while having to hold back the explosion.

This same patient made clear whence came the concern over "control." It was an externalization and displacement of his failing struggle to control his own powerful impulses. The experiences with mother had so stimulated his sexual drives at an age when he would not manage them that he felt helpless to tame them. The impulse would become so strong, the urgency of the sexual drives so great that it would incite an explosive rage, and hurting sadistic fantasies would take over. The patient's resultant fear of inflicting pain, his fantasies of mutilating his objects (always mother or one of her substitutes) paralyzed him sexually and then invaded all decision making. He would go through frequent periods of having to test himself—testing his ability to control his own impulses (by not eating, by exercises, etc.), which then spread to controlling other people's actions. All this was stimulated by the displaced need to reassure himself that he did have control of his earlier, prematurely stimulated impulses.

Such acting out became in increasing source of his self-esteem and now began to contaminate his outside life. He would seek to control or manipulate others, provoking and testing authority figures, chairmen of departments, school officials, employers. He was extremely skilled at such provocations. Their responses of anger or guilt (similar to what he was trying to provoke in me) were the desired reactions, evidence that he was in control, that he could "beat" them. Such behavior is similar to that of the exhibitionist, who requires the response of anger or revulsion from the victim, to reassure himself of *his* power, of *his* control, even if it is destructive to him in reality.

This patient would grin and mock my "defeat." His parents and I were helpless to get him to look for a job, to prevent him from ruining his interviews for professional school, and so on. "I guess I'm diggin in my heels," he said with a smile as he persisted in coming late, 15 minutes or more, to our sessions.

The glee exhibited by the patient during such masochistic "orgies" in the transference when he felt he was "beating" me was similar to the glee of the toddler as he defeats his parents with his negativism— "I will have a bowel movement where and when *I* want." Not always aware of their delight, patients may deny it even while the lilt of smug condescension in their voice is pointed out. But it often helps when the patient can recognize that the gratification does exist despite his self-destructive push. However, the gratification does not lie in the overt sexual excitement found in the perversion. Rather, it is a response to great increase in self-esteem. The suffering is arranged so that the person will be loved. It is also because realistic gratification, including sexuality, has been replaced by pride and pleasure in the ability to control impulses and to control objects and make them submit.

Eventually it was no longer possible for him to work in the analysis and maintain a therapeutic alliance. A fixed negative therapeutic reaction had taken over. Finally, analysis had to be terminated before the intensification of his conflict in the transference became too destructive.

Case II: A Patient with Moral Masochism Demonstrating the Need for Enslavement

This patient behaved as if his role were to shoulder ever increasing responsibilities. He thus preserved a fantasy relationship with his long-dead mother, who had constantly made such demands on him. He had married twice, both times to demanding, ungiving women. The divorce of his first wife was accomplished only after he had agreed to unrealistic and burdensome support payments ("I'll have to support her now for the rest of my life"). Like his marriages, his business was unconsciously not for profit or pleasure, but rather had the aim of adding some burden.

Case III: A Patient with Moral Masochism Where
Childhood Developmental Factors Have Contributed to
Incomplete and Fragile Integration of Internal Objects

This patient, a 32-year-old man, had become very successful by devoting all his time to his work, including weekends. He came to treatment because of a pervasive unhappiness over his inability to form personal relationships. Whenever he would begin to experience closeness to someone, he would panic, feeling that he was becoming an evil, destructive person, "a harpy." He would then abruptly break off the relationship. When he was a boy, his mother would compete and interfere with his relationships with others. She would intrude herself into his games with friends, demanding that he leave the sport and come and "talk" with her. At the end of the day, when he would prepare for sleep, she would come and sit on his bed and "debrief" him on the day's events. In the course of these talks, she would have him detail the contacts he had had during the day and then denigrate the people. These people were all bad, she would say. The only one who loved him fully was she. Only after he had reassured her that she was the most important one to him would she offer her love, and only then could he fall asleep comfortably. It soon became apparent that when attracted to another person, he felt that the important relationship with his mother was endangered, and he would partially identify with her, so as not to lose her. The "harpy" image of himself was a composite of a devouring, hostile image of her, coupled with his own unconscious rage at her.

In each of these last two examples, the need to hold onto the "evil" introject was the significant resistance to treatment. Interpretations directed toward the fear of being angry at the old object were experienced as a threat. They aroused intense anxiety (and usually denial) at the danger of losing the object.

The severe separation anxiety and unwillingness to give up an exclusive but destructive attachment is similar to the dynamic of many battered children and their relationship with the battering mother (Asch, 1981). Most beaten and even mutilated children will not give up their sadistic mother. Such children do all they can to show their love for the batterer and can even become seriously depressed if they are separated from her. Despite this observation, the present pattern in managing battering behavior is to place the child away from home to protect the child from serious physical damage. It is difficult to avoid this choice even though we know that such separations are in some way even more destructive to the emotional life of the child. The "abandonment" that is created is usually a temporary one, the hope being that the resulting psychological damage will be less severe and permanent than the physical damage to the child would be. It has yet to be proven that such environmental manipulation will somehow ameliorate masochistic needs that are in the service of preserving an important object relationship.

It is helpful to conceptualize the perversion in contrast to moral masochism in terms of object relations. Although both phenomena may occur in the same individual (e.g., T. E. Lawrence) in a sort of continuum, they usually are part of two different personality types.

Perversion may appear in an otherwise intact, high functioning person, capable of good and warm object relations. The perversion itself usually appears only in certain specifics of those object relationships, that is, during sexual activity. It is usually fairly well encapsulated and may not contaminate other aspects of functioning, exclusive of sexuality. As a result, there may be little suffering. which is why perversions are so seldom brought to analysis.

By contrast, the moral masochist has a pervasive personality difficulty that may skew attitudes toward relationships and life in general. As a result, these unhappy people *do* seek help.

The extent of other disturbances of ego functions is not necessarily related to the masochism per se. Both forms of masochism are seen in ego organizations that are relatively intact. The exception is the pervasive ego pathology associated with the more destructive forms of perversion—self mutilations and lust murders. These are manifestations of a more general disturbance of ego pathology of which the perversion is only a part.

MASOCHISM AND DEPRESSION

The close clinical association of moral masochism with depression is a familiar one. The perversion does not seem to have this affinity. Both masochistic and depressed patients have internalized their significant objects. This is most obvious in the depressive, who is preoccupied with internal self-esteem regulation, using part of the self in lieu of a lost object, or trying to appease guilt aroused by his superego.

The importance of internal objects is less obvious in the masochist since much of his pathology reveals itself in interactions with the outside world. Nevertheless, much of his functioning has the aim of placating or pleasing some fantasized internal object. With some exceptions, both groups of patients have difficulty in expressing overt aggression in their interpersonal relations. Both function under heavy burdens of guilt; they suffer from an overtly severe, self-critical, and demanding conscience. They try to appease this guilt by their own distinctive ways of seeking punishment. The masochist projects his superego and arranges for the environment to "punish" him. The depressive retains most of the conflict internally and does his own attacking of himself. It is, however, true that both depression and masochism are relieved if some outside agency takes over the punishing. When life introduces its own suffering, such as illness, both conditions seem to lose their intensity and urgency.

Manifestations of depression and masochism are often intermingled. Since the dynamics are so similar, it is not surprising that there is a tendency for one to flow into the other as different aspects of the conflicts shift. Many masochistic personalities manifest depression at different times, and they may even progress to an overt clinical depression later in life. Conversely, some dysthymic disorders and even major depressions may merge into a masochistic life style when the affective disorder is in remission. It is as if as the depression improves and becomes more object oriented, the previous *self*-punitive dynamics shift to punishment by outside objects.

The perversion, in contrast to the masochist character, does not seem to have an overt affinity for depression. A failure of the perversion results usually in anxiety rather than depressed affect.

THERAPY

There are multiple grounds for the development of a masochistic character structure. Oedipal guilt, fear that aggression will destroy one's objects, castration anxiety, and the like are the more familiar ones. Treatment strategies first require delineation of the significant basic conflict. These then become part of classical analytic work.

The most difficult technical problems occur with the more profound, "malignant" masochist. These masochistic characters are extremely resistant to analyzing behavior and attitudes that they maintain in order to perpetuate a primitive attachment to an internal object, a preoedipal conflict. The attachment is a residual of incomplete separation-individuation from the early mothering object. Although an early internalized object, this is not a symbiotic mechanism and is usually not a significant part of the self-representation. That is, it is not mainly a narcissistic object, in the older terminology. The patient's images unconsciously involve more of an ego ideal or critical internal object from whom he is unable to separate.

The analyst must first succeed in demonstrating that the patient is maintaining a fantasized love affair, a private, internalized relationship with an imago of a devouring, sadistic mother. Again, this dynamic helps explain why a negative therapeutic reaction is so common in the analysis of the masochistic patient, especially if depression is a significant part of the clinical picture. The aim is not to succeed in treatment but rather to appease the critical internal object and remain attached to it while at the same time taking revenge on the significant other—the analyst as the transference object. Successful interpretation is often antagonistic to this important aim of the patient's since it is usually directed against the power of the ambivalently loved object (Asch, 1976).

As is familiar in the treatment of many classical depressions, the internalized image must be delineated before it can be "exorcised." By working with the transference and accumulating descriptions of the patient's attitudes toward the analyst, one may be able to recapture the image of the mother (as the patient identifies with her). The aim of the identification, a need to hold onto her, can then be demonstrated.

Teasing out this image may be difficult with the masochistic patient because the therapeutic alliance so necessary for such work is often experienced by the patient as submission. "Patients who have had difficulties in their separation-individuation phase tend to react to the invitation by the analyst to work together as if they were being *forced* to do it the analyst's way. The struggle against the analyst is a defense against their passive submissive wishes. It is one of the defensive aims of the negativism of the toddler during the period of separation and individuation" (Asch, 1976).

The gratification in failure, with its associated aim to make the therapist or parent or surrogate helpless to stop the patient, is often tied to a specific fantasy. The primary love object, usually the preoedipal mother, is somehow aware of this jousting and is watching and approving of the defeat of the analyst. The patient experiences it as *reuniting him with his preoedipal object.* The negative therapeutic reaction in these instances is intended to defeat the analyst's aim of disengaging the masochist from his death embrace with the internalized preoedipal, engulfing mother figure. This early figure is often remembered from childhood as belittling all relationships other than the one with her (see case III). The patient is recreating and preserving this passive, cannibalistic relationship with the fantasized internalized mother by identifying with the aggressor and acting out her role as he remembers experiencing it with her.

It is these powerful ties to preoedipal objects that are responsible for many of the difficulties and the failures in analytic work that occur when the patient's character structure includes a large element of this more primitive and destructive form of masochism.

COUNTERTRANSFERENCE PROBLEMS

An additional and difficult element in the analysis of masochism of any origin is the moral masochists' need to defend against their own expressions of anger and to incite it rather in the analyst. They often do accomplish this by stubborn passivity in treatment, by denigrating the analysis with negative therapeutic reactions, and the like. These are the bases for some of the serious countertransference problems so usual with these patients and the almost inevitable burgeoning of anger in the therapist.

A further source of serious difficulties in the analysis of masochistic personalities can, I believe, be traced to the affinity between maso-chistic patients and the personality of many analysts. This may also help explain why countertransference problems are probably more prominent in the analysis of masochism than in the treatment of most other emotional disorders. It is reasonable to suppose that many people in the healing professions have their ambitions strongly influenced by a "need to cure." Not infrequently this need has been stimulated by a wish to undo some serious illness in a significant figure from their past. Although it has become a cliche to speak of the ubiquitous depressed mother as fueling the specific therapeutic zeal that is so often a factor in the analyst's choice of profession, it is often a valid factor.

Olinick (1978) has suggested that such powerful incentives in the analyst may derive from residua of powerful rescue fantasies that have remained intact since childhood. "The depressed mother in particular has an unwitting but remarkable ability to evoke and include such fantasies, and, in fact, to generate mothering behavior in her child" (p. 173). Such early experience can stimulate patterns of behavior whose aim is to repair the injured narcissism arising from the early object's psychological or physical dependence. Olinick goes on to suggest, "The youth's subjective justification for existence in the course of further growth and development, will be in the direction of service as an imperative ideal . . ." (p. 173).

Brenman (1952) has described a masochistic character whose "pro-jections of her own needy and exploitative impulses is seen in her view of all her relationships as a situation in which she must "give" limitlessly and/or be dropped when her usefulness comes to an end.

. . . the projection of insatiable demands is the masochist's assumption that all people are imperiously needy as he, and therefore he must be exhaustively giving" (pp. 272–73). Masochistic patients have a special valence for evoking sympathetic vibrations in the analyst. This can lead to a more or less transient regression to the analyst's childhood experiences of being required to provide ego supplies for a needy significant object. Case II, described earlier, is an example of this kind of enslavement to an internalized object. If this is accompanied by the feeling that only *he* can provide these supplies, the lesson taught that his object's existence depends on his own self-abnegation and providing nurturance, then the patient-doctor relationship is compromised and the analysis may be placed in jeopardy.

Masochistic patients all try to arouse guilt, especially in the transference. The analyst whose development has been skewed into the path of *needing* to give is prone to guilty responses when his suffering patient complains he has not helped enough. The analyst often responds to these complaints with silence or passivity. He may have the analytic aim of stimulating the patient to reflect on what he is doing or to facilitate the patient mobilizing his repressed anger. Often, however, his behavior reflects his need to suppress his own annoyance for fear of creating a sadomasochistic collaboration. As expected, this can only complicate the analytic work.

If the analyst remains silent or passive, the masochistic patient now *must* raise his self-destructive ante until the desired response is obtained. However, if the analyst is now too giving (out of guilt that is rationalized as a "corrective emotional experience") rather than interpreting, this is also destructive to treatment. The patient hears this response of the analyst as confessing, "Mea Culpa, I am guilty for what I have done (or withheld from you). *I* am the helpless person that I once made you feel *you* were."

Racker (1968, p. 179) has emphasized how the masochistic analyst may be inclined toward submission to the patient, particularly to his resistances. Such a therapist tends to allow the patient to be in charge, even letting himself be tortured and used, so as not to frustrate the patient.

However, all incentive for therapeutic zeal should not be disparaged, even if it does stem from a core of masochism in the analyst's personal history. It can also serve a positive therapeutic value in fueling the patience and devotion necessary for the long and difficult tasks of analytic work. Since we cannot expect much positive reinforcement by praise of out relationships, our zeal can have a powerful value in preserving our own self-esteem regulation, in providing inner resource of gratification and pride in our work, that is, approval by the ego ideal. Olinick (1969) uses similar reasons to explain the baffling phenomenon of the analyst's dedication to this "impossible profession" (p. 46).

Nevertheless, the countertransference dangers should not be minimized. Racker (1968) also describes a kind of negative therapeutic reaction of analysts that may be instigated by an "unseen collaboration between the masochism of the analyst and that of the patient" (p. 177). It is not uncommon to witness in supervision how an analyst may make several errors, after a period of good work with useful interpretations, undoing what has just been accomplished.

It is important that we study such countertransference reactions. They may be one explanation of the fascinating and relatively unexplored ability of certain masochists to contaminate and then to arouse similar masochistic actions in their objects—even their analysts. I have elsewhere (1985) described just such a relationship, which was clearly and poignantly developed in Fowles' "The French Lieutenant's Woman."

DISCUSSION

The term moral masochism refers to the masochist's internal conflict among various aspects of his own personality that require him to fail and restrict his gratification and to seek subjugation and punishment. These aspects of his personality are identifications with significant figures from early life. In some character structures, they remain more or less intact, as internalized objects, like flies trapped in amber. Some people never fully separate from these early objects, who remain as important internal arbiters of what is valuable and what is bad. With regression, these internal clusters of ideals and rules, which we have called superego, become more pronounced, and the person may feel desperately driven to please and be loved by them. In the masochist, these internal relationships are usually more important than relationships with external objects.

A clinical hierarchy of masochistic personality does seem to exist and may be divided into two main groups: (1) those derived from oedipal conflicts including guilt, castration anxiety, etc.; (2) those with separation-individuation problems resulting in fragile and incomplete integration of internal objects. The first group is relatively analyzable using usual analytic techniques. The second group is much more difficult, and treatment is characterized by severe self-destructive behavior, negative therapeutic reactions, and a general reluctance to work through what are essentially preoedipal conflicts that would lead to change.

In the masochistic perversion, the relationship to superego elements is mainly externalized and thus is more easily recognizable, since a chosen partner is usually required to act out the role. Freud's (1916) "Criminals Out of a Sense of Guilt" similarly try to force an outside object to play the role of punisher. By contrast, the moral masochist's internal conflict remains with internal objects for the most part. Enactment is not required as it is with the perversion. The depressive externalizes least of all, is sufficient unto himself, with less involvement with outside objects.

Threatened loss of love is a common precipitating element to masochist behavior. The narcissism that is integral to masochism (Asch, 1985), wards off depression by de-emphasizing the loss of the external object, while re-emphasizing the love relationship with the internal object. The narcissistic gratification derives from acting out and provoking the object, now displaced to the outside world, to be reinvolved (even though the involvement is overtly through aggression rather than love). Such control aims in the masochist were strikingly present in Case I, malignant masochism. A specific example of this dynamic can often be found in suicide, the ultimate masochistic act. The suicide often has the fantasy that he is *passively* experiencing the act, that it is being carried out by the loved person, the "hidden executioner" (Asch, 1980). It has the aim of forcing a reunion with an abandoning loved object by enslaving the "executioner" through his act and binding him tightly to the suicide. The masochism serves its frequent aim of control, of preserving or creating a primitive attachment.

Too early stimulation by overly seductive or gratifying parents can arouse and nurture drives before the child is mature enough to deal with their increased urgency and demandingness (viz. Case I). Early environmental problems that may limit development of one's own ability to be in control, such as an overly restrictive childhood or a severe illness, can have a similar effect. The terrifying feeling of being overwhelmed by dark forces that cannot be controlled by the child is often dealt with by shifting the struggle for *internal* control over these impulses to control over the *external* object, who is experienced as stimulating the impulse. As was demonstrated in Case I, the treatment becomes a struggle by the patient to control the analyst while experiencing him as someone who is trying to dominate and enslave the patient. The struggle not only was with the analyst as the transference figure (the seductive incestuous mother) but was also the struggle against the embodiment of the patient's *own* projected frightening desires.

We recognize internalization as an important and necessary element in all human development. In some or all masochists the incomplete and fragile integration of internal objects becomes the core of their special pathology. This is often a result of early mothering that was frequently characterized by incomplete individuation from the controlling, angry, depressed mother figure. Throughout the lives of these patients, their dominant object relationships remain reflections of this internalized duality. Frequently the mother had not satisfactorily separated from her own mother, and she emphasized her own suffering, requiring the child to repair the mother's defective self-representation by re-creating early primitive attachments. The attempt to resolve this problem requires that the child sacrifice to the mother as she sacrificed herself (as she may well have been required to do in a similar way with her mother). These too are etiological elements in the forms of masochism that make treatment difficult and are responsible for many of the analytic problems with masochism that derive from oedipal guilt, castration anxiety, and so forth.

It can be difficult to empathize with some masochistic acting out, especially when the patient is clearly setting up a situation that *must* interfere with a gratification in the real world. It helps to consider that there is an unconscious gratification, one not sought in the real world. It is a choice made to submit to a depriving but loved internal object and to demean the object at the same time. The mechanism is similar to the familiar dynamic of those depressives who attack the part of their self-representation that is identified with the ambivalently felt object. The masochist, by splitting and externalizing, gets the *world* to attack or deprive him.

Eschewing gratification in the real world is a special morality of masochism. It is reminiscent of the Church's teaching in the middle ages—that deprivation and renunciation in *this* world is unimportant. All rewards will accrue after death, in heaven. The Church has institutionalized this particular dynamic of masochism. As with all systems of morality, once it has been integrated, obedience not only assuages guilt, it also produces a narcissistic gratification that becomes an end in itself. Pride, with an increase in self-esteem, has been created by renouncing pleasure. The ego ideal *lovingly* approves of suffering. "The narcissistic gratification lies in being the love object of the approving ego ideal" (Hartman and Lowenstein, 1962, p. 62). The frustration of realistic goals and the appearance of suffering no longer conflicts with narcissism because a new form of narcissistic gratification has evolved—moral masochism.

REFERENCES

American Psychiatric Association (1980), *Diagnostic Statistical Manual of Mental Disorders*, 3rd ed. Washington, DC: American Psychiatric Press.

Alvarez, A. (1972), *The Savage God*. New York: Random House.

Asch, S. S. (1976), Varieties of negative therapeutic reactions. *J. Amer. Psychoanal. Assn.*, 24:383–407.

——— (1980), Suicide and the hidden executioner. *Internat. Rev. Psycho-Anal.* 7:51–60.

——— (1981), Beating fantasies: Symbiosis and child battering. *Internat. J. Psychoanl. Psychother.*, 8:653–658.

——— (1984), Book review: Autoerotic fatalities. *J. Psych. & Law.*, winter:563–571.

——— (1985), Depression, masochism and biology. *J. Clin. Psychiat. Hillside Hosp.*, 7:34–53.

Bak, R. C. (1974), Distortions of the concept of fetishism. *The Psychoanalytic Study of the Child*, 29:191–215. New York: International Universities Press.

Brenman, M. (1952), On teasing and being teased: And the problems of "moral masochism," *The Psychoanalytic Study of the Child*, 7:264–285. New York: International Universities Press.

Brenner, C. (1959), The masochistic character: Genesis and treatment, *J. Amer. Psychoanal. Assn.*, 7:197–226.

Eliott, T. S. (1964), *Murder in the Cathedral*. New York: Harcourt, Brace, Jovanovich.

Fenichel, O. (1945), *The Psychoanalytic Theory of Neurosis*. New York: Norton.

Freud, S. (1916), Some character types met with in psychoanalytic work. *Standard Edition*, 14:311–333. London: Hogarth Press, 1957.

——— (1924), The economic problems of masochism. *Standard Edition*, 19:159–170. London: Hogarth Press, 1959.

Grossman, W. I. (1986), Notes on masochism: A discussion of the history and development of a psychoanalytic concept. *Psychoanal. Quart.*, 40:379–413.

Hartman, H., & Loewenstein, R. (1962), Notes on the superego. *The Psychoanalytic Study of the Child*, 17:42–81. New York: International Universities Press.

Hazlewood, R. R., Dietz, P. E., & Burgess, A. W. (1983), *Autoerotic Fatalities*. Lexington, MA: Heath.

Krafft-Ebing, R. F. von (1895), *Psychopathia Sexualis*. London: F. A. Davis.

Lax, R. F. (1980), The rotten core: A defeat in the formation of the self during the rapprochment subphase. In: *Rapprochement: The Critical Subphase of Separation-Individuation*, ed. R. E. Lax, S. Bach, J. A. Burland. New York: Aronson.

——— (1977), The role of internalization in the development of certain aspects of female masochism. Ego, psychological considerations. *Internat. J. Psycho-Anal.*, 58:289–300.

Loewenstein, R. M. (1957), A contribution to the psychoanalytic theory of masochism. *J. Amer. Psychoanal. Assn.*, 5:197–234.

Mack, J. (1976), *A Prince of Our Disorder*. Boston: Little, Brown.

O'Connor, F. (1962), *Wise Blood*. New York: Farrar, Straus & Giroux.

Olinick, S. S. (1978), The negative therapeutic reaction: A retrospective 15 years later. *J. Phila. Assn., Psychoanal.*, 5:165–176.

——— (1969), On empathy and regression in service of the other, *Brit. J. Med. Psychol.*, 42:41–49.

Racker, H. (1968), *Transference and Countertransference*. New York: International Universities Press.

Rattigan, T. (1960), *Ross: A Play in Two Acts*. London: S. French.

Reik, T. (1941), *Masochism in Modern Man*. New York: Strauss.

Sacher-Masoch, L. von [1870], *Sacher-Masoch: An Interpretation by Gilles Deleuze, together with the entire text of "Venus in Furs,"* trans. J. M. McNeil. London: Faber & Faber, 1871.

Sadger, J. (1926), A contribution to the understanding of sadomasochism, *Internat. J. Psycho-Anal.*, 8:484–491.

Stein, M. (1956), Panel report—the problem of masochism. *J. Amer. Psychoanal. Assn.*, 4:526–538.

Stolorow, R. D. (1975), The narcissistic function of masochism and sadism, *Internat. J. Psycho-Anal.*, 56:441–448.

7 / The Narcissistic-Masochistic Character

Arnold M. Cooper

THERE IS AN OLD CHINESE CURSE: "May you live in interesting times." These are analytically interesting times, in which, more than ever before in the history of psychoanalysis, accepted paradigms have been called into question, and a congeries of new and old ideas compete for attention and allegiance. In intellectual history, such periods of enthusiastic creative ferment have led to the development of new ideas. Sciences make their great advances when new techniques lead to new experiments, when new data contradict old theories, and when new ideas lead to new theories. Since the early 1970s, much of the interesting creative tension in psychoanalysis has focused on the crucial role of preoedipal experiences and the centrality of issues of self or narcissism in character development. I propose that masochistic defenses are ubiquitous in preoedipal narcissistic development and that a deeper understanding of the development of masochism may help to clarify a number of clinical problems. I suggest that a full appreciation of the roles of narcissism and masochism in development and in pathology requires that we relinquish whatever remains of what Freud referred to as the "shibboleth" of the centrality of the Oedipus complex in neurosogenesis. I further suggest that masochism and narcissism are so entwined, both in development and in clinical presentation, that we clarify our clinical work by considering that there is a narcissistic-masochistic character and that neither appears alone.

The problem of reformulating our ideas was foreshadowed over half a century ago, when Freud (1931), in speaking of the intensity and duration of the little girl's attachment to her mother, wrote:

> The pre-Oedipus phase in women gains an importance which we have not attributed to it hitherto. Since this phase allows room for all the fixations and repressions from which we must trace the origin of the neuroses, it would seem as though we must retract the universality of the thesis that the Oedipus complex is the nucleus of neurosis. But if

anyone feels reluctant about making this correction, there is no need for him to do so [p. 225].

Freud then went on to reveal some of his own difficulties in accepting his new findings by stating that those who are reluctant to make this clearly necessary revision need not do so, if they are willing to accept a redefinition of the Oedipus complex to include earlier events. He said:

> Our insights into this early pre-Oedipus phase in girls comes to us as a surprise like the discovery, in another field, of the Minoan-Mycenean civilization behind the civilization of Greece. Everything in the sphere of the first attachment to the mother seems to be so difficult to grasp in analysis—so gray with age and shadowy, and almost impossible to revivify, that it was as if it has succumbed to an especially inexorable repression [p. 226].

Perhaps this is an indication of Freud's and our own difficulty in accepting the breadth of theoretical revision that our data may require. The fact is that in his posthumous work, "The Outline of Psychoanalysis," (1938) he again stated without reservation that the Oedipus complex is the nucleus of neurosis.

It is questionable whether it was ever the case that most analytic patients presented with primary oedipal pathology. Edward Glover in his "Technique of Psychoanalysis," published in 1955, was already lamenting the scarcity of cases of classical transference neurosis. He referred to "those mild and mostly favorable cases which incidentally *appear all too infrequently* in the average analyst's case list" (p. 205). I suspect that few of us have ever seen many cases of "classical transference neurosis," and yet it has been difficult for us to give up the accompanying clinical idea, so dear to Freud, that the nucleus of neurosis is the Oedipus complex. I in no way depreciate the immensity of the discovery of the Oedipus complex and its vital role in human affairs. But we need not share Freud's reluctance to place the Oedipus complex in perspective as one of a number of crucial developmental epochs, and not necessarily the one most significant for our understanding of narcissistic and masochistic pathology, and perhaps not even for understanding neurosis generally.

Kohut's (1971) self psychology represented the most radical attempt to date to address, and resolve, the various dissonant elements in psychoanalytic developmental research, clinical experience and general theory. As I have written elsewhere (1983), I believe it is this exposure of some of the major unresolved problems of psychoanalytic work that accounts for much of the passion—positive and negative—that was generated by self psychology. For more than a decade, psychoanalysis has been productively preoccupied with developing a new understanding of narcissism in the light of our newer emphasis on preoedipal events. The scientific and clinical yield of this investigation has been high, and it should prompt us to apply these methods to other of our metapsychological and clinical formulations that are a bit fuzzy. Prominent among these are the concepts of masochism and the masochistic character.

Our major ideas concerning masochism date to an earlier period of psychoanalytic thinking, when the focus was on the Oedipus complex. The cultural climate of psychoanalysis was different then. A reexamination of masochism at this time, using our newer ideas of separation-individuation, self-esteem regulation, the nature of early object relations, and so on, might help clarify our understanding of masochistic phenomena.

REVIEW OF THEORIES AND DEFINITIONS

The literature is vast, and I will mention only a few salient points. The term *masochism* was coined by Krafft-Ebing in 1895 with reference to Leopold von Sacher-Masoch's (1870) novel, *Venus in Furs*. The novel described, and Krafft-Ebing referred to, a situation of seeking physical and mental torture at the hands of another person through willing submission to experiences of enslavement, passivity and humiliation. Freud (1920) used Krafft-Ebing's terminology, although in his early writings on masochism he was concerned with perversion masochism with clear sexual pleasure attached to pain, and only later was he concerned with the problems of moral masochism in which humiliation and suffering are sought as part of the character formation and without evident sexual satisfactions. Freud postulated several explanations for these puzzling phenomena:

1. It is the nature of physiology that an excess of stimulation in the nervous system automatically leads to experiences of both pain and pleasure.

2. Masochism is a vicissitude of instinct; sadism or aggression, a primary instinct, turns against the self as masochism, a secondary instinctual phenomenon.

3. Masochism is defined as "beyond the pleasure principle," a primary instinct, a component of the death instinct, a consequence of the repetition compulsion, and thus an independent, automatically

operating regulatory principle. Masochism as a primary instinct is, in the course of development, directed outward, and as a tertiary phenomenon, is redirected inward, as clinical masochism.

4. Moral masochism is the need for punishment, consequent to the excessive harshness of the superego. Persons feeling guilty for sexual, generally oedipal, forbidden wishes seek punishment as a means of expiation.

5. Masochistic suffering is a condition for pleasure not a source of pleasure. That is, masochists do not enjoy the suffering per se; rather they willingly endure the pain as an unavoidable guilty ransom for access to forbidden or undeserved pleasures.

6. Masochism is related to feminine characteristics and passivity.

I think it is fair to say that Freud struggled throughout his lifetime for a satisfactory explanation of the paradox of pleasure-in-unpleasure. In "Analysis Terminable and Interminable," (1937) he wrote:

No stronger impression arises from resistances during the work of analysis than of there being a force which is defending itself by every possible means against recovery and which is absolutely resolved to hold on to illness and suffering. One portion of this force has been recognized by us, undoubtedly with justice, as a sense of guilt and need for punishment, and has been localized by us in the ego's relation to the super-ego. But this is only the portion of it which is, as it were, psychically bound by the super ego and thus becomes recognizable; other quotas of the same force, whether bound or free, may be at work in other, unspecified places. If we take into consideration the total picture made up by the phenomena of masochism immanent in so many people, the negative therapeutic reaction and sense of guilt found in so many neurotics, we shall no longer be able to adhere to the belief that mental events are exclusively governed by the desire for pleasure. These phenomena are unmistakable indications of the presence of a power in mental life which we call the instinct of aggression or of destruction according to its aims, and which we trace back to the original death instinct of living matter. It is not a question of an antithesis between an optimistic and pessimistic theory of life. Only by the concurrent or mutually opposing action of the two primal instincts—Eros and the death-instinct—never by one or the other alone, can we explain the rich multiplicity of the phenomena of life [p. 242].

The death instinct, as we all know, is an idea that never caught on.

The vast subsequent literature on masochism was well summarized by Brenner (1959), Stolorow (1975), Maleson (1984), and Grossman (1986), and a Panel of the American Psychoanalytic Association, in which I participated (Fischer, 1981). I will not repeat these summaries, which succinctly convey the large array of functions and etiologies ascribed to masochism. Stolorow's paper deserves special note because he also concerned himself with the narcissistic functions of masochism, pointing out that sadomasochistic development can aid in maintaining a satisfactory self-image. I will, through the remainder of this paper, confine my discussion to so-called moral masochism, or, as some have referred to it, "psychic" masochism. I will not discuss perversion masochism, which I believe to be a developmentally different phenomenon. (See Maleson, 1984, p. 350, for a brief discussion of this issue.) Perverse fantasies, however, are common in persons of very varied personalities.

While many definitions of masochism have been attempted, Brenner's (1959) definition has remained authoritative. He defined masochism as "the seeking of unpleasure, by which is meant physical or mental pain, discomfort or wretchedness, for the sake of *sexual* pleasure, with the qualification that either the seeking or the pleasure or both may often be unconscious rather than conscious" (p. 197). Brenner emphasized that masochism represented an acceptance of a painful penalty for forbidden sexual pleasures associated with the Oedipus complex. He agreed that masochistic phenomena are ubiquitous in both normality and pathology, serving multiple psychic functions including such aims as seduction of the aggressor, maintenance of object-control, and the like. Brenner believed that the genesis of the masochistic character seemed related to excessively frustrating or rejecting parents.

A somewhat different, highly organized view of masochism was put forth in the voluminous writings of the late Edmund Bergler. Because his theories seem to me relevant to topics that are currently of great interest, because they have influenced my own thinking, and because they are so little referred to in the literature, having been premature in their emphasis on the preoedipal period and narcissism, I will present a brief summary of his work. As long ago as 1949, Bergler stated that masochism was a fundamental aspect of all neurotic behavior, and he linked masochistic phenomena with issues of narcissistic development, or development of self-esteem systems. Bergler described in detail a proposed genetic schema out of which psychic masochism develops as an unavoidable aspect of human development. I will mention only a few elements that are particularly germane to the thesis of this paper.

1. Bergler assumed that the preservation of infantile megalomania or infantile omnipotence (we today would say narcissism) is of prime importance for the reduction of anxiety and as a source of satisfac-

tion—on a par with the maintenance of libidinal satisfactions. This formulation is not dissimilar to Kohut's many years later.

2. Every infant is, by its own standards, excessively frustrated, disappointed, refused. These disappointments always have the effect of a narcissistic humiliation because they are an offense to the infant's omnipotent fantasy.

3. The infant responds with fury to this offense to his omnipotent self, but in his helplessness to vent fury on an outer object, the fury is deflected against the self (what Rado (1969) termed retroflexed rage) and eventually contributes to the harshness of the super ego.

4. Faced with unavoidable frustration, the danger of aggression against parents, who are also needed and loved, and the pain of self-directed aggression, the infant nonetheless attempts to maintain essential feelings of omnipotence and self-esteem, and in Bergler's terms, he "libidinizes" or "sugarcoats" his disappointments. He learns to extract pleasure from displeasure for the sake of the illusion of continuing, total, omnipotent control, both of himself and of the differentiating object. "No one frustrated me against my wishes; I frustrated myself because I like it." It was Bergler's belief that some inborn tendency made it easy and inevitable that a pleasure-in-displeasure pattern would develop. He insisted that this develops at the very earliest stages of object differentiation and perhaps, I would add, becomes consolidated during the disappointing realization of helplessness that occurs during the rapprochement phase of the separation-individuation process as described in Mahler (1972).

According to Bergler, these hypothesized early events of psychic development resulted in the "clinical picture" of psychic masochism, which was characterized by the "oral triad." The oral triad, a phrase he used many years before Lewin (1950) used the term for a different purpose, consists of a three-step behavioral sequence that is paradigmatic for masochistic behavior.

Step 1. Through his own behavior or through the misuse of an available external situation, the masochist unconsciously provokes disappointment, refusal, and humiliation. He identifies the outer world with a disappointing, refusing, preoedipal mother. *Unconsciously*, the rejection provides satisfaction.

Step 2. Consciously, the masochist has repressed his knowledge of his own provocation and reacts with righteous indignation and *seeming* self-defense to the rejection, which he consciously perceives as externally delivered. He responds, thus, with "pseudo-aggression," that is, defensive regression designed to disclaim his responsibility for, and unconscious pleasure in, the defeat he has experienced.

Step 2 represents an attempt to appease inner guilt for forbidden unconscious masochistic pleasure.

Step 3. After the subsidence of pseudoaggression, which, because often ill-dosed or ill-timed, may provoke additional unconsciously wished for defeats, the masochist indulges in conscious self-pity, feelings of "this only happens to me." Unconsciously he enjoys the masochistic rebuff.

This clinical oral triad, or, as Bergler calls it, the mechanism of "injustice collecting," is, I think, an excellent description of a repetitive sequence of events observable in almost all neurotic behavior. The term "injustice collector" was coined by Bergler, and later used by Louis Auchincloss (1950) as the title of a collection of stories. In Bergler's view, all human beings have more or less masochistic propensities. The issue of pathology is one of quantity.

THEORETICAL ISSUES

I would like now to explore some of the theoretical issues that have been raised in previous discussions of masochism.

Today there is little disagreement that we can explain masochism in terms of its defensive and adaptive functions without recourse to a primary drive. The extraordinary ease with which pleasure-in-displeasure phenomena develop, and their stickiness, suggests a psychic apparatus that is well prepared for the use of such defensive structures, but there is no theoretical need to call on a primary instinctive masochism.

What is the nature of the pleasure in masochism? The generally accepted formulation that the pleasure is the same as any other pleasure and that the pain the necessary guilty price, has the great merit of preserving the pleasure principle intact. There has always been a group of analysts, however, including Lowenstein (1957) and Bergler, who insisted, to quote Lowenstein, that "in the masochistic behavior we observe an unconscious libidinization of suffering caused by aggression from without and within" (p. 230). The operating principle seems to be, "If you can't lick 'em, join 'em." Perhaps, more simply, one may speculate that the infant claims as his own, and endows with as much pleasure as possible, whatever is familiar, whether painful experiences or unempathic mothers. The defensive capacity to alter the meaning of painful experience so that it is experienced as egosyntonic has also been described in certain circumstances in infancy by Greenacre (1960) and Jacobson (1964). Greenacre reported that babies under conditions of extreme distress will have genital, orgasticlike responses, as early as the second half of the first year, and that these early events may result in ego distortions creating sexual excitation arising from self-directed aggression. This is similar to Freud's original formulation, and I think we must leave open the possibility that there is a dialectic here of excessive quantity changing quality.

From a different point of view, we may ask, What are the gratifying and constructive aspects of pain? We do not dispute every mother's observation that painful frustration, disappointment, and injury are inevitable concomitants of infancy. It is rare that any infant goes through a 24-hour period without exhibiting what we adults interpret at least to be cries of discomfort, frustration, and need. Even the most loving and competent mother cannot spare the infant these experiences, and, indeed, there is good reason to believe that no infant should be spared these experiences in proper dosage. It seems likely that painful bodily, particularly skin, experiences are important proprioceptive mechanisms that serve not only to avoid damage, but also, developmentally, to provide important components of the forming body image and self-image. There are many cases in the literature, summarized by Stolorow (1975), of persons who experience a relief from identity diffusion by inflicting pain upon their skin.

A typical pattern for borderline self-mutilators is to cut or otherwise injure themselves in privacy, experiencing little pain in the process. They later exhibit the injury to the usually surprised caretaking person, be it parent or physician, with evident satisfaction in the demonstration that they are suffering, in danger, and beyond the control of the caretaking person. A prominent motivation for this behavior is the need to demonstrate autonomy via the capacity for self-mutilation.

Head banging in infants, a far more common phenomenon than is usually acknowledged and quite compatible with normal development is also, I suggest, one of the normal, painful ways of achieving necessary and gratifying self-definition. Skin sensations of all kinds, and perhaps moderately painful sensations particularly, are a regular mode of establishing self-boundaries.

Hermann (1976) stated:

> In order to understand masochistic pleasure, one has to recognize that it is quite closely interwoven with the castration complex but behind this link is the reaction-formation to the urge to cling—namely the drive to separate oneself. At this point, we have to go far back to early development. Our guess is that the emergence of the process of

separation of the mother and child dual unit constitutes a pre-stage of narcissism and painful masochism; normal separation goes along with "healthy" narcissism [p. 30].

Hermann then went on to describe that pain is a necessary concomitant of separation but is a lesser evil than the damage and decay of the self, which would result from failure of separation in infancy. He referred to a healing tendency within the psyche and the erotization of pain, which facilitates healing of a damaged psychic area. Hermann viewed all later self-mutilations, such as self-biting, tearing one's cuticles, pulling hair, tearing scabs, and the like as attempts to reinforce a sense of freedom from the need to cling: ". . . pain arises in connection with the *separation that is striven for*, while its *successful accomplishment* brings pleasure" (p. 30). Hermann viewed masochistic character traits as a consequence of failure of successful separation with reactive repetition of separation traumas.

Pain, it is suggested, serves the person's need for self-definition and separation-individuation and is part of a gratifying accomplishment. Mastery—not avoidance—of pain is a major achievement in the course of self-development; mastery may imply the capacity to derive satisfaction and accomplishment from self-induced, self-dosed pain. The tendency for such an achievement to miscarry is self-evident. The pleasurable fatigue after a day's work, the ecstasy of an athlete's exhaustion, the dogged pursuit of distant goals, the willingness to cling to a seemingly absurd ideal—all of these represent constructive uses of pleasure in pain and a source of creative energies.

All cultures at all times have idealized heroes whose achievement involves painful and dangerous feats, if not actual martyrdom. The achievement is not valued unless it is fired in pain. No culture chooses to live without inflicting pain on itself; even cultures seemingly devoted to nirvana-type ideals have painful rituals. Rites of passage and experiences of mortification, "baptism by fire," are means of assuring essential aspects of cultural and individual identity, and their effectiveness may be proportional to their painfulness and sharpness of definition. A circumcision ceremony at puberty is obviously a clearer marker of a stage in self-development and onset of manhood than is a Bar Mitzvah ceremony.

The question of aggression in the induction of masochism is interesting but, I think, not satisfactorily answerable at this time. Regularly in the course of development, aggression is distributed in at least five directions: 1) in legitimate self-assertion; 2) in projection; 3) turned against the self; 4) toward the formation of the superego;

and 5) used defensively as "pseudoaggression." The proportions vary, but in the narcissistic-masochistic character legitimate self-assertion is in short supply. I will not discuss here the many issues of the relationship of sadism to masochism, double identifications with both aggressor and victim, and so forth. It seems clear that experiences of frustration and the absence of loving care, whether in infant children or infant monkeys, induce self-directed aggression and mutilation. The usual explanations involve ideas of retroflexed rage or failure of instinct fusion. These concepts are convenient, but not entirely adequate. Stoller (this volume) states that hostility, in retaliation for and in disavowal of early experiences of passivity and humiliation at the hands of a woman, is the crucial motivation in *all* perversions, not only masochistic perversion. (Hostility, in his view, is an important aspect of all sexuality.) Referring to the risks that perverts take, he says, "But the true danger that perversion is to protect him from—that he is insignificant, unruly—is not out there on the street but within him and therefore inescapable. It is so fundamental a threat that he is willing to run the lesser risk, that of being caught." Dizmang and Cheatham (1970), discussing the Lesch-Nyhan Syndrome, have suggested a psychobiological basis for masochistic behavior in the postulate of a low threshold for activation of a mechanism that ordinarily controls tendencies toward repetitive compulsive behaviors and self-inflicted aggression.

At what stage of development do the decisive events leading to masochistic character disorder occur? It is clear from what I have been describing that I feel it is now evident that the masochistic conflicts of the Oedipus complex are reworkings of much earlier established masochistic functions. In the later character development, these defenses, by means of the mechanism of secondary autonomy (Hartmann and Loewenstein, 1962) function as if they were wishes.

AN ATTEMPT AT CLARIFICATION

If even part of what I have been suggesting is correct, then masochistic tendencies are a necessary and ubiquitous aspect of narcissistic development. I think there is convincing evidence that Freud was right—the pleasure principle alone is inadequate to explain masochism, nor does the dual instinct theory add sufficient heuristic power. If we add an instinct or tendency toward aggression, we still lack heuristic power. Our knowledge of early development and our knowledge derived from the studies of borderline and psychotic disorders make it abundantly clear that a newer theoretical perspective requires that issues of self-development and object relations be accorded their proper weight as crucial factors in early psychological development. Libidinal pleasures and aggressive satisfactions will be sacrificed or distorted if necessary to help prevent the shattering disorganizing anxieties that arise when the self-system is disturbed or the ties to the object disrupted. Whether one refers to Kohut's (1972) narcissistic libido, or Erikson's (1963) basic trust, or Sullivan's (1953) sense of security, or Rado's (1969) basic pride and dependency needs, or Sandler and Joffee's (1969) feelings of safety, or Bergler's (1949) omnipotent fantasy, or Winnicott's (1971) true self—all are ways of addressing the crucial issues of the organism's primary needs for self-definition out of an original symbiotic bond. In fact, Freud, under the unfortunately termed "death instinct" was making the same point. The organism will give up libidinal pleasure for the safety, satisfaction, or pleasure of maintaining a coherent self.

Let me summarize my view of the relevant issues:

1. Pain is a necessary and unavoidable concomitant of separation-individuation and the achievement of selfhood. Perhaps "Doleo ergo sum" (I suffer, therefore I am) is a precursor of "Sentio ergo sum" (I feel, therefore I am), and "Cogito ergo sum", (I think, therefore I am).

2. The frustrations and discomforts of separation-individuation, necessary events in turning us toward the world, are perceived as narcissistic injuries—that is, they damage the sense of magical omnipotent control and threaten intolerable passivity and helplessness in the face of a perceived external danger. This is the prototype of narcissistic humiliation.

3. The infant attempts defensively to restore threatened self-esteem by distorting the nature of his experience. Rather than accept the fact of helplessness, the infant reasserts control by making suffering ego-syntonic. "I am frustrated because I want to be. I force my mother to be cruel." Freud (1937), of course, often discussed the general human intolerance of passivity and the tendency to assert mastery by converting passively endured experiences into actively sought ones. The mastery of pain is part of normal development, and this always implies a capacity to derive satisfaction from pain.

4. Alternatively, one may consider that the infant, out of the need to maintain some vestiges of self-esteem in situations of more than ordinary pain, displeasure, failure of reward, and diminished self-esteem, will still attempt to salvage pleasure by equating the familiar with the pleasurable. Survival in infancy undoubtedly depends on retaining some capacity for receiving pleasurable impressions from

the self and object. We may theorize that the infant makes the best adaptation he can—familiar pains may be the best available pleasure.

5. What I am terming narcissistic-masochistic tendencies are compatible with normal development and with loving, although never unambivalent, ties to objects.

6. Where the experience of early narcissistic humiliation is excessive for external or internal reasons, these mechanisms of repair miscarry. The object is perceived as excessively cruel and refusing; the self is perceived as incapable of genuine self-assertion in the pursuit of gratification; the gratifications obtained from disappointment take precedence over genuine but unavailable and unfamiliar libidinal, assertive, or ego-functional satisfactions. Being disappointed, or refused, becomes the *preferred* mode of narcissistic assertion to the extent that narcissistic and masochistic distortions dominate the character. Nietzsche, quoted by Hartmann and Loewenstein (1962), said, "He who despises himself, nevertheless esteems himself thereby as despisor" (p. 59). One can always omnipotently guarantee rejection—love is much chancier. If one can securely enjoy disappointment, it is no longer possible to be disappointed. To the extent that narcissistic-masochistic defenses are used, the aim is not a fantasied reunion with a loving and caring mother; rather it is fantasied control over a cruel and damaging mother. Original sources of gratification have been degraded, and gratification is secondarily derived from the special sense of suffering.

7. It seems clear that the pleasure sought is not genital-sexual in origin, is preoedipal, and is the satisfaction and pride of a more satisfying self-representation, a pleasure in an ego function, the regulation of self-esteem. Psychic masochism is not a derivative of perversion masochism, although the two are often related. Exhibitionistic drives, pleasures of self-pity, and many other gratifications play a role secondarily.

8. Inevitably, when narcissistic-masochistic pathology predominates, superego distortions also occur. The excessive harshness of the superego is, in my view, a feature of all narcissistic and masochistic pathology and often dominates the *clinical* picture.

9. In any particular instance, the presenting clinical picture may seem more narcissistic or more masochistic. The surface may be full of charm, preening, dazzling accomplishment, or ambition. Or the surface may present obvious depression, invitations to humiliation, and feelings of failure. However, only a short period of analysis will reveal that both types share the sense of deadened capacity to feel, muted pleasure, a hypersensitive self-esteem alternating between

grandiosity and humiliation, an inability to sustain or derive satisfaction from their relationships or their work, a constant sense of envy, an unshakable conviction of being wronged and deprived by those who are supposed to care for them, and an infinite capacity for provocation.

Trilling (1963), in his brilliant essay "The Fate of Pleasure," based on Freud's "Beyond the Pleasure Principle," spoke of the change in cultural attitude from the time of Wordsworth, who wrote of "the grand elementary principle of pleasure," which he said constituted "the named and native dignity of man," and which was "the principle by which man knows and feels, and lives, and moves." Trilling referred to a

> change in quantity. It has always been true of some men that to pleasure they have preferred unpleasure. They imposed upon themselves difficult and painful tasks, they committed themselves to strange "unnatural" modes of life, they sought after stressing emotions, in order to know psychic energies which are not to be summoned up in felicity. These psychic energies, even when they are experienced in self destruction, are a means of self definition and self-affirmation. As such, they have a social reference—the election of unpleasure, however isolated and private the act may be, must refer to society if only because the choice denies the valuation which society in general puts upon pleasure; of course it often receives social approbation of the highest degree, even if at a remove of time: it is the choice of the hero, the saint and martyr, and, in some cultures, the artist. The quantitative change which we have to take account of is: what was once a mode of experience of a few has now become an ideal of experience of many. For reasons which, at least here, must defy speculation, the ideal of pleasure has exhausted itself, almost as if it had been actually realized and had issued in satiety and ennui. In its place or, at least, beside it, there is developing—conceivably at the behest of literature!—an ideal of the experience of those psychic energies which are linked with unpleasure and which are directed towards self-definition and self-affirmation" [p. 85].

The model for Trilling here is Dostoevsky's "Underground Man," the provocateur without peer. One could add Melville's "Bartleby" as the other pole of the masochistic-narcissistic character who dominates through his seeming passivity. I believe that Trilling was, with his usual extraordinary perspicacity, describing at the level of culture the same shift we have experienced in psychoanalysis at the level of clinical practice. This new type that he described was the same new type with which psychoanalysis has been struggling now for years, the so-called narcissistic-masochistic character. Trilling clearly perceived that this character type struggles to achieve self-definition through the experience of unpleasure. When this occurs within socially acceptable limits we have 'normal' narcissistic-masochistic character development. The narcissistic-masochistic character as a pathological type, of varying severity, is marked by the preferential pursuit of suffering and rejection with little positive achievement. Every quantitative gradation occurs between normal and severely pathological or borderline. The mildly neurotic "plays" with self-torture, while the borderline or psychotic may cause irreparable self-damage.

CLINICAL EXAMPLES

I would like now to illustrate this thesis with a clinical vignette and a condensed account of an analysis. Once again, I emphasize that I will not in this brief presentation elaborate a great many significant elements but will focus on a few of these relevant to the view I am suggesting.

Clinical Vignette 1

Miss A., a 26-year-old student, entered treatment with complaints of chronic anxiety and depression, feelings of social isolation, and a series of unfortunate relationships with men. She was the younger by three years of two sisters, who were the children of an aloof, taciturn, successful businessman father and a mother who was widely admired for her beauty and who devoted herself almost full time to the preservation of her beauty. Miss A. recalled having had in childhood severe temper tantrums that would intimidate the family, but in between tantrums she was an obedient child and an excellent student. Although she always felt cold and distant in her relationships, she recalled that almost up to puberty she had continued to make a huge fuss whenever the parents were going out for an evening. She couldn't bear their leaving her alone. When she began to date at age 14, this middle class Jewish girl chose lower class black boys for her companions and insisted on bringing them home to meet her parents. As a consequence, she and the father fought and literally did not speak to each other from that time until the father died when she was 16. By the time that she entered treatment, she had repeated several times the following pattern with men: she would become intensely involved with a man who she knew from the start was unsuitable. He might be married, or someone who was intellectually her inferior, or someone she really didn't like. From the beginning of the relationship, she would be aware that this could not last. She would project this feeling and become intensely angry at the man because he, in her view, was unreliable and threatened to leave her. She would in her fury become increasingly provocative, finally bringing about the separation she both desired and feared. She would then become depressed and feel abandoned.

The repetition of this pattern was a major element in the transference. She was never late for an appointment, paid her bills on time, tried hard to be a "good patient," although she found it difficult to talk. She was convinced that I eagerly awaited the end of every session, the break for the weekend, or the start of a holiday because I was delighted to be rid of her, and she felt that she could not survive without me. (She had dreams of floating in space, isolated, and dreams of accidents.) On the surface, her idealization of me was complete, but dreams and other data revealed the anger and devaluation which permeated that seeming idealization. Idealization in the transference is, in fact, never in the adult pure idealization but is always merged with the hidden rage that the child experienced in the course of separation-individuation. She would never allow herself to take a holiday or miss an appointment, obviously to maintain the clear record that I was the one who did all the abandoning. This was analyzed at length. Midway in the analysis, in the spring of the year, she planned her summer holiday before knowing precisely what my holiday dates would be. We discussed her plan at length, and for the first time she felt confident and pleased about being able to go away on a self-initiated separation. Several weeks later, I mentioned in the course of a session that the vacation dates had worked out well because in fact my holiday would coincide with hers. She immediately was enraged and self-pitying that I would go away and leave her, and it became utterly unimportant that she had previously made her own arrangements to go away. Several things became apparent in the analysis of this episode.

1. A major portion of her self-esteem and self-knowledge consisted of her representation to herself of herself as an innocent abandoned martyr.

2. She felt a comfortable familiarity and control of her intimate objects only in the context of her ability to create a feeling of abandonment or to provoke an actual abandonment by the object. This was at its basic level preoedipal in nature and clearly reflected her sense of being uncared for by her narcissistic mother.

3. Additionally, this constellation represented the repetition of

oedipal issues, and in the transference she was also reliving aspects of her oedipal relationship to her father. All preoedipal constellations have another reworking during the oedipal phase, but that latter does not constitute all the recoverable content of the genetic constellation.

4. The intolerable frustration of the original infantile demands for love and union had led to narcissistic-masochistic defenses. What she *now* sought in her relationships, disguised as an insatiable demand for attention, was the repetition of the painful abandonment, but with the hidden gratification of narcissistic control and masochistic satisfaction. The demand for love had been given up in favor of the pleasure of rejection.

This is the paradigmatic sequence for narcissistic-masochistic pathology.

Clinical Vignette 2

A 40-year-old, successful corporate executive entered analysis because he had plunged into a deep depression following an accusation of minor wrongdoing in some financial maneuvers. In fact he was innocent of the charge, which had arisen out of an equally innocent error of one of his assistants. He had been officially cleared of any taint, and the whole matter was minor to begin with. However, this was one in a lifelong series of actually, or potentially, self-damaging provocations in important situations, which were further characterized by his inappropriate failure to defend himself with sufficient vigor in the face of the attack that followed his provocation. These incidents had regularly been followed by feelings of depression and self-pity, but this time the feelings were severe. He could not rid himself of the feelings that he had shamefully exposed himself to his colleagues, that his entire career would collapse, and that he would turn out to be a laughingstock with fraudulent pretensions to greatness. The presenting symptom thus combined masochistic, provocative self-damage, and self-pity with a sense of narcissistic collapse. I will present only a few relevant aspects of the history and treatment course. I will deliberately neglect much of the oedipal material that arose during the course of the analysis and that was interpreted; instead I will concentrate on earlier aspects of development. This will be a sketch, and many significant issues will not be elaborated.

He was the youngest of three children, the only boy and, as he acknowledged only later, the favorite child. He viewed his own childhood with great bitterness. He felt he had received nothing of value from his parents and that they had played no positive role in his life. He regarded himself as a Phoenix—born out of himself, his own father and mother. These feelings of bitter deprivation—nobody ever gave me anything—had formed a masochistic current throughout his life. His mother had been a powerfully narcissistic woman, who saw in her son the opportunity for realizing her ambitions for wealth and status, cravings she unceasingly berated the father for not satisfying. The patient recalled little affection from his mother and felt she had used him only for her own satisfaction and as an ally against his weak, passive father. His father had been a modest success until the depression hit, when the patient was four, and both he and his business collapsed, never to recover. This probably provided a serious blow to whatever attempts at idealization may have been underway. The parents fought constantly, mother reminding father daily of his failure, and the boy remembered great anxiety that they would separate and he would be abandoned.

The sharp edge of his depression lifted shortly after analysis began, revealing a level of chronic depression and a character of endless injustice collecting and self-pity, covered by a socially successful facade of charm and joviality. He felt that although many people regarded him as a friend and sought him out, he had no friends and felt no warmth toward anyone. Perhaps he loved his wife and children, but he arranged his work schedule so that he would never have to be near them for any length of time. He felt isolated and lived with a constant dread that some disaster would befall him. The incident that precipitated his depression bothered him partly because he felt he was being hauled down by something trivial rather than by an episode fittingly grandiose. He battled endlessly with his associates in business, making wildly unreasonable demands and feeling unjustly treated when they were not yielded to. At the same time, he maintained a killing work pace and never asked for the readily available help that might have reduced his work load. He had a mechanically adequate sex life with his wife and fantasied endlessly about the beautiful women he wanted to sleep with. In fact, he was convinced that he would be impotent with anyone except his wife, and he never dared to attempt an affair.

Early in the treatment, he expressed two major concerns with regard to me. First, that it was my goal to make him "like everyone else." "I couldn't bear to live if I thought I was like everyone else. I'd rather be bad or dead than not be a somebody. Before I give up the feeling of awful things happening to me, I want to be sure I won't be giving up my sense of being special." Second, he was convinced that I had no interest in him, that I saw him only because I wanted the fee.

That suited him fine because he had no interest in me, but it worried him that I might not need the fee badly enough so that he could count on my availability for as long as he might want me. Interestingly, convinced then that I only saw him for the money, he was regularly late in paying his bills and would worry about the consequences but not mention it himself. When I would bring up his tardiness, he would feel a combination of terror that I was now going to be angry with him and throw him out and fury that I had the nerve to dun him for money, when everyone knew he was an honest man. Quickly, then, the transference, like his life, developed a variety of narcissistic and masochistic themes.

The early transference combined both idealizing and mirror forms. These narcissistic transferences are, in my view, always equally masochistic, since they are regularly suffused with rage and the expectation of disappointment. The idealization often is the façade for constructing larger, later disappointments. As adults, narcissistic-masochistic characters no longer have genuine expectations of their grandiose fantasies being met. Rather, grandiose fantasies are the occasion for re-enactment of unconsciously gratifying disappointments. The seeming insatiability of so many of these patients is not due to excessive need; instead, it represents their raising the demand for love, time, attention, or whatever to the level necessary to be sure it cannot be met. This man, for example, seemed to look forward to sessions, was friendly, felt that my most obvious remarks were brilliant, seemed happy to attribute to me all of the intelligent ideas that he had in the analysis. The other side of this coin, however, was his angry conviction that I used my intelligence totally in my own behalf and had no interest in helping him. He felt that all the work in analysis was being done by himself. A typical dream was of him and a guide scaling a high mountain, making remarkable progress but never speaking, and with him in the lead. In discussing this dream, he said, "All you do here is nudge me along. Why don't you help me more? The work is all mine. I can't bear the thought that anyone else has a part in anything I do." Fantasies of this sort have the double purpose of maintaining a grandiose, omnipotent image of himself and of maintaining an image of the totally refusing mother. The narcissistic portion of the fantasy requires the masochistic portion. "I give myself everything; my mother gives me nothing." A sense of grandiosity and a sense of self-pitying deprivation paradoxically are sides of the same coin, and neither can exist without the other. The narcissistic grandiose self as seen in the adult can never be the original germ of narcissism but is always tempered by the experiences of frustration, which then become part and parcel of the narcissistic fantasy. "I am a great person because I overcome the malice of my refusing mother."

At a later stage of treatment, when I insistently brought up the issue of his feelings about me, he reacted fiercely, saying, "This is a process, not a human relationship. You are not here. You are not. There is just a disembodied voice sitting behind me." As I persisted and discussed how difficult it was for him to acknowledge that he received something from me and felt something for me, he reported, "I feel creepy. I have a physical reaction to this discussion." He was experiencing mild depersonalization, related to the disturbance of self and narcissistic stability, which resulted from the revival of remnants of the repressed affectionate bond toward his mother. The acknowledgment of this bond immediately induced feelings of terrifying weakness, of being passively at the mercy of a malicious giant. On the other hand, this masochistic, passive, victimized relationship to a maliciously perceived mother was an unconscious source of narcissistic gratification (I never yield to her) and masochistic gratification (I enjoy suffering at the hands of a monster). One could see much of this man's life as an attempt at narcissistic denial of underlying, passive masochistic wishes.

As further memories of affectionate interactions with his mother were recovered, he began to weep, was depressed, and dreamed that I was pulling a big black thing out of the middle of him, a cancer that wouldn't come out but that would kill him if it did come out. The analysis, which had been pleasant for him before, now became extremely painful, and he insisted that I was deliberately humiliating him by forcing him to reveal his stupidity, because I knew the answers to all the questions that I was raising with him and he did not. I enjoyed making a helpless fool out of him. He dreamed he was in a psychiatrist's office in Brooklyn, which for him was a term of derogation, and receiving a special form of treatment. "I was hypnotized and totally helpless. People are ridiculing me, screaming guffaws like a fun house. Then I run down a hill through a big garage antique shop." In another dream at this time he was driving a huge shiny antique 1928 Cadillac in perfect condition. "As I am driving, the steering wheel comes apart, the right half of it comes off in my hand, then the big black shiny hood is gone, then the radiator cap is gone." He was born in 1928. At this time he also developed a transitory symptom of retarded ejaculation, which was a form of actively withholding the milk he insisted was being withheld from him.

The revival of repressed positive ties to his mother threatened his major masochistic and narcissistic characterological defenses. His entire sense of being exceptional depended on his pride in having suffered unusual deprivation at the hands of mother, and his entire experience of being loved and favored by his mother had been perceived by him as a threat of passive submission to a superior malicious force. He perceived this turn in the treatment as endangering his life of narcissistic and masochistic satisfactions and exposing him to the hazards of intimacy, mutual dependence, and a genuine recognition of the extent of his unconsciously sought-for bittersweet pleasure in self-damage and self-deprivation. The increasing recognition of a bond to me was accompanied by an exacerbation of the fantasy that I was the all-powerful, withholding mother and he was the victimized child. Lowenstein (1957) has remarked, "Masochism is the weapon of the weak—of every child—faced with the danger of human aggression." I would only emphasize that, indeed, every child, in his own perception, faces the danger of human aggression.

At this stage in treatment his injustice collecting surged to new refinements. Frequent requests for appointment changes, complicated dreams to which I did not have magical, brilliant interpretations, the fact that he was not already cured, my insistence that sessions had to be paid for—all of these were proof of my malicious withholding and of his innocent victimization. The injustice collecting, partly a result of fragile and fragmented self- and object representation, is also a guilt relieving, rage empowering, reinforcement of masochistic, and narcissistic defenses. These patients are indeed singled out for mistreatment by especially powerful figures to whom they have a special painful attachment.

After a great deal of working through, two incidents occurred that signaled a change in the transference. The first was that I had made an error in noting the date of an appointment he had cancelled. Instead of his usual reaction of outrage and indignation, he sat bolt upright on the couch, looking at me as if this were the first mistake I had ever made and said, "You mean, you make mistakes too?" The second incident occurred a few weeks later. After a particularly resistant session, I said, "I wish we could better understand your relationship to your mother." He was again startled and said, "You mean you really don't know the answer?" I assured him that I did not and that we would have to work it out together. He now began to acknowledge my reality as a human being, fallible and yet concerned for his welfare. Increasingly from this point the case tended to resemble that of a classical neurosis, although with many, many detours to deep masochistic and narcissistic issues.

One could further discuss the nature of the Oedipus complex in this type of patient, from this point of view, but that is beyond the scope of this paper.

SUMMARY

I have attempted in this chapter to suggest, on the basis of genetic hypotheses and clinical data, that the themes of narcissism and masochism, crucial in all human psychic development, achieve their particular individual character at preoedipal stages of development. Furthermore, narcissistic tendencies and masochistic defenses are intimately and inevitably interwoven in the course of development; so interwoven, in fact, that I further suggest that the narcissistic character and the masochistic character are one and the same. I think the vast literature on these entities may become more coherent when considered from the point of view of a single nosological entity—the narcissistic-masochistic character.

In any particular person either the narcissistic or masochistic qualities may be more apparent in the lifestyle, as a result of internal and external contingencies that may be traced and clarified in the course of an analysis. A closer examination, however, will reveal the structural unity and mutual support of the two characterologic modes, despite the surface distinctions. Neither can exist without the other. Interpreting masochistic behavior produces narcissistic mortification, and interpreting narcissistic defenses produces feelings of masochistic victimization, self-pity, and humiliation.

The analysis of the narcissistic-masochistic character is always a difficult task. I hope that our changing frame of reference and the beginning elucidation of the genetic and clinical unity of the seemingly disparate pathologies may help to make our efforts more consistent, coherent, and successful.

REFERENCES

Auchincloss, L. (1950), *The Injustice Collectors*, Boston: Houghton Mifflin.

Bergler, E. (1949), *The Basic Neurosis, Oral Regression and Psychic Masochism*, New York: Grune & Stratton.

——— (1961), *Curable and Incurable Neurotics*, New York: Liveright.

Brenner, C. (1959), The masochistic character: Genesis and treatment. *J. Amer. Psychoanal. Assn.*, 7:197–226.

Cooper, A. (1983), *Psychoanalytic inquiry and new knowledge. Reflections on Self Psychology*, ed. J. Lichtenberg & S. Kaplan. Hillsdale, NJ: The Analytic Press.

Dizmang, L., & Cheatham, C. (1970), The Lesch-Nyhan Syndrome. *Amer. J. Psychiat.*, 127(5):131–137.

Erikson, E. (1963), *Childhood and Society*. New York: W. W. Norton.

Fischer, N. (1981), Masochism: Current concepts. *J. Amer. Psychoanal. Assn.*, 29:673–688.

Freud, S. (1914), On the history of psycho-analytic movement. *Standard Edition*, 14:7–66. London: Hogarth Press, 1957.

———— (1920), Beyond the pleasure principle. *Standard Edition*, 18:3–66. London: Hogarth Press, 1955.

———— (1931), Female sexuality. *Standard Edition*, 21:223–246. London: Hogarth Press, 1961.

———— (1937), Analysis terminable and interminable. *Standard Edition*, 23:250–251. London: Hogarth Press, 1964.

———— (1938), An outline of psychoanalysis. *Standard Edition*, 23:141–208. London: Hogarth Press, 1964.

Glover, E. (1955), *Technique of Psychoanalysis*. New York: International Universities Press.

Greenacre, P. (1960), Regression and fixation: Considerations concerning the development of the ego. *J. Amer. Psychoanal. Assn.*, 8:703–723.

Grossman, W. I. (1986), Notes on masochism: A discussion of the history and development of a psychoanalysis concept. *Psychoanalytic Quarterly*, 54:379–413.

Hartmann, H., & Loewenstein, R. M. (1962), Notes on the superego. *The Psychoanalytic Study of the Child*, 17:42–81. New York: International Universities Press.

Hermann, I. (1976), Clinging going in search. *Psychoanalytic Quarterly*, 44:5–36.

Jacobson, E. (1964), *The Self and The Object World*, New York: International Universities Press.

Kohut, H. (1971), *The Analysis of the Self*, New York: International Universities Press.

———— (1972) Thoughts on narcissism and narcissistic rage. *The Psychoanalytic Study of the Child*, 27:360–400. New Haven: Yale University Press.

Krafft-von Ebing, R. F. (1895), *Psychopathia Sexualis*. London: F. A. Davis.

Lewin, B. (1950), *Psychoanalysis of Elation*, New York: W. W. Norton & Company.

Lowenstein, R. (1957), A contribution to the psychoanalytic theory of masochism. *J. Amer. Psychoanal. Assn.*, 5:197–234.

Mahler, M. (1972), Rapprochement subphase of the separation-individuation process. *Psychoanalytic Quarterly*, 44:487–506.

Maleson, F. (1984), The multiple meanings of masochism in psychoanalytic discourse. *J. Amer. Psychoanal. Assn.*, 32:325–256.

Rado, S. (1969), *Adaptational Psychodynamics*, New York: Science House.

Sacher-Masoch, L. von [1870], *Sacher-Masoch: An Interpretation by Gilles Deleuze, together with the entire text of "Venus in Furs"*, trans. J. M. McNeil, London: Faber and Faber, 1971.

Sandler, J., & Joffee, W. G. (1969), Towards a basic psychoanalytic model. *Internat. J. Psycho-Anal.*, 50:79–90.

Stolorow, R. D. (1975), The narcissistic function of masochism and sadism. *Internat. J. Psycho-Anal.*, 56:441–448.

Sullivan, H. S. (1953), *The Interpersonal Theory of Psychiatry*, New York: W. W. Norton.

Trilling, L. (1963), *Beyond Culture*, New York: Viking Press.

Winnicott, D. W. (1971), *Playing and Reality*, New York: Basic Books.

8 / Masochism and the Repetition Compulsion

John E. Gedo

IN RECENT YEARS, psychoanalysts have devoted much thought to the question of *how* analysis cures (e.g., Kohut, 1984), without paying similar attention to the more basic problem of *what* exactly needs to be cured through psychological measures. More than 60 years have passed since Ferenczi (Ferenczi and Rank, 1924) proclaimed that the analysis of both symptoms and "complexes" had been superseded by a technique giving equal weight to all aspects of the personality, but our nosology has not kept pace with advances in other areas of psychoanalytic theory. To be sure, those who undergo analytic treatment are self-selected individuals seeking to improve their adaptation—by obtaining profit or pleasure, if you will, or through the avoidance of pain or loss. Hence, for the practitioner, diagnostic considerations seem to have little pragmatic significance and have generally been subordinated to concerns about analyzability (e.g., Erle, 1979; Erle and Goldberg, 1979, 1984).

A basic postulate of psychoanalytic psychology is that of exceptionless psychological determinism (Freud, 1901); from this it follows that avoidable pain or loss comes about only through the operation of preexisting mental dispositions. In other words, in a fundamental sense, any maladaptation is "masochistic." It may be pertinent to note in this connection that in his late work, beginning with "Beyond the Pleasure Principle" (1920), Freud assumed the operation of a permanent force he called "primary masochism." Although he defined this term narrowly as the operation of entropy, in a clinical context it is understood as a self-damaging "drive" that prevents the attainment of pleasure aims. Although recently theoreticians have seldom classified masochism as a drive, Freud's concept still appears to be useful in focusing on the inevitability of conflict between certain innate dispositions and one's conscious adaptive goals.

In everyday discourse, we tend not to take primary masochism into account; we are more likely to speak of masochism when we encounter repetitive maladaptive behaviors that strike patient and observer alike as motivated by a need to *seek* pain or loss. As I have described at greater length elsewhere (Gedo, 1984, chap. 1), such behaviors run the gamut of functional possibilities from the ability to make constructive sacrifices in behalf of others, through fantasies of being victimized, masochistic perversions, and addictions to painful experiences, to the literal infliction of self-injury.

Patients vary considerably in their readiness to acknowledge responsibility for the causation of their perceived misfortunes; it takes some therapeutic work for agreement to be reached that everyone to a very large extent determines one's own unfavorable destiny. Yet it is seldom very difficult to undo the rationalizations that may cover the self-restrictive or self-damaging enactments that can be stopped only if patients recognize that alternative choices are available to them. Analytic patients frequently are keenly aware of their masochism but tend to confuse it with self-punishment. I do not mean to imply that it is ever easy to differentiate clinically between the expiation of guilt and the need to seek unpleasure, based on other motives; I am merely suggesting that people tend to be humiliated by their masochistic propensities and may just as readily defend against recognition of the real nature of their inclinations by conceiving of them as superego conflicts as they may claim that the consequences of their "proclivities are the result of intractable external realities.

It is characteristic of most varieties of masochism that one who compulsively repeats the behaviors that bring about unpleasure does not understand the motives for doing so. The major exception to this rule is the person who behaves masochistically as part of an identification with someone, generally a primary caretaker, who served as a model of masochism in the person's childhood. Very often such an identification is founded on ambivalence—sometimes the protagonists are actually engaged in a competition about who has suffered more. (I have described such a circumstance in some detail in a family of death-camp survivors [Gedo, 1984, chap. 5].) In such cases it is generally clear that the child could gain self-esteem only by following the thorny path of the parent's masochistic proclivities. Even in less unusual family settings, masochistic behaviors by one or both parents may become idealized by a child or children and thus acquire the status of the only avenue leading toward true worth. Later life experience may very likely result in the adoption of conscious ideals more acceptable to the community at large, but such a change often leaves the original identification unaltered, although the archaic ideal may be disavowed or repressed and therefore continue to influence behavior unconsciously.

Instances of masochism based on early identifications probably cannot be classified as behaviors "beyond" the pleasure principle, for their actual aim is the achievement of what was once understood as excellence—in other words, the excessive cost of these inconvenient adaptive patterns is merely an incidental byproduct of the attainment of childhood self-esteem. Occasionally, this may be buttressed by masochistic behaviors that do not stem from identifications with a similarly masochistic caretaker. I should like to illustrate the formation of such a pattern on the basis of a different mechanism through a more detailed case history.

Case 1:

A patient I had treated in intensive psychotherapy—a treatment that would have qualified as an analysis except that the frequency of sessions never exceeded three per week—returned to see me in late middle age, after a hiatus of some 25 years. He began by announcing the good news—in the intervening years he had accumulated a fortune of tens of millions of dollars. He attributed his success to the mastery, as a result of our successful collaboration, of his castration anxiety and to the release of his previously inhibited aggression. His bad news consisted of an obsessional symptom, very similar to that of the Rat Man, wherein he brooded anxiously about losing his business through prosecution for racketeering. He ultimately revealed, however, that although he had occasionally engaged in ethically questionable activities, he had carefully made certain never to violate any laws. His obsession was with an eventuality that could not actually come about. He dreaded persecution by a merciless fate—otherwise he could not tolerate the continued enjoyment of prosperity.

We soon discovered that, behind this empty obsessional façade, the patient was moderately depressed. He began to complain about the rigors of his life: his endless working hours, the long drive back and forth between his downtown office and his exurban home, the boring and meaningless religious observances necessitated by his wife's Orthodox Jewish belief system, the constriction of his existence to unvarying routines lacking in joy, humor, or intellectual content. I made obvious inquiries about the exigencies that may have compelled the patient to live in this way and learned that his arrangements were intended to accommodate his wife, a chronically disturbed person unimproved despite many years of psychotherapy.

He had married this attractive and well-educated woman about two years after he terminated his previous treatment with me—a therapy in the course of which he overcame a preference for affairs with very young women he could depreciate. He and his wife had several children in short order, a circumstance that provided a rationale for their seeking the assistance of his mother-in-law to run the household. In this context, his wife became progressively more helpless and hostilely dependent on her mother. He encouraged her to seek therapy from a nearby analyst, but this effort reached a stalemate; only joint participation in ever more complex and financially successful business ventures could pull his wife out of her regressive symbiosis with her mother. She insisted on their exurban domicile, their participation in religious affairs, and their immersion in the business, and he did not dare to frustrate her because of her brittleness and propensity to lapse into paranoia.

In the course of an extended series of consultations, I explored various possibilities for improving the quality of their existence and gradually learned that ultimate responsibility for the choices they made rested on my patient—his wife insisted on nothing; she merely became distressed if her preferences were ignored. At the price of becoming known as the "Hungarian *Hund*" who allegedly led her husband astray, I was able to encourage my patient to moderate his fear about damaging his wife by choosing alternatives that he would find more palatable. Within a relatively brief interval, he delegated to subordinates most of the work on which he had spent his days, established a second home in the city, hired a chauffeur, shifted his business into a holding pattern that permitted him to procure a vast expansion of disposable income, and so on. Not only did his wife get used to these changes, she also confessed that she had pushed for the previous status quo via emotional blackmail in order to ward off what she experienced as the overwhelming influence of her husband.

The patient naturally was pleased by these results and became intrigued with the mystery of the genesis of his masochism. Why did he allow himself so to be bamboozled by his wife? And why were his children so insolent, so oblivious of his generosity, kindness, and unfailing courtesy? Why did various tradesmen take advantage of his prosperity and his good nature by attempting to cheat him? Why was he endlessly patient with unsatisfactory employees, compensating for their deficiencies by stepping into the breach to perform even the most menial of jobs within his organization? When I indicated that we could find answers to such questions only by exploring the unconscious, the patient decided to undertake an analytic effort in order to free himself of these characterological constraints.

The analysis revolved around issues about which we failed to reach consensus during the first period of treatment. The patient had always regarded himself as a victim of child abuse at the hands of his merciless mother and an older brother who was her henchman. In our earlier contact, I was convinced—I no longer know on what precise grounds—that he had provoked these savage punishments in order to expiate the guilt of an oedipal victory: when the patient was five, his father absented himself for a number of years, ostensibly because of some legal difficulties. (Was the patient's obsession an echo of his father's alibi for leaving an impossible marriage?) The transference in the second analysis rapidly recreated the complex family situation that had prevailed while the father was absent: the patient's wife and oldest son now played the roles of the abusive mother and brother, and I was assigned that of the fugitive father whose influence could be defied.

Indeed, I was made to feel like a Hungarian *Hund* barking at the moon. The lessons of the period of our consultative work were now jettisoned. Not that the patient went back to his previous external arrangements; he merely redoubled his efforts to please his wife and to appease his son. In this context, he recollected his rejection of his father when the latter returned from exile. He now repeated with me the provocativeness about which his father had commented that it seemed to be calculated to elicit a beating! Clearly a seemingly magical triumph had taken place at the climax of the patient's oedipal period—but the resultant guilt, albeit important, did not constitute his only long-term reaction. He gave his father (or fate, or his analyst) every opportunity to punish him, but insofar as the dreaded catastrophe was not yet upon him, the patient continued his relentless campaign to compel his mother's (or wife's, or daughter's) admiration.

The many behaviors that originally seemed to be self-sacrificing or self-restrictive now took their place as aspects of the patient's grandiosity—his insensate effort to be the sole effective agent in keeping a quasi-psychotic woman afloat. It became equally obvious that many of the cruel punishments he had incurred in childhood came his way because he was continually stepping forward to help, to show off, to take as important a part in the action as he could, whereas elementary prudence would have dictated a policy of self-effacement. But how could he efface himself? Throughout life he had thought of himself as a performer, a raconteur, a clown, a sage. He was raised to be a superstar; before his father fled the country, he made the rounds with my patient as a putative child prodigy. How can you keep them down on the farm after they've seen Paree?

I trust that this clinical example is detailed enough to demonstrate that a whole variety of childhood ideals or ambitions may become unconscious and then in adult life give rise to repetitive behaviors that will be seen as "masochistic" by the affected person himself. As many authors have noted with regard to a gamut of specific syndromes (e.g., Valenstein, 1973; Weill, 1985), the mental dispositions that produce later masochism may, in fact, originate much earlier than did those I have described in the foregoing case illustration. To state this point differently, as masochists go, this energetic multimillionaire, whose "self-sacrificing" exhibitionism proved to be so costly, is a rather mild case, with a favorable prognosis.

In my experience, the compulsion to repeat self-damaging enactments is much more difficult to modify in instances where this pattern of behavior was formed earlier in life, especially in cases with a preverbal genesis. In such people, the masochistic pattern did not initially buttress self-esteem, although it may later become drawn into the maintenance of narcissistic equilibrium, in accord with the principle of multiple function. I presented the analysis of such a personality in a recent book (Gedo, 1986, chap. 12)—the history of a man forever molded by infantile experiences of overstimulation caused by eczema. In that case, the sequence of pleasurable stimulation changing to painful tension, rage, aggression directed against his own person, and depressive exhaustion came to characterize the patient's very core of being. Whenever a pattern of this kind is built into the basic organization of the personality (of "the self" [Gedo, 1979], if you will), the most we can hope to accomplish through treatment is to bring about a "change of function" (Hartmann, 1939) for the behaviors in question.

It is relatively unusual to uncover preverbal experiences the particular qualities of which are as easy to discern as those of a patient with infantile eczema. In most instances, we do well to reconstruct the subjective nature of the child's experience at a considerably later phase of infancy, generally in the second half of the second year of life. By that time, whatever the constitutional basis of such experiences may have been, they are almost invariably drawn into the complex web of the toddler's relations with the caretakers. Consequently, most authors (for outstanding exceptions, see Basch [1975] and Weill [1985]) have emphasized the origins of later behaviors within the matrix of archaic object relations. Although this is a valid conclusion for many cases, if not most, the exceptional instance which demonstrates that subjectivity may conform to a template formed by the constraints of the infant's own physiology proves that, *in principle*, it is patterns of sensations and affects that form the core of later masochistic enactments—as, indeed, they constitute the core of the self-organization itself.

The nature of the typical preverbal experiences that find their echo in adult masochism is illustrated in the following case example.

Case 2:

An academician in her late thirties entered analysis because of chronic dysphoria, unrelieved by professional success or the birth of the three children she had always desired. Nor had her distress been mitigated by a lengthy psychotherapy, discontinued during her first pregnancy; she was angry at her former therapist because he did not take responsibility for the disappointing result of this treatment. She was convinced, at the same time, that she had botched all her enterprises: she expected her fellow scholars to discover that her academic work was derivative or worse, she felt helpless to raise her children properly, and she thought she had poisoned the atmosphere of her marriage because of her unceasing attacks on her less than adequate husband.

Nor could one contradict her about any of these self-accusations. As the story unfolded, it revealed that she owed her rapid advancement in the academic world to her skill in making herself into the protégée of several prestigious senior scholars. She was now rapidly approaching a tenure decision that would involve a review of her work by an unbiased committee, and she had reason to fear that her lifelong posture of submissiveness and eager discipleship would not suffice in their eyes. Her children were showing the expectable results of having been brought into the world to undo their mother's deficiency in self-esteem; moreover, the patient understood that her participation in their upbringing was simultaneously too intense and too intrusive. While an undergraduate at a prestigious university, she had met her sophisticated and promising husband. Although she had never been able to respond to him sexually, she felt very fortunate to have captured his interest despite her gaucherie, her utter lack of experience with dating, and her obesity. Following their marriage, she allowed him to transform her into a fashionable young woman, and this relationship did not deteriorate until she began to achieve success in her graduate work. His own career in business did not fulfill its early promise; when he failed in a private venture as a result of his own personality problems, the patient's mounting dissatisfaction burst into the open. Her disappointment took the form of terrible scenes; in these disputes, she generally got the worst of things because he was able to label her reactions as irrational.

This volcano of smoldering resentment was the younger child of parents who lived the conventional upper middle class life of successful Jewish professionals in New York. Her father was a busy physician whose lucrative practice did not fully satisfy his aspirations and who deferred to his wife's superiority in intellectual matters. The patient's mother was an imperious woman who had left a teaching career for marriage and considered herself to have been wasted on family life. She was unable to cope with her first child, a wild and rebellious boy of extraordinary spirit. Apparently it was the success of her son in asserting his independence that had led her to conceive the patient, whom she called her "depression baby." The patient recalled her early years as a continual but unavailing effort to win the favor of her mother, who preferred a prodigal son to an obedient daughter. One of the ways in which the brother asserted himself was to be physically assaultive toward the patient, who was able neither to protect herself nor to convince her mother of the reality of her complaints about this persecution. On the other hand, she began to experience his assaults as sexually exciting, and she was also able to take revenge by outdoing her brother as a student. However, this triumph also lost its savor when he made it clear that he was not interested in intellectual matters at all. He became a financially successful businessman, in marked contrast to the patient's husband, and he never showed any concern about his sister's activities as an adult.

As one might expect, the analysis was characterized from the first by a sadomasochistic flavor. My interventions were misperceived as intrusions and putdowns, alerting me to the possibility of provoking an unmanageable brother transference. If I avoided this pitfall, however, the patient experienced me as an echo of her passive and self-involved father. In either case, she might attack me verbally but put her hostile assault in the guise of complaints of mistreatment. At other times, she would see me as the mother who was overly eager to help her out in childhood—she had even rewritten the patient's homework, so that some of the daughter's excellent grades were undeserved. In the developing mother transference, the patient gradually reenacted a pattern of requesting some intervention to relieve her perplexity, only to push me away angrily in order to protect her autonomy. It took several years of analytic work, dealing mostly with the patient's regressive retreat into grandiosity, to establish a silent, idealizing transference (see Gedo, 1975)—or, if you will, a "holding environment" that allowed the patient to reexperience certain early childhood transactions, involving mostly her mother, wherein the patient functioned as an animate extension of the other.

In this context, she began unmistakably to violate the basic rule of free association, escalating these episodes of withholding until I complied with the requirements of the transference pattern she was wordlessly enacting; I did so by commenting on her ostensible delinquency as analysand. She reacted to these matter-of-fact descriptions of the realities of her behavior as if they constituted an irresistible force that compelled her compliance, only to resume in short order her provocation of this alleged insistence on her obedience. This cycle of hide-and-seek persisted until we succeeded in reconstructing its childhood antecedents, the enemas administered by her mother in response to the patient's failure to move her bowels with regularity, starting late in the second year of life. It became clear that if the mother neglected to intervene in this manner, the child's obtrusive noncompliance with the mother's expectations soon invited mother, masochistically, to do so once again. This game eventually became erotized (several years before the same thing had happened in relation to the aggressive interactions with her brother). During the oedipal years, the patient developed it, in fantasy, into the enactment of anal rape. When this fantasy was repressed in its turn, the patient became sexually frigid. In other words, her neurotic inhibition was designed to control a tendency toward masochistic perversion. As her mother lost interest in the child's bowel habits, the patient developed chronic constipation. Following the reconstruction of these childhood transactions, the constipation was relieved. Her frigidity did not yield, however, until she became aware of her envy of her partner's phallic performance as well. Needless to say, this insight was achieved only as a result of transference interpretation.

The most interesting aspect of these transference developments, however, was that the patient continued to feel that her symbiotic adaptation was at least as important to me as it was to her. She experienced our relationship as completely interdependent, particularly in the intellectual sphere: she felt obliged in some manner to achieve a distinction that would bring great credit upon me. These transference attitudes permitted us to reconstruct her childhood ambition to cure her mother's chronic depression by becoming her mother's (phallic) representative in some public arena. It was in this sense that she felt herself to be her mother's animate tool. Mother and daughter formed but one mind, so that the child could not function without the continual participation of the mother. When she left home for college, this symbiotic need was lived out with her future husband; after her husband failed to live up to the requirements of this role, the patient was ready to reexperience the pattern in a therapeutic context. When her first therapist also disappointed her, she began to enact the problem with one of her children.

Be it noted that learning about her childhood symbiosis with her mother, including its anal manifestations, did not bring to an end the patient's symbiotic need in the transference. Moreover, her dysphoria persisted; if anything, it became more intense within the analytic sessions, which turned into occasions for more or less continuous weeping. The persistence of this primitive bond with me, despite my inability to mitigate the patient's distress, alerted us to the probability that she was now reliving certain crucial preverbal experiences. At this juncture, the patient recalled a story often repeated by her father, to the effect that he had been the only person able to pacify her in infancy. She would be crying in great distress when he arrived at home; he claimed that he would then refuse to rest until he calmed her down, carrying her on his shoulder, if necessary for hours at a time. It appeared that she was reenacting in the transference the very same pattern with me. She had no capacity to soothe herself: it was imperative to induce a caretaker to initiate effective action on her behalf.

I have described only those facets of this complex, difficult, but ultimately successful treatment that throw light on the meaning of the patient's addiction to painful feelings. I realize that it is less than fully convincing to put into words, within a brief paragraph, the affective reverberations on which our conclusions were based—at the same time, I scarcely know how I could say more about them. It is important to mention, however, that the foregoing insight into the patient's need to draw someone else into her system of regulating tension or reducing distress initiated the process of her learning to perform these functions for herself. Episodes of dysphoria recurred from time to time, but eventually she became able to bring them to an end without external assistance.

It is unusual to encounter clinical contingencies that require the clarification of patterns of affectivity established in the preverbal era in order to relieve the patient's presenting complaints, in the manner illustrated by the foregoing case. As a consequence, the earliest anlagen of the mental dispositions that cause what is perceived in adult life as maladaptation are generally unknown; in the past, such predispositions were attributed to constitutional givens and were not regarded as amenable to psychological scrutiny. In "Beyond the Pleasure Principle" (1920), Freud simply lumped such tendencies together as a force he named the "repetition compulsion" (pp. 20ff).

Two generations later, we are in a position to use the analytic method to investigate how "masochistic" patterns that are endlessly repeated by almost everyone are established in the early phases of self-formation. As a result, our therapeutic effectiveness has been vastly enhanced.

REFERENCES

Basch, M. (1975), Toward a theory that encompasses depression: A revision of existing causal hypotheses in psychoanalysis. In: *Depression and Human Existence*, ed. E. Anthony & T. Benedek. Boston: Little Brown.

Erle, J. (1979), An approach to the study of analyzability and analysis: The course of forty consecutive cases selected for supervised analysis. *Psychoanal. Quart.*, 48:192–228.

———— & Goldberg, D. (1979), Problems in the assessment of analyzability. *Psychoanal. Quart.*, 48:48–84.

———— (1984), Observations on assessment of analyzability by experienced analysts. *J. Amer. Psychoanal. Assn.*, 32:715–738.

Ferenczi, S., & Rank, O. (1924), *The Development of Psycho-Analysis*. New York: Nervous and Mental Disease Pub., 1925.

Freud, S. (1901), The psychopathology of everyday life. *Standard Edition*, 6. London: Hogarth Press, 1960.

———— (1920), Beyond the pleasure principle. *Standard Edition*, 18:3–64. London: Hogarth Press, 1955.

Gedo, J. (1975), Forms of idealization in the analytic transference. *J. Amer. Psychoanal. Assn.*, 23:485–505.

———— (1979), *Beyond Interpretation*. New York: International Universities Press.

———— (1984), *Psychoanalysis and Its Discontents*. New York: Guiford.

———— (1986), *Conceptual Issues in Psychoanalysis*. Hillsdale, NJ: The Analytic Press.

Hartmann, H. (1939), *Ego Psychology and the Problem of Adaptation*. New York: International Universities Press, 1958.

Kohut, H. (1984), *How Does Analysis Cure?* Chicago: University of Chicago Press.

Valenstein, A. (1973), On attachment to painful feelings and the negative therapeutic reaction. *The Psychoanalytic Study of the Child*, 28:365–392. New Haven: Yale University Press.

Weill, A. (1985), Thoughts about early pathology, *J. Amer. Psychoanal. Assn.*, 33:335–352.

9 / On Masochism:
A Theoretical and Clinical Approach

Herbert A. Rosenfeld

THE SUBJECT OF MASOCHISM, which I prefer to call sadomasochism because sadism and masochism are so often intricately related, has become so vast that in this chapter I want to concentrate on some of my own observations that may be of interest to the reader. First of all, I want to say that there are both masochistic and sadomasochistic processes and character resistances that are very difficult to diagnose and that may cause an impasse in the analysis for a very long time. These masochistic reactions are frequently combined with destructive narcissistic structures that dominate the patient, whom they even appear to imprison and paralyze. But obviously there must also be reasons and tendencies in those parts of the self that submit to the domination and imprisonment. I have described (1971a) the pathology of destructive narcissism in some detail and related it also to severe depression and to the person's determination to satisfy his desire to die and to disappear into nothingness.

On the surface we seem to be dealing with the death drive in complete defusion, but on detailed analysis we observe that this state is caused by destructive, often envious, parts of the self that are severely split off and diffused from the caring libidinal self, which seems to have disappeared. The whole self becomes temporarily identified with the destructive omnipotent self, which aims to triumph over life and creativity presented by the analyst as the parent. Simultaneously in this attack, the dependent libidinal self, presented as a child, is also injured or destroyed. This is one of the central aspects of destructive narcissism.

I also observed that destructive narcissism attempts to control the analysis by withholding the dependent libidinal parts of the self, which would want to cooperate with the analyst. This situation is often obscured by a tricky or false cooperation.

Just as the destructive drive is directed not only against any tie or bond to significant objects but also against the dependent, libidinal part of the self, a sadomasochistic situation is created where the infantile self of the patient is left to painful suffering, starvation, and poisoning. The attacks on the infantile self and its suffering are obviously increased to triumph over the important objects that have to watch the infant suffer without being able to help him and save him from death.

The problems of destructive narcissism and masochism are illustrated by material from the analysis of Simon. Simon told me that his mother had told him that he was an exceptionally difficult child to feed from the first six months onward. When he was a year and a half he seemed to be an expert in throwing all his food on the floor. When he had succeeded in making a proper mess on the floor, he looked triumphantly at his mother, who obviously was by that time rather worried. These scenes occurred again and again. His father criticized his mother as being ineffective in looking after the child. So an expert nurse was employed. After a year the nurse told the mother that she had to admit that her work with this child was a complete failure. She had never had any child before who had so persistently and cleverly, but also with obvious satisfaction and pleasure, foiled all her attempts to feed and look after him. Then she resigned, leaving the mother to struggle alone again with this difficult situation.

The striking symptoms of the patient were impotence and a rather obscure perversion. He was very schizoid. I was the patient's second analyst. I felt that the patient was obviously very narcissistic, but he kept relations to external objects and myself empty by constantly deadening any part of his self that attempted object relations. After some years in analysis, he dreamed of a small boy who was in a comatose condition, dying from some kind of poisoning. The boy was lying in a bed in a courtyard and was endangered by the hot midday sun, which was beginning to shine on him. The patient was standing near to the boy but did nothing to move or protect him. He only felt very critical of and superior to the doctor treating the child; the doctor should have seen that the child was moved into the shade.

The patient's previous behavior and associations made it clear that the dying boy stood for his dependent libidinal self, which he kept in a dying condition by preventing it from getting help and nourishment from the analysis. I showed him that even when he came close to realizing the seriousness of his mental state, experienced as a dying condition, he did not lift a finger to help himself or to help me make him move toward saving himself because he was using the killing or torturing of this infantile dependent self to triumph over me and show me up as a failure. I thought the dream illustrated clearly that the destructive narcissistic state is maintained in part by keeping the libidinal infantile self in a constant dying condition.

Occasionally the analytic interpretations penetrated the narcissistic shell, and the patient felt more alive. He then admitted that he would like to improve; but soon he felt his mind had drifted away from the consulting room, and he became so detached and sleepy that he could scarcely keep awake. There was an enormous resistance, almost like a stone wall, that prevented any examination of the situation. But gradually it became clear that the patient felt pulled away from a closer contact with me because as soon as he felt helped there was both the danger that he might experience a greater need and a fear that he would attack me with sneering and belittling thoughts. Contact with me meant a weakening of narcissistic omnipotent superiority and the experience of a conscious feeling of overwhelming envy, which was strictly avoided by the detachment.

Frequent interpretation and firm confrontation of the patient's destructive narcissistic thoughts and behavior gradually brought about, to my complete surprise, a considerable change in the patient's personality and attitude toward other people. He seemed helped by my understanding and interpretation that a part of himself, particularly his infantile self, had masochistically colluded and accepted this paralyzed dead state by submitting to torture rather than admitting the need and hunger for life. I thought that his impotence and perversion had greatly decreased or disappeared when he ended treatment. But he remained reluctant to tell me about the improvements while the analysis went on. When we stopped he said that he was quite sure he would show how much better he was some time after he had stopped treatment. About a year after termination, I heard that he had become sexually normal and potent. About eight years after the patient's analysis, he was offered a very important position where he had to deal with a very large staff and was obviously very efficient in this work.

At this point, I want to discuss the relationships among masochism, the destructive, narcissistic structures and the negative therapeutic reaction. Often a patient who has made progress during the analysis is suddenly overcome by a strong, almost hypnotic force that impels him to give up. Freud (1924) suggested that such negative therapeutic reactions are caused by an unconscious sense of guilt which pushes the patient back into a retreat and suffering, but this has not been so in my experience. The force exerting such powerful regression is often experienced by the patient as a friendly force, like a mother who persuades him to give up his wish for development and to become a small child again. Sometimes a state of fusion with an object occurs, which may be pleasant but paralyzing and imprisoning. These negative reactions, which may occur again and again, are at first puzzling and completely resistant to treatment.

Detailed investigation over the years reveals that the seductive force is an omnipotent, destructive narcissistic organization that creates a threatening climate when the patient resents, or resists, the pull away from life into a narcissistic world. This destructive world is generally misrepresented delusionally as something very pleasant or life-saving. As a result, these patients, who should be regarded as potentially psychotic, are not aware that the pull into the psychotic state implies a pull toward death, whereas the melancholic depressed patient is fully aware of the attraction of death and his desire for it. The following case example illustrates the negative therapeutic reaction and the masochistic withdrawal state in a borderline patient.

Jill had been in psychotherapy in another country for many years when she developed what appeared to be an "acute psychotic state." For some time she had had a violent impulse to cut her wrists, and after she succeeded in doing so she was kept in a private hospital for over three years. Here the staff attempted sympathetically to understand her psychotic behavior and thinking. She felt glad to be in the hospital, because for the first time in her life her sickness, as she called it, was being taken seriously. She had felt that her parents could not stand her being ill and would therefore not believe how ill she was, and her manifest psychotic state was an attempt to be more open about her feelings. She previously had felt so encased by her rigidity that to make her blood flow out seemed to her not so much to be a wish to die as an attempt to become more alive.

Jill made progress in the treatment but was constantly pulled back into her withdrawal state. Finally her therapist felt that the treatment could not get any further. Jill decided that she wanted to go on on her own and accepted a job in another country, where at first she felt interested and excited. After a year, however, she was again overwhelmed by severe, paralyzing anxiety. She felt forced to withdraw from life, stayed in bed for days on end, and sat in front of a fire, eating, and drinking alcohol, popping tranquilizers and reading detective stories. She felt helpless against the forces that prevented her from living and hopeless about any possibility of improving. She was also uncertain about her identity. After her breakdown she had felt that she had an identity of being psychotic. She idealized this state and often longed to return to being the rebellious patient in the disturbed ward of the hospital, where one could smash windows, cut one's wrists, and fight against the forces demanding that one should be part of life, a demand to which she contemptuously referred as conforming or being "goody-goody." She attempted another analysis, which failed, and then she reluctantly came to me in England.

Very soon after starting analysis with me she made it quite clear that she felt it was dangerous to improve because as soon as she improved she became more and more terrified. So in order to appease the frightening forces within, she would give up life and again withdraw to the paralyzed state, which was sometimes described as an infantile state, or one where she felt fused with another object, partly the mother. These states, never lasting more than a fortnight, repeated themselves frequently in the early stages of the analysis, but then she could again turn toward life though only in a very limited way. I observed that she had to obey a narcissistic principle of self-sufficiency that demanded that she should be able to do everything for herself and not accept any kindness, care, food, or sexual satisfaction from anybody. To take anything in was bad, dirty, or weak, and subsequently she felt she had to be physically sick to rid herself of what she had taken in. During childhood, and even much later, she had not been able to bear her mother's giving her food or presents, and her mother's attention and interest in her were felt to be an intrusion into her privacy. But she also found it unbearable that her mother was anxious when the patient behaved aggressively with her. The difficulties with the mother had obviously existed from early infancy.

In the analysis it became clear that the patient was dominated by a psychotic, destructive narcissistic structure or self that threatened her whenever she attempted to come closer to life or to any living person. This self posed as a friend who pretended to take care of her and give her whatever warmth and food she wanted so that she would not have to feel lonely. This situation was acted out during the withdrawal state. In fact, however, this so-called friend spoiled any contact she was trying to make with work or other people. During analysis she gradually became aware that this exceedingly tyrannical and possessive friend was an omnipotent, destructive part of herself posing as a friend who became very threatening if she attempted to continue cooperation in analysis and any progress in her life situation. For a long time she felt too frightened to challenge this aggressive force, and whenever she came up against this barrier she identified herself with this aggressive narcissistic self and became aggressive and abusive towards me. In the transference I seemed sometimes to represent her mother and at other times her infantile self, which she projected into me. However, the main reason for her violent attacks was my challenging the domination of her aggressive narcissistic state, my impudence in wanting to help or even cure her. She demonstrated that she was determined to do anything to defeat me. But after a few days of these attacks, I also noticed that there was a secret hope that I—and the self that was directed toward life—might win in the end. I also began to realize that the only alternative to a violent attack on me was her admission that she really wanted to get well, and this exposed her to the danger of being killed by the omnipotent destructive part of herself.

After we had worked on this situation for many months, the patient had a dream that confirmed and illustrated the problem. In the dream the patient found herself in an underground hall, or passage. She decided she wanted to leave and go upstairs into the open air, but she had to go through a turnstile to get out. The turnstile was obstructed by two people, but when the patient investigated she found they were both dead. In the dream she decided that obviously they had recently been murdered. She realized that the murderer was still about and that she had to act quickly to save herself. Nearby was an office of a detective, and she rushed in unannounced but had to wait in the waiting room for a moment. Even while she was waiting, the murderer appeared and threatened to kill her because he did not want anybody to know what he was doing and what he had done and he feared that the patient would give him away. She was terrified and burst into the detective's room and so was saved.

The patient realized immediately that the detective represented me, but the rest of the dream was quite a surprise. She had never allowed herself to think how frightened she was of being murdered if she were to trust me and come for help, giving me all the information and cooperation she was capable of. Particularly, of course, this meant the information about the nature of her own murderous self. In fact, the two people in the dream reminded her of two previous unsuccessful attempts to get better. I took the dream to mean that a part of her had decided to get well and leave the psychotic narcissistic state that imprisoned her and that she equated with death. But then the deadly part became actively murderous because of this decision.

It is interesting that since this dream the patient has in fact turned much more to life, and her fear of death has lessened. Theoretically and clinically the work with this patient seems to confirm the importance of the destructive aspect of narcissism, which in the psychotic state completely dominates and overwhelms the patient's object-related sane parts of the self and tries to imprison them. This paralyzed imprisoned state often appears clinically as a masochistic condition. In this patient the masochistic excitement in the paralyzed state was not severe. But in other patients similar to her we find sadistic or masochistic or sadomasochistic perversions. This omnipotent withdrawal state is very often filled with exciting, perverse phantasies that produce the constant temptation to masturbate. I have observed patients who are pulled into states of fusion with the mother. But it is important to differentiate "benign" states of fusion from those where the sane self is pulled into the psychotic self or object and is subjected to a delusional influence through the strong hypnotic pressure that either compels the patient to submission or stimulates cruel, sadistic, and masochistic phantasies.

It is, of course, essential to understand not only the structure of the destructive omnipotent part of the patient's personality but all the circumstances of the patient's life situation that contributed to the masochistic attitude or masochistic perversion. We usually find in the history of the patient a sadomasochistic pattern both in very early infancy and later on. Jill seemed to have been a lively baby and child, enjoying physical activities greatly. One had the impression that her mother felt very anxious and was not able to cope with this very lively and, at times, aggressive child, and so she became rather defensive and controlling and dominating with the child. Jill felt disturbed that her mother behaved as if she were her victim; and she also felt that to satisfy her mother, she had to get rid of her liveliness and aggression. As a child Jill had always been put to bed after lunch for over an hour and her bedtime was very early. She very much resented having to go to bed, because she wanted to roam around and to enjoy herself. Always to be put to bed against her will made her feel she was being overpowered, and this contributed to her masochism. I had the impression that Jill was certainly not a passive or phlegmatic child. One generally gets a picture of the patient's fundamental object relations only after the narcissistic structures and the splitting off of aggression, which is the basic problem in destructive narcissism and sadomasochism, has been understood and emotionally worked through in the transference.

Robert is a patient suffering from a sadomasochistic character structure. He has sadomasochistic perverse phantasies and masturbates frequently by scratching his anus until it bleeds profusely.

He reported that his mother had told him that when he developed teeth as a baby he started to bite her breast regularly and so viciously that it always bled, and consequently her breast was very scarred. In the analysis he remembered this biting of the mother's breast quite vividly. His mother did not withdraw her breast when she was bitten and seemed to be passively suffering. He thinks he probably was breast fed for a year and a half. Robert also remembers having very painful enemas from very early childhood onward. He does not remember being constipated but felt that these painful enemas were probably revenge from mother for biting her. It is interesting that his mother would not allow his father to stay in the flat where she and Robert were living; he had to stay in the cellar of the same house. The patient felt that his father had to submit to this humiliation and did not seem to be strong enough to fight against his wife.

The patient is married and has several children. He is highly intelligent and holds a valued position as a scientist. He was consciously very determined to have analysis and to cooperate in it. He was in analysis with a well-known analyst in another country for five years, but there apparently was no improvement and the analyst told him that his masochistic character structure was not analyzable. He did his best to cooperate with me and improved considerably for several years, but then his progress slowed down. He was at times elusive, which undermined the therapeutic effort.

In the fourth year of the analysis, Robert had to leave London occasionally for short professional trips, and he often returned late on Mondays and so missed part or all of his session. He frequently met women during these trips and brought to analysis many of the problems that arose with them. It was clear that some acting out was taking place, but only when he regularly reported murderous activities in his dreams after such weekends did it become apparent that violently destructive attacks against the analysis and against me were hidden in the acting out behavior. He was at first reluctant to accept that the acting out over the weekend was killing and blocking the progress of the analysis, but gradually he changed his behavior, and the analysis became more effective. He reported considerable improvement in some of his personal relationships and his scientific activities. At the same time, he began to complain that his sleep was frequently disturbed by violent palpitations and anal itching, which kept him awake for several hours. During these anxiety attacks he felt that his hands did not belong to him; they seemed violently destructive as if they wanted to destroy something. He scratched at his anus violently until it bled profusely: he felt his hands were too powerful for him to control so that he had to give in to them.

He then had a dream of a very powerful arrogant man who was nine feet tall and who insisted that he had to be obeyed absolutely. Robert's associations made it clear that this man stood for part of himself and related to the irresistibly destructive, overpowering feelings in his hands. I interpreted that he regarded the omnipotent destructive part of himself as the superman who was nine feet tall and much too powerful for him to disobey. He had disowned this omnipotent self, related to anal masturbation, which explained the estrangement of his hands during the nightly attacks. I further explained that this split-off self was an infantile omnipotent part of himself which claimed that it was not an infant but stronger and more powerful than all the adults, particularly his mother and father and now the analyst. His adult self was so completely taken in and therefore weakened by this omnipotent assertion that he felt power-less to fight the destructive impulses at night, and so he had submit-ted to them.

Robert reacted to the interpretation with surprise and relief and reported after some time that he felt a little more able to control his hands at night. He gradually became more aware that the destructive impulses at night had some connection with the analysis, because they increased after any success that could be attributed to the analysis. He saw the violent scratching as a wish to tear out and destroy the part of himself that depended on me. Simultaneously, the aggressive narcissistic impulses that had been split off became more conscious during analytic sessions, and he sneered, saying, "Here you have to sit all day wasting your time." He felt that he was the important person and he could be free to do anything he wanted to do however cruel or hurtful this might be to others and himself. He was particularly enraged by the insight and understanding that the analysis gave him. He hinted that his rage was related to wanting to reproach me for helping him, because this interfered with his omnip-otent acting-out behavior.

He then reported another dream: He was running a long-distance race and was working very hard at it. However, there was a young woman who did not believe in anything that he was doing. She was unprincipled and nasty and did everything to interfere and mislead him. There was a reference to the woman's brother, who was called "Mundy." He was much more aggressive than his sister. He appeared in the dream snarling like a wild beast even at her. In the dream this brother had had the task of misleading everybody during the pre-vious year. Robert thought that the name Mundy referred to his frequent missing of the Monday sessions the year before, and he realized that the violent, uncontrolled aggressiveness related to him-self; but he felt that the young woman was also himself. During the last year he had often insisted in his analytic sessions that he felt he was a woman and was very contemptuous of and superior to me. Lately, however, he occasionally dreamed of a little girl who was receptive and appreciative of her teachers, which I had interpreted as a part of him who wanted to show more appreciation of me but was prevented from coming into the open by his omnipotence. By the dream Robert admitted that the aggressive omnipotent, misleading part of himself represented as male, who had dominated the acting out until a year before, had now become quite conscious. The identification with the analyst was expressed in the dream as a determination to work hard at his analysis, the long-distance race. The dream, however, was also a warning that he could continue his aggressive acting out in analysis by asserting in a misleading way that he could present himself omnipotently as a grown-up woman who did not believe in the analytic work and could nastily work against me and the part of himself that was trying to work hard in the analysis. In this way there was a danger that he would prevent himself from responding to the work of the analysis with receptive feelings, which were experienced by a positive infantile part of himself, the little girl.

The dream revealed the structure of the patient's masochistic anal perversion. The male self, "Mundy," was particularly destructive and overpowering and was also attacking his female self, which was the sister of Mundy in the dream. She was also perverting and nastily and omnipotently misleading and was therefore obviously colluding with Mundy. Thus a sadomasochistic couple is formed who are not identical but who both have the desire to pervert and mislead and obviously have some satisfaction in preventing improvement by holding on to the sadomasochistic perversion. It is clear that the only positive cooperative part of the patient was felt to relate to the infantile little girl self, which was receptive and wanted to grow. But the perverse female and male sadomasochistic couple were still trying, by the anal tearing, to destroy this normal self so that the perversion could be continued. The patient improved a great deal over the years, but when he had to stop the analysis it was still not quite certain whether the perversion was cured.

If we try to trace the genesis of the patient's sadomasochistic character structure, we find that the destructive "Mundy," a male part of the patient, was the most omnipotent, aggressive and misleading feature. He was described as snarling like a wild beast, completely untamed. It seems likely that the patient's early infantile biting impulses when he attacked his mother's breast unrestrictedly relates to Mundy. These primitive impulses were split off and were acted out violently at weekends until I restrained the patient by pointing out his destructive behavior against the analysis that was revealed in his dreams. I insisted that the violent acting out had to stop because it was destroying the analysis, and I felt I should not submit to his behavior. He responded very well to this constraint, and it must have been clear to him that in this way I became a stronger father than he had had in the past. As a result, the receptive little girl self who wanted to learn from me was gradually allowed to appear, which was an experience he never had in childhood with his father.

Simultaneously, however, the omnipotent sister figure, who was misleading and did not believe in normal development, was probably an identification with his omnipotent mother, who both devalued the father—which was a misleading attitude—and misled herself by allowing herself to be bitten and maltreated by the patient when he was a biting baby and child.

However, Mundy was not only the biting child. In the analysis he nastily wanted to interfere in the analysis by deliberately trying to mislead me, to be superior to me and defeat me. But these attacks were also directed against his self who wanted to get well and was trying to work hard in the analysis. In this way there was a danger that he would prevent himself from responding to the work of the analysis with receptive feelings that were located mainly in a positive infantile part of himself experienced as the little girl. So there was still a struggle ahead. Mundy and his sister were a false male and a false female self who were omnipotently only posing as grown ups and were trying to pervert and confuse his sexual identity, particularly his normal feminine self, which contained his capacity to love and appreciate and to grow up normally. It was clear that the anal masturbatory attacks were created both by the sadistic omnipotent male self and the perverted masochistic omnipotent female self, who were both colluding to keep his sexuality perverted. The perverting male and female parts of the patient belonged to the destructive narcissistic organization I described at the beginning of the paper. The perverse sadomasochistic experience in the present situation repeated the sadomasochistic experience with Robert's mother that had both stimulated his destructive omnipotence and his sadomasochistic excitement. Technically I find it useful not only to work through the sadomasochistic experiences in the here and now situation but to help the patient to link these experiences as precisely as possible to his early infantile experiences. The detailed linking makes it much easier for the patient to get out of the sadomasochistic addictive trap that so often exerts enormous pressure to suck the patient back again into the original perverse, sadomasochistic experience.

Sometimes the masochistic perversions are linked to autistic problems. In these cases the masochistic perversion has the more defensive function of covering up, by the exciting masochistic phantasy, the painful blockage and the inability to grow up. Fred has a sadomasochistic perversion whose origin apparently lies in a childhood experience that overwhelmed and disorganized him. When Fred started treatment with me his predominant masturbation phantasy was of a powerful Amazon woman—who had a phallus—fighting with him and overpowering him. The woman then forced her penis into his rectum.

The patient had been very attached to his mother in early childhood and went into her bedroom as soon as he could walk and slept close to her at night. His father had a separate bedroom, so it was easy for Fred to deny that the parents ever had any sexual relations. When Fred was four, a sister, Ella, was born. Fred has no memory whatsoever of her birth or his mother's pregnancy. He apparently had a good relationship with his father until his sister was born. He was told of this by his parents; he himself has not the slightest memory of this. The patient remembers that when Ella could walk she often wanted to come into his room, but he generally locked his bedroom door to keep her out. When Fred was eight years old, Ella was killed accidentally. Fred remembers that he was touched and saddened by her death for a very short time, perhaps some hours, but then he put the whole tragic situation completely out of his mind and felt quite detached about it.

A number of features in his analysis point to Ella's birth being enormously traumatic to Fred, yet he still has no memory about this event. He does, though, have often the feeling that Ella is about, as if she follows him around. When he wanted to apply for an important position a while ago, he had an overpoweringly strong feeling that Ella was standing behind him, insisting that she should have the job instead of him; he was inclined to agree with her. To his great surprise he was accepted for the job. In some part of himself Fred has a very strong feeling that he cannot grow up, that his development has been arrested, that he is still a small boy. This feeling is accompanied by a strong conviction that another younger sibling will overtake him.

Fred has improved a great deal in a variety of situations. For example, he is now capable of having a girlfriend with whom he has sexual relations, but for a long time he preferred his sadomasochistic phantasy that a very powerful, muscular young girl, much younger than he, fights with him, overpowers him, and then inserts her penis into his anus.

The patient's autism centers on a preoccupation with a special small place that he is trying to find and that he often feels compelled to enter even if the space has become a very desolate one. Sometimes he speaks of feeling very frustrated that there is no warm, secure place for him. He often wants to stay in a warm, pleasant place without ever coming out into the open. At other times he has negative feelings of being pulled back to his own flat, which then represents the small place that is so overpoweringly compulsive that Fred has a feeling of being impossibly frustrated. At first he could not say very much more about this, but it was clear that these phantasies related to the inside of the mother's body. In discussing these feelings one day, he suddenly remembered that he very often stood in his little bed and looked through a hole he had bored in the wall. He remembered clearly that he didn't want just to look through it; he felt he wanted to get inside it even if it was a dark place. Occasionally this little place inside felt completely deserted and dirty, but he still felt he had to cling to it, closed in and shut out from the world, even when he felt starving.

He sometimes complained that after a particularly good session he forgot everything. He observed himself grinding his teeth and biting something as if he were destroying everything. He was also biting his nails at that time and felt full inside, but food was not appealing. I had the impression that there was at first an omnipotent phantasy of entirely dominating his mother and father, particularly his mother's inside by intruding into her and preventing anything from coming inside her. It is likely that the shock of Ella's birth aroused over-whelmingly furious feelings against both his mother and his father, with violently destructive feelings against mother's inside. This rage created an overwhelming guilt associated with a phantasy of masoch-istically being pulled inside her.

It was only very gradually that very intense feelings appeared, not so much in the sessions but in relationship to friends and people he was working with. He could control this intense rage so that his good relationships were not spoilt. He was also aware of the unreality of his feelings. He noticed he could not tolerate being with couples and was constantly thinking of separating them, even when he was on very good terms with each of the friends separately. He also experi-enced, during one weekend, intense feelings of being rejected by a friend whom he had known for many years who came to stay with him. This intense feeling of rejection arose because this friend did not introduce him specifically to other friends when they took part in a rally. He suffered agonies for about an hour, but when he suddenly met another good friend he felt completely all right. Next morning, when he saw his boss, who was particularly friendly and protective to him, he felt that he wanted to shout at him that the boss had probably had a good weekend but that he himself had had an awful weekend. At the same time, he knew that all this was not true, but nonetheless he felt extremely angry with his boss and wanted to leave his job. At that moment his boss offered some very interesting and important work; he realized that he wanted to exclude his boss, and that he had not been excluded.

He seemed now to be aware of the part of him that was extremely dominating and suggestive and caused certain feelings in him, and he recognized that he was going to spoil life for himself if this omnipotent self had its way. At this time, breathing difficulties, which had not disturbed him for a long time, came back and he felt afraid, as if threatened with death. I suggested that the omnipotent little boy in him wanted to force him to stop analysis and withdraw into his room, which represented his mother's inside, where he could assert the complete right to control and exclude me entirely. He realized that there was a danger that he would forget our work in the session, which he felt was extremely important for him now and in the future. When his memory failed, his omnipotent self could force him to pull back into his phantasies, which were trying to control and completely pervert his thinking. It seemed to me that at that moment he was more aware of his perverting destructive omnipotence than at any time previously. It was clear that this destructive little boy did not mind lying to distort reality and was trying to mislead his boss completely, and obviously me too, by believing that I was excluding and neglecting him, as if I had promised him a session on Saturday. I thought the problem of not having been introduced to the other people in the group could give me an important clue to what I had to do now in order to assist him. It was becoming essential that I introduce the various aspects of himself to one another so that he could get to know himself better and so prevent him from sinking back into a state of isolation where he could cut himself off entirely from the saner part of himself and other people.

The genesis of this patient's problems seemed to be quite clear. He had felt he was controlling his mother and keeping his parents separate so that they could have no sexual relations. He had felt completely safe in this omnipotent assertion until he was four, when he noticed his mother's pregnancy, which then led to the appearance of his sister. He then withdrew entirely from his father, with whom he had had very good relations until that time. In his omnipotent rage, he tried to get rid of his father completely and exclude him. At the same time, he obviously omnipotently withdrew inside his mother in order to control her inside. So a split in his personality occurred at that time and this omnipotent autistic self and his normal self seemed no longer able to meet. I recognized that if I, through my interpretations, linked his autistic self to his normal self, there could be a chance that he would no longer feel left out and isolated.

In my report on this patient I have tried to illustrate the severe splitting and increase of destructive omnipotence that can take place at the height of the Oedipus complex. It is of course obvious that the omnipotent structures must have been at work much before his mother's pregnancy and Ella's birth, but such traumas can greatly reinforce the patient's destructive omnipotence and it is clear that he was in danger of suffering from a severe psychosis.

His masochistic perversion is now very seldom mentioned. He predominantly struggles to be more sure of growing up gradually to be a man. What is still disturbing to him in analysis and also occasionally in social relations is the complete blockage of this thinking and feelings that can suddenly occur. Blocking had mainly been due to splitting of his self into many contradictory selves. But there is now sometimes the realization that he has to curb his intense destructive feelings against his parents, his boss, and me, particularly as he has now become more aware that he needs all of us to help him to grow. This recognition implies that he appreciates having been introduced by me to the good relationships from whom he had cut himself off, a situation that had created his intense feeling of being isolated and excluded. This sadomasochistic character structure seems gradually to have become more balanced. His masochistic perversion seemed a reversal of the omnipotent phantasy of intruding with his masculine self into his mother and his sister and overpowering and triumphing over them, which led to a reversal, probably through intense feelings of guilt. The guilt created the need to be humiliated and overwhelmed by the strong sister figure who was allowed to have masculine superiority over him and deprive him of his male attributes; a relationship he had masochistically submitted to.

It is interesting that this patient's omnipotent narcissistic organization seems to have originated early in life and was reinforced by his controlling mother, who apparently encouraged him to come to her bed. But the shock of being faced, through Ella's birth, both by the parents as the couple in intercourse and by the appearance of the rival sister threatened his complete domination of the household. His now severely destructive narcissistic organization was increased, bringing his development to a standstill. As the split in his personality developed, this autistic self remained split off while some aspects of the patient's personality seemed to develop but were constantly threatened by the autistic situation under the domination of destructive narcissism. These complicated autistic, narcissistic, and masochistic character structures are not easily treatable. It seems to be technically essential to be able to address in the analysis the different aspects of the patient's personality, at first isolate them, and then introduce them to one another so that a more harmoniously functioning self can be created that can resume the interrupted normal growth of the patient's personality.

I have stressed so far the main perverting force, the "hidden destructive narcissism." I shall now consider how the rest of the masochistic patient's personality, the more normal parts, may come under the influence of the perverting force as well as those aspects of the patient's personality which might resist the perversion. I must begin with an important aspect of normal development, which Melanie Klein called the "depressive position," that never functions normally and effectively in masochistic perversions and masochistic character disturbances.

The depressive position generally starts in the middle of the first year of life, but the important integrating force of the depressive position goes on all through life.

> In the early months of life the infant relates predominantly to part objects and splitting of objects into good and bad is the rule. The central importance of the "depressive position" is the fact that the infant recognizes a whole object and relates himself to this object and he begins to notice that his good and bad experiences do not proceed from a good or bad breast or mother, but from the same mother who is the source of good and bad. Simultaneously with this important change in his object relations the infant's ego develops into a whole ego and is left split into good and bad components [Segal, 1964, pp. 55–56].

It is important to understand that in the depressive position introjective processes are intensified, owing mainly to the infant's discovery of his dependence on his objects, which he has come to perceive as independent and liable to leave him. This increases his need to possess his object, keep it inside, and if possible protect it from its own destructiveness.

It is particularly with Fred that I could illustrate the severe split in the patient's self and the integrating drive in one session, where he could reconcile his hatred against and his need for his parents, his boss, and me and where he was able to feel less aggressive because he was so strongly aware that he needed them and did not want to lose them.

In perverse patients, where splitting of the self and objects is marked, integration proceeds very slowly. Again and again the destructive forces try to interfere in the integrating process through suggestion, seduction, and by being disguised as advisers who mislead the patient. This was clearly illustrated in Robert's dream with Mundy, whose job it was to mislead everybody and his sister, who was similarly described by the patient. This accusation of being misleading is exceedingly common in sexual perversions, particularly the sadomasochistic ones.

Meltzer (1973) observed, as I did (1971b), that "the destructive part of the self presents itself to suffering good parts first as protector from pain, second as a servant to its sensuality and vanity, and only covertly in the face of resistance to regression—as the brute, the torturer" (p. 97), which opens the way to severe sadomasochistic suffering. When depressive anxiety can be borne, slipping off into perverse, sadistic, and masochistic perversions can be avoided; but when "trust is loosened by aggravation of depressive anxiety through jealousy, then depression and persecution often become indistinguishable" (p. 97), and this is a dangerous weakening of the resistance. I have often observed that when depressive and persecutory anxieties become confused—generally along with confusion of libidinal and aggressive parts of the self—the depressive integration stops and leaves the personality vulnerable to the interfering destructive forces that pull the patient into exciting masochistic suffering.

The perverting influence of split-off, destructive, disguised forces interfered with the working through of the "depressive position"— the important integrating force in the patient Antonio. Antonio had to return to his Southern European homeland some years ago after a long analysis. He had made considerable progress in his analysis, but throughout the last year of analysis he had begun to torture himself almost continuously with doubts about his mental strength and integrity. He felt particularly concerned that by returning to his country he would lose all he had gained in the analysis, and he had many nightmares about this theme. His torturing doubts consisted mainly in something inside him constantly questioning him about all sorts of problems, insisting that he did not perfectly understand them and demanding that he should have the complete answer. This torturing seemed always to get worse when he had done something very well, for example, when he had been praised by his teachers for excellent work. He felt that it was important to scrutinize himself carefully, but his torturing doubts exhausted and depressed him.

His doubts obviously were creating such a strong masochistic suffering, such torture, in him that it was impossible for him to enjoy looking forward to anything in the future. I pointed out to him that he seemed to relate to the part of him that constantly instructed and questioned him as though it were a good, helpful figure. I thought he was mistaken in this thinking. This internal figure seemed to me to be very destructive, perhaps even deadly. I pointed out that there was considerable cruelty in this part of himself which was directed against himself and probably also against what he had gained from me in his analysis. Antonio was very thoughtful and quiet after this interpretation. He said only that he could not think any further at the moment because he so often gets blocked.

In the next session Antonio said he had been very much preoccupied with death. He could not understand why he constantly thought about death and dying, of himself or others. These thoughts were very torturing, but he could not connect them with anything, apart perhaps from my having pointed out to him that there was something destructive lurking inside him. In fact, thoughts about death and fear of death had occurred from time to time during the previous few years, but it had not been possible to understand them clearly before. Antonio said he was, for example, preoccupied with being dead and unable to get in touch with anybody. The idea of death had always been terrifying for him. I pointed out to him that there seemed to be an incapacity to mourn, which was disturbing him greatly and which had something to do with the ending of his analysis. He replied that the feeling of lack of communication and of being incommunicative himself seemed to torture him most.

He suddenly became quite animated and told me something he had never explained to me before. He said that there was one analyst whom he always thought about as somebody probably much stronger than I and who made much more aggressive interpretations. In his imagination, that analyst would point out to him, for example, how delinquent he was. He always had the idea that he would feel much safer with this analyst. Interestingly, despite his characterizing this analyst as apparently very sadistic, he had idealized him in his mind; I, on the other hand, seemed to be rather weak and friendly but ineffective by comparison.

Antonio explained that this Dr. G. was obviously a very cruel person. Outwardly he appeared to be kind and friendly, but Antonio and some of his friends had clear evidence that there was a great deal of cruelty going on in Dr. G. all the time. Antonio mentioned two patients who had been analyzed by Dr. G. some years before. Antonio had had letters from them indicating that they were quite disturbed and even slightly delinquent, which had come to him as a great surprise. He again emphasized that Dr. G. had always seemed superficially very nice, so one could not easily recognize how aggressive and disparaging he was.

The hidden secret figure in Antonio's mind had been identified all the time with Dr. G., and he had been prevented from telling me before. Now, suddenly, he could inform me in this very detailed account that I had been correct in my observations that there was a destructive or deadly figure hidden in his mind. He remembered that his father's attitude and preoccupation had been very similar and that there had always also been some masochistic torturing in his father which he could never quite clearly identify. This revelation was very meaningful to him.

In a session just a few days later, Antonio reported the following dream: He was already back in his own country, and he had finished his analysis. He found himself in his father's house in his own bedroom. He felt that he was eight years old again, playing with his younger brother soon after his mother's death. He noticed that the window was rather weak and was afraid that bandits could get inside fairly easily. In the dream he suddenly missed England very deeply—the England he sometimes disliked—even the cold weather. He also missed some eating places in a particular street in London.

In his associations, he was aware that the two eating places were good but not excellent. The cold was something he disliked, but he still felt that in the dream he missed it very much. He remembered from the dream that he could also have missed his mother a great deal more than he had at her death. He realized that in the dream he could miss a mother who was not perfect. He said that he was also afraid that he might be denigrating me by saying these eating places were not perfect. Then he remembered confusing and conflicting feelings in this dream, feelings of strongly missing something that is both good and not so good.

I told Antonio that he obviously recognized in the dream that in his mourning for his mother and for me there was a capacity to feel sad and to miss somebody who is not perfect—something not usually possible for him. It is only the good/bad confusion that he fears, which causes the tension and anxiety in him and that makes this painful situation unbearable. He said he understood that his depression was very strong and there was much suffering in it.

Then he talked about the window and the bandits. He felt very anxious and worried about them and feared that the bandits would spoil everything and take everything important away from him. I explained that he had been achieving, in the dream, an approach to mourning normally, an accomplishment that is very painful and disturbing. The idealization had lessened so that he could think of good and bad things; but when the good and bad things came close together, there was a great feeling of confusion. This was confusion not only about the past and present, but also about good and bad things. He was afraid that the good would be denigrated and lost. I pointed out that it was the confusion that always arises at the moment of coming close to the depressive situation which causes this painful and disturbing situation in the attempt to move forward. There was the danger that destructive feelings would enter at that moment and use this uncertainty to take all the good things he had achieved away from him and destroy everything. The emergence of these feelings would drive him again into a very fixed position to which he then would have to cling. He was afraid that in the end he would be driven back to masochism and suffering and feeling invaded by a destructive, punishing force—the deadly force that we were talking about before.

In other words, the weak point in experiencing and working through the integrating mourning process was the intense feelings of confusion, which occur when loving and aggressive feelings come close together. Normally, the feeling of confusion in mourning is not intense and longlasting. In the process of integration, some neutralizing (Hartmann, Kris, and Loewenstein, 1949) or binding (Klein, 1958) of the destructive feelings can take place, considerably strengthening the ego. However, when the destructive feelings are very strong, there is a danger that the binding process will miscarry; and rather than fusion of the destructive and libidinal impulses resulting in neutralization of the danger, these two contrasting forces become confused. There is then the danger of a prolonged confusional state (of libidinal and destructive impulses), which is quite unbearable, and this makes the patient most vulnerable. The destructive narcissistic structure, posing as helper and rescuer from the confusion, tries at that stage to invade the confused self to make a takeover bid. Simultaneously it kills the good libidinal self and so ends the confusion, the end being a falsely claimed a "cure." This invasion completely destroys the possibility of mourning.

I explained to Antonio that at the moment of confusion and doubt, he generally allowed the destructive organization standing for Dr. G. to take over; this blocked his mourning and made him hopeless and feeling dead. But in the dream, he seemed to hold on to the mourning situation and felt it was good fundamentally, but he was aware of the weakness (the weak window) and was aware that he had to guard against the attack of the bandits, the destructive narcissistic organization.

This dream illustrates very clearly both the depressive anxiety and the early feeding situation; he missed the two breasts and even the occasional coldness of his mother's absence, which seemed fully accepted in the dream. The dream related also to his mourning in childhood, at the age of 8, when his mother died; mourning he was not able to do at that time. Mourning, of course, related also to the ending of analysis. All these important depressive circumstances were connected and accepted in the dream. At the same time, he warned himself that there was still the danger of certain weaknesses and that he had to ward off the destructive narcissistic organization; the bandits that could make an assault on his present stability and on all his progress and on his memory of the good position he seemed at last to have achieved. He still feared that he could be pulled back to the painful destructive masochism that would be experienced as constant, painful doubts and suffering, which would then keep him imprisoned. During the following months many anxiety situations still had to be worked over, and it seemed that he was giving me an opportunity to help and strengthen him, so that he would feel fully restored. Interestingly, this was illustrated in a dream related to his teeth, indicating a connection with the early oral situation.

During a session he told me that he again felt blocked and silent. He was waiting for a catastrophe. Then he told me a dream. Somebody had to do a restoration of his teeth, but in the dream this was mainly related to a gold crown that had to be replaced. He was keen that this should be done in England, where it would be much cheaper; he feared that in his own country it would cost five times as much, which would be too expensive. In fact, his teeth had been fully restored by his dentist in England, but he was afraid that some items, such as buying a house, could be quite expensive at home. Suddenly he said that he felt awful because he realized that he would not again see any of the blossoms on the trees in this country because he would be returning home before spring. But then it suddenly occurred to him that he would remember those blossoms, those beautiful blossoms, very well and not to see them again would not be a calamity. He realized that he was creating a panic inside himself unnecessarily. He recognized that the destructive, sadistic organization worked by creating a propaganda of panic, which he listened to and felt terribly frightened of, as if something terrible would really happen. If he kept calm, he would realize this was not true. It seemed clear that listening only to his destructive part—which was trying to frighten him by vastly exaggerating his problems or which falsely proclaimed danger (when in fact the only danger lay in listening to the destructive organization that tried to frighten him)— would diminish his strength and prevent his normal mourning from occurring. This tendency to create trouble and panic, which disturbs the patient's peace of mind by exaggerating the problem, as in the dream about the enormous cost of a house in his own country, is typical of the disturbing assault on the security and peace of mind of patients working through depressive anxieties. These disconcerting panic reactions and a tendency to frighten himself must be worked through with the patient to make him aware of this false assault and distortions, which seem to be created by a part of the patient that still seems to resent his ability to be better and reach health and security in the future.

It is very important for the analyst to know about the highly suggestive, almost hypnotic, panic-spreading propaganda of the destructive narcissistic organization. The patient very easily is paralyzed by it, and there is a real danger that the patient, weakened by the panic, will fall back on the false, seductive "help" that is often offered by the destructive organization in disguise. The perverting influence of this maneuver is very powerful, and this has to be shown to the patient by the analyst again and again. This weakening influence is often used by the destructive masochistic organization to create addictive perversions, drug addiction, alcoholism, and even delusional psychosis. These problems are often very confusing to the analyst, who needs much experience and skill to avoid being misled by the patient's material.

The worst mental and physical result occurs when the misleading addictive influences succeed in confusing the patient about good and bad to the extent that good and bad actually become reversed. This addictive influence in the perversion has been investigated by Meltzer (1973), who wrote:

> The bad, destructive, evil, Satanic—whatever degree of malevolence may characterize this part of the infantile structure of the self in an individual—this part of the self is in eternal opposition to good objects, in the first instance the combined object, breast-and-nipple of the mother. It seeks to pervert the good relation of other parts of the self to the object and to bind them in addictive passivity to itself. To this end it utilizes every means at its disposal: seduction, threat, coercion, confusion, intolerance of the good parts to depressive pain, to separation, to jealousy, etc. It seeks to pervert and to addict. [p. 133].

There is, of course, a danger that even with very detailed knowledge of these processes we cannot succeed in freeing patients from the threat and imprisonment of the addictive perversion when the sexual pressure in the sexual/masochistic perversion is particularly intense. Joseph (1982) described an addictive perversion—addiction to near death. She observed a few patients who were addicted not only to masochistic pleasure but to death or near death. In the analysis,

> these patients go over and over their unhappinesses, failures, things they feel they ought to feel guilty about. They talk as if they are attempting unconsciously to pull the analyst into concurring with the

> misery or with the descriptions or they unconsciously try to make the analyst give critical or disturbing interpretations . . . Such patients feel in thrall to a part of the self that dominates and imprisons them and will not let them escape. . . . The point I want to add here is that the patient experiences sexual gratification in being in such pain. [p. 451].

Joseph described a patient where "no ordinary pleasure, genital, sexual or other, offered such delight as this type of terrible and exciting self-annihilation which annihilates also the object" (p. 451).

The patient had great difficulty making any progress in the analysis, essentially sadomasochistic, which operated also as a negative therapeutic reaction" (p. 451).

Joseph also stressed that the aggressive part of the patient is not only sadistic to the analyst and waits to triumph over him, but is actively sadistic towards another part of the self which is masochistically caught up in this process and this has become an addiction.

Meltzer's (1973) Joseph's (1982), and my own observations (1971a, b) have many important factors in common. Interestingly, while we were working on these issues, we were not in contact with one another. So this triple research seems to confirm the value and truth of the phenomena we observed.

There are obviously still many processes related to the masochistic perversions that have to be studied in much greater detail. There are only very few books and papers in the English literature to which I could draw attention. Of the incredibly large collection of papers on masochism from the United States I shall mention only that the relationship of narcissism to the masochistic perversions has been described by Glenn (1981) and particularly Cooper (1981). I have also come across patients whose narcissism was characterized by feelings of omnipotence and intense desire to be looked after by a powerful person with whom they could experience a sense of symbiotic union. These patients sometimes react with intense rage against the frustrating person and a sadomasochistic pattern may develop around these experiences. I agree with Cooper on a number of points. For example, the aim of the masochistic perversion is not a union with the loving mother but a phantasy of controlling a cruel and damaging mother. But I think it is not only control. There is always a collusion when such a pull toward union with the damaged but destructive object takes place. I have the impression that most American writers are not aware of the omnipotent destructive narcissism, which is so difficult to uncover as it frequently works disguised as a helpful figure. This factor is crucial to understanding the negative therapeutic reactions as well as the masochistic perversions.

REFERENCES

Cooper, A. (1981), Summary of Panel Discussion on "Masochism: Current concepts." *J. Amer. Psychoanal. Assn.*, 29:673–668.
Freud, S. (1924), The economic problems of masochism. *Standard Edition,* 19. London: Hogarth Press, 1961.
Glenn, J. (1981), Masochism and narcissism in a patient traumatized in childhood. *J. Amer. Psychoanal. Assn.*, 29:677–680.
Hartmann H, Kris E, & Loewenstein, R. M. (1949), Notes on the theory of aggression. *The Psychoanalytic Study of the Child.* 314:9–36. New York: International Universities Press.
Joseph, B. (1982), Addiction to near-death. *Internat. J. Psycho-Anal.*, 63:449–456.
Klein, M. (1958), On the development of mental functioning. *Internat. J. Psycho-Anal.*, 39:84–90.
Meltzer, D. (1973), *Sexual States of Mind.* Perthshire: Clunie Press.
Rosenfeld, H. (1971a), Contribution to the psychopathology of psychotic states. In: *Problems of Psychosis. Volume 1,* ed. P. Doucet & C. Launin. Amsterdam: Excerpta Medica.
Rosenfeld, H. (1971b), A clinical approach to the psychoanalytic theory of the life and death instincts: an investigation into the aggressive aspects of narcissism. *Internat. J. Psycho-Anal.*, 52:169–178
Segal, H. (1964), *Introduction to the Work of Melanie Klein.* London: Heinemann.

10 / A Consideration of Treatment Techniques in Relation to the Functions of Masochism

Helen Meyers

THE TREATMENT OF MASOCHISTIC character problems has long been considered one of the more difficult analytic challenges. The fixity of masochistic trends and their self-defeating nature in life and treatment, as well as the related countertransference reactions, are major constituents of this difficulty. But a part is also played by the complexity of the genesis and variety of functions of masochism. Thus, to my way of thinking, the very differences in the many contributions to the theory of masochism, rather than being obscuring and contradictory (Maleson, 1984), add valuable components to the whole picture. Each contribution, clinically valid, yet addressing a different function of masochism derived genetically from a different developmental level, adds another piece to the puzzle, enriching and filling in the theoretical understanding that informs our clinical interventions. Each piece is necessary for completion of the puzzle. The relative dominance of a particular meaning or function may vary from patient to patient, but often all the pieces play a part, and need to be addressed in the same treatment at different times. In this essay I hope to address some of these issues of application of theoretical understanding to the clinical situation.

Treatment considerations of masochistic features seem of particular importance to me, since I believe that some degree of masochism is universal as long as there is a superego, and helplessness and frustration in childhood, a need for object relatedness and self-definition, for separation and individuation, or a need for repair of the loss of infantile omnipotence. The difference, of course, is one of degree and quality of maladaptation. I recall no analytic treatment during which masochistic issues did not arise. Certainly, in every treatment, resistance to getting well contains masochistic goals as well. This resistance is exemplified par excellence in the masochist in the "negative therapeutic reaction", where the patient gets worse instead of better as a result of a "correct interpretation" or after some longed-for success. In a way, all defenses have a masochistic aspect in that they cling to a miscarried repair (Rado, 1969); masochistic features appear in the treatment of all character pathologies; in the masochistic character disorders, masochistic compromise formations predominate.

SOME COMMENTS ON THE TREATMENT OF CHARACTER TRAITS IN GENERAL

In this essay, then, I shall address characterologic masochistic problems, masochistic character traits, and their treatment. Before focusing on masochism per se, a few words on the treatment of character traits in general, with its inherent difficulties and complexities, are in order. Whether we argue that character is synonymous with the ego or ego ideal, or one of its functions, or is a supraordinate concept synonymous with psychic structure as a whole, character results from compromise formations involving identifications and counteridentifications, early endowment, and conflict solution. Consolidated in late adolescence, character has been defined as the habitual mode of bringing into harmony the tasks presented by internal demands and by the external world; the habitual way for achieving synthesis and integration, involving id, ego, and superego pressures and identifications, and internal object relations. Although, in significant measure originating in conflict, character is removed from conflict by its codification of conflict solution and patterned fixity, this fixity being represented by distinctive traits or qualities and by typical ways of conducting oneself. Its function involves the maintenance of psychosomatic homeostasis, patterned self-esteem regulation, stabilization of ego identity, and automatization of threshold and barrier levels, both levels shifting in accordance with the intensity of internal and external stimuli (Blos, 1968). Character traits are consciously ego syntonic but not necessarily adaptive or "healthy". What makes us consider a character trait as pathological is its degree of rigidity and compulsory nature, the resultant degree of constriction, and interference with desired function and gratification. While it is developmentally the best compromise solution available under the circumstances, its current use is maladaptive.

Character traits are difficult to change in treatment because of the multiple determinants that reinforce them and contribute to their relative fixity; letting go of them means giving up the secondary gain inherent in the traits as well as the primary gain involved in the original compromise formation or conflict solution. It may mean giving up a mode of functioning that provided early approval, self-esteem and self-definition, or may even mean the loss of an idealized introject—as well as facing the original danger. This ego syntonicity and relative distance from conflict and relative efficacy in protecting from anxiety lessens motivation for change and increases resistance to change. In the masochistic character we may have a small ally in that, although there is pleasure in pain, there also is pain.

Turning to the analytic situation, some authors have distinguished between characterologic defenses, inherent in character traits, as nonspecific defenses against the establishment and recognition of transference in general, particularly early in treatment, and the specific resistances that appear in the transference during treatment, the transference resistances. This differentiation has led to a technical debate between those who suggested an approach to character analysis of "breaking through the character armour" first in order to get to the analysis (Reich, 1953), and those who recommend waiting until later stages to analyze character traits, and then only if they serve resistance. This distinction between character resistance and transference resistance is, however, somewhat misleading. Characterologic defenses continue to appear as resistance against further transference throughout treatment. And the resistances, as they appear in specific transferences, are apt to use the same defense mechanisms as the character defenses. Both use the same armamentarium of available ego techniques to deal with the patient's same infantile drive pressures, infantile object relations and superego identifications, and infantile conflict solutions, transferred in a somewhat altered form to the present treatment relationship. Of course, as regression proceeds, earlier constellations are uncovered and more primitive defenses may come into play. Later, after working through, it is to be hoped that new, more adaptive and flexible defensive compromises will replace the old pathologic, rigid characterologic ones. Thus, just as character traits, in order to be analyzed, first have to become ego dystonic, all resistances similarly need first to be isolated, confronted by the observing ego, and clarified before being interpreted.

THE MEANING OF MASOCHISM

A number of authors have felt that the concept of masochism has become too broad to be meaningful. They have advocated a return to a more limited definition of masochism as states of suffering with a clear linkage to sexual (genital) pleasure, conscious or unconscious.

For myself, I see much merit in the broader concept, which I find extraordinarily useful both clinically and theoretically. It embraces phenomena that are found throughout our clinical experience and defines a constellation that has specific clinical manifestations and implications and an essential core mechanism. That we recognize this constellation to be multidetermined, and to serve different defensive and narcissistic functions arising from different developmental levels, adds to our ability to understand and deal with it clinically.

The essence of masochism is the intimate connection between pain and pleasure. It has been conceptualized as pleasure in pain. It is the seeking or pursuit of psychic or physical pain, discomfort or humiliation, where the unpleasure becomes gratifying or pleasurable; but either the seeking or the pleasure, or both, may be unconscious. Indeed, frequently the masochist, unaware of his own agency and satisfaction, is conscious only of the suffering that is experienced as imposed from the outside by fate or others, who are angrily blamed for the pain. And yet there frequently is no mistaking the evident satisfaction in the sufferer's voice, or the gleam in his eyes, as he asserts yet another failure or humiliation, as he snatches defeat out of the jaws of victory. And it is only after much work that the sufferer may get in touch with his part in the painful play. There is pursuit of the pain—pleasure in the pain—because the pain is unconsciously considered the necessary, indispensable condition for need satisfaction or "pleasure", and becomes inextricably associated with it.

But the gratification need not be only sexual. There are other pleasures and excitements. It may indeed be gratification of sexual or aggressive drives or their derivatives; or it may be an ego gratification, such as maintenance of object relations or self-definition or self-esteem enhancement; or it may be appeasement of the sadistic superego's need to punish. In the compromise formation of masochism, the price of pain pays for gratification and avoids attendant anxiety and dangers of damage, object loss or loss of self-esteem or identity. Whether the pain itself also is experienced as pleasure, either by libidinization of the destructive instinct or simply based on the physiologic prototypes of excitement associated with any strong stimulus (Freud's, 1924, "erotogenic masochism"), or whether the pain is only the prerequisite for pleasure is still a matter of debate. But it is close enough for the pursuit of pain to become an apparent end in itself. Not all pain or humiliation in life, of course, is masochistic; pain may be inflicted from the outside without a choice, or unavoidable discomfort may be consciously accepted for the sake of an ideal or conscious goal. It is the motivation of *seeking of the unpleasure* and the satisfaction in it that is the key. Compare one war hero's acceptance of danger to achieve a vital objective with another's repetitive seeking out of life-threatening situations for their own sake. Or compare a woman's tolerance of labor pains in order to have a desired child with seeking the pain of labor as the goal and taking pleasure in its severity. It is not masochistic if a mother enjoys her child's pleasure in eating the last piece of chocolate cake; it is masochistic if this enjoyment is heightened because of her own deprivation.

THE FUNCTIONS OF MASOCHISM AND TREATMENT APPROACHES:

Masochism, then, is a complex configuration, multiply determined from different developmental levels, and serves various functions. In this motivational hierarchy, one or another of these components may have played a dominant part in the formation of a particular masochistic phenomenon in a particular patient, but the other components are likely to have taken part, though only a minor one, as well. Ultimately, of course, it is the fact that pain serves an unconscious function in achieving some need satisfaction that gives us our therapeutic leverage to uncover this continued unconscious purpose and its genesis. In treatment, one or another of these functions may take center stage, be dominant at any given point in the transference; but sooner or later the other functions will have to be dealt with as well and sometimes all are operating together in a condensed fashion. Understanding this will determine our interpretations and other interventions, their timing and content.

The following outline is an attempt to relate various technical emphases to our understanding of each function of masochism. Clearly these points are overlapping and cannot be neatly separated, but the outline is offered in the hope of providing some theoretical structure.

(A) Masochism and Guilt: The pain and suffering of masochism are payment for forbidden, unacceptable oedipal desires and aggression, to avoid danger of retaliation—damage and abandonment. The sadistic superego needs to punish, and the masochistic ego submits to punishment out of an excessive unconscious sense of guilt (Freud, 1924). The pain and humiliation unconsciously are both payment and permission for further transgression—"pay as you go" (Rado, 1969) or like a "lay-away plan." The self-directed aggression is libidinized. The sadistic superego is appeased and feels pride in its punishing, the ego feels pleasure in its suffering—moral masochism. At the same

time, aggression is directed outward as the masochist provokes and invites hurt and anger from others and with his pain tries to play on their guilt. In this context, one meaning of a negative therapeutic reaction during treatment is the patient's guilty refusal to accept anything good, which he does not deserve, or to have pleasure without pain, which is without punishment. He needs to defeat both himself and the analyst. .

Insofar as we are addressing this dynamic, the relevant classical technique, well known of course, involves: (1) confrontation of the unconscious active seeking of unpleasure in and out of the transference, a quest that is often consciously misperceived as a search for pleasure that failed; (2) clarification of the projection of this destructive activity onto the outside world, analyst or other, in a kind of "injustice collecting"; and (3) interpretation of the motivation of the unconscious sense of guilt in its reconstructed genetic context and its current transference manifestations. Here, then, we focus on the oedipal conflict and the role of guilt. The mechanism for change predominantly involves mutative interpretation with lessening of severity of the superego. Clearly, it is mainly the third step, that is, the content of the interpretations and reconstructions, that will vary with the elucidation of other functions of masochism; but to some degree also the relative reliance on other mechanisms for change will differ.

(B) *Maintenance of Object Relations:* Maintenance of object relations is, of course, involved in the oedipal conflict as well, but I would like to focus here on preoedipal issues. Preoedipal aggression against mother in the face of infantile helplessness and frustration is turned against the self (Bergler's 1961, "psychic masochism") to gratify aggression yet avoid retaliation. But here the emphasis is on the maintenance of the all-important object relationship with mother, appeasing the aggressor mother, and buying her love with suffering. This has been referred to as "seduction of the aggressor" in childhood, a precursor of masochism (Loewenstein's, 1957, "protomasochism"). For the masochist, because of traumatic fixation in this period, pain and discomfort become equated with getting love and become established as the mode for maintaining vital object relations (Berliner, 1958). Unconsciously, the masochist continues to "seduce" his internalized, critical, maternal object and repetitively reenacts, in current relationships and in the transference, the old scenario learned at his mother's knee. A poor way of getting love, but the masochist knows not, nor trusts, another way. Unconsciously he is convinced he will get love only if he submits to pain and humiliation and will loose his objects if he stops suffering. In this context, a negative therapeutic reaction in treatment also represents the patient's fear that getting better would mean loss of a vital object relationship.

In addressing this dynamic, the relevant technique includes the same three steps as described in the previous section except that the interpretations and reconstructions would focus on preoedipal issues of helplessness, aggression, and maintenance of object relations. But it involves more: namely, the fact that, in the analysis, the relationship does not stop in the face of each success or each sign of pleasure on the patient's part; nor is the relationship destroyed by the patient's aggression. This new experience provides a temporary base of trust on which the patient can build—a base from which to try out further steps toward a different adaptation without the threat of object loss. Confidence in the continuity of a relationship is, of course, also a factor in working out the oedipal transgressions discussed earlier. Indeed it is a factor in all analyses, though of relatively different importance.

Maintenance of object relations is of particular importance in masochism in the presence of more severe pathology. Excessive frustration and aggression due to early experience with a primitive or narcissistic, nonempathic mother may lead to relatively impaired internal object relations and self-images. Defensively, to keep the bad from destroying the good, the bad is split off from the object image, which, for survival, must be maintained as all good, while the self becomes all bad in a kind of "identification with the aggressor." Aggression and punishment is then directed against the bad self. The defensively idealized, omnipotent, all-good object or self-object is needed to merge with and shore up a defective or bad self. When masochism serves this function, the double-pronged treatment approach described earlier assumes added dimensions. The aggression and defensive split must be addressed vigorously by interpretation, and eventually the split must be healed and the defensive all good and all bad images replaced by more complete and stable self and object images. On the other hand, for these interventions to work, the patient must first experience a different object relationship in the treatment with an empathic, accepting analyst who validates the patient's feelings and perceptions of earlier experience, in order to establish the necessary trust to permit internalization of different object and self representations (Berliner, 1968; Stolorow, 1975). Thus, in addition to interpretation in the transference and reconstructions, the added mutative mechanism here is in the diatrophic patient–

therapist relationship (Loewald, 1960), and in the empathic self–object function of the analyst who accepts both the patient's anger and his pleasure.

(C) Masochism and Self-Esteem: Implied in the concept of psychic masochism is a narcissistic function of masochism. In the face of unavoidable frustration and helplessness and loss of magical infantile omnipotence, the child attempts to repair this injury to his self-esteem by asserting some sense of control. He cannot gratify his own needs or control the environment, but he can pain himself; he can, by turning passive into active, assume responsibility for his disappointments, and he can provoke rejection, and extract some pleasure from that: "No one frustrates me against my wishes; I frustrate myself because I like it." This narcissistic function of masochism may be consolidated during separation-individuation, with its attendant frustrations and pain (Cooper, this volume), and, if being disappointed and pained becomes the preferred mode of gratification, the adult masochist feels pride in his own agency and sense of control in creating his own displeasures—"victory in defeat" (Reik, 1941). This narcissistic investment in masochism comes from various developmental levels. There is pride in undoing early helplessness and being in control, in manipulating others into sadistic, guilty or helpless responses, in being in charge of the desired degree of discomfort (Smirnoff's, 1969, "masochistic contract"). There is superego pride in the ability to control one's instincts, in self-abnegation, in the mastery of pain. There is pride in pursuing one's own course even if it is painful. There is pride in being special as a victim of fate. "I am in control. I want to be pained. I asked for it. I enjoy it. I can handle it. I have more discomfort than anyone."

In relation to the narcissistic function of masochism, certain technical directions are indicated. Step 1 in the earlier described sequence—confrontation of the patient with his own activity in unconsciously but purposefully seeking unpleasure—assumes special importance. Done tactfully, it enhances the patient's self-esteem by underlining his control rather than his helplessness and being a victim of external forces (Eidelberg, 1959). Of course, it also involves the other steps of clarification and interpretation, so that, understanding the infantile reasons and origins for his search for and pleasure in pain, the patient does not feel helplessly victimized from within either. The patient can then use his sense of control and understanding to obtain more direct and better gratification, pleasure *without* pain, with a now more mature and competent ego.

At the same time, care must be taken to protect the patient's narcissistic vulnerability. Such interventions must be done with tact and empathy. Otherwise, confrontations of his aggression may be experienced as further proof of worthlessness and badness by the masochist, already burdened by a severe superego, a further support for the critical internalized object leading to further masochistic submission. Indeed, these patients often react with increased "mea culpa" after such an interpretation. Or such a confrontation can be experienced by the patient as a sadistic assault by the analyst—a reaction indeed frequently provoked in others by the masochist. This elicits further anger and further guilt and further masochistic behavior in the patient.

Insofar as masochism is a component of the narcissistic personality disorder as such, an additional function of the negative therapeutic reaction (Kernberg, 1975) has to be considered. The idealized object and omnipotent self-representations—the ego ideal—are defensively condensed with the real self image to bolster the real self and form the grandiose self, while the internalized objects are left fragmented and with only a negative valence. This defensive balance is maintained by narcissistic withdrawal, entitlement, and devaluation, preventing the punitive objects from effectiveness but also preventing the internalized objects from being invested with anything good. If these objects were to be seen as good, it would upset the balance, increase the sense of badness of the self, and lead to further intolerable envy and greed, the basic archaic affects that needed to be defended against in the first place. The narcissist, thus, cannot permit anything "good" in the object. In the transference, then, the patient has to destroy the "good analyst" and cannot accept a good or helpful interpretation. Instead he has to get worse. This is a self-defeating move that not only is destructive to himself but also destroys the good within the object and thus satisfies his aggression, his defensive need to maintain his grandiose self, as well as his sense of control, discussed earlier. In treatment, this has to be interpreted, as the role of primitive aggression, greed, and envy is confronted and worked on and the defensive nature of the grandiose self is analyzed.

(D) *Masochism and Self-Definition:* Frustration and unpleasure are necessary aids in an infant's self–other differentiation and in the establishment of boundaries during the separation-individuation process. The child's need for separateness is tied to the unpleasurable feelings of loss, anger, and guilt toward the "mother of separation" during rapprochement. The "no" of the two-year-old toddler helps him define himself, even when it involves getting into trouble. Unpleasure is experienced as a necessary accompaniment or condition for the pleasure in and drive for separateness and individuation. The adult masochist's "I will, too, be self-destructive and you can't stop me" asserts his control, but also defines him as an independent agent, separate, autonomous, and individuated. "I am the sufferer" defines his identity, though a negative one. He needs to do his own painful thing to feel individuated. Thus masochistic phenomena appear in the transference, at times, in the service of the need for separateness: throughout treatment in patients who have to struggle against their wish for and fear of merger, and only toward the end of treatment in other patients in the pursuit of separation from the therapist. In certain patients with very early pathology, of course, pain itself can serve the function of self-definition and self-reality.

Technically, this masochism in the service of separation-individuation requires interpretation in the transference and genetic reconstruction, though early reconstruction to that phase of separation-individuation may be difficult. But at times it is necessary for the patient to act out painfully in order to establish his sense of autonomy, even though it may be a self-defeating, masochistic act. As difficult as this may be for the therapist, it may be necessary for the patient to fail on his own, before he can give up this masochistic stance without fear of merger.

Case Illustration

The patient was a bright, good looking, talented young public interest lawyer who was pursuing her goal of "serving those in need." She was married to a successful newspaper man whom she "loved" and idealized, but with whom she was engaged in a painful sadomasochistic relationship in which he abused her physically in frequent fights, humiliated her publicly with frequent affairs, and generally neglected her. It quickly became clear how she masochistically provoked these attacks, knowing just how to stir up this vulnerable man whom she had unconsciously selected in the first place for his narcissistic and sadistic aspects. It took, however, some time and much work for her to accept her active part in this pursuit of pain rather than experiencing herself as the victim. She used this insight into her activity, of course, to further flagellate herself emotionally. As treatment progressed, guilt over oedipal conflicts emerged as the dominant theme in her masochism. She had been her admired, seductive father's "golden girl," and was in angry competition with her "sexy" mother, who preferred her brother. She had fled from (yet acted out) this conflict early by moving into several sexual escapades with unacceptable partners, which led to several guiltfilled abortions; one of these partners became her husband.

In treatment, at this point, interpretation of oedipal issues was the main tool. She improved, lessened her provocations. The husband first reacted by ceasing to abuse her physically, then stopped his affairs. Things were going better. The patient followed with a series of new provocations and an orgy of self-defeating, humiliating behavior both in relation to her husband and at work. She reported each episode triumphantly with tears and anger. These episodes were multiply determined: Guiltily she could not tolerate success and felt she did not deserve anything good; in the transference, she expressed her rage against her mother-therapist and tried to provoke her by failing and defeating the therapist's efforts—mother was revealed as narcissistic and distant, yet competitive; the patient asserted her control and independence by not getting better. As these issues were worked through, she slowly revealed her conviction that she needed to suffer to seduce her analyst, to maintain this important sustaining relationship, as she had appeased her critical mother with her painful failures. When neither the aggression nor her slow improvement seemed to interrupt the treatment relationship, the patient permitted herself less pain and more pleasure. When the husband entered his own treatment, which she had dearly hoped for, she acted out with self-defeating sabotage by initiating a move to California. The plan almost to completion, analysis revealed that she had felt she needed to fail once again to retain her identity and prove her separateness from the analyst. This was again interpreted and treatment proceeded to a relatively good termination.

This case, while predominantly oedipal, involved many preoedipal issues as well. The masochism was multiply determined and served various functions. At times, one or another function was dominant in the transference; at times, they all operated simultaneously. Analysis of all the functions with relevant interventions, as discussed in the previous sections, helped in bringing this case to a successful conclusion.

MASOCHISM AND GENDER

There can be no discussion of treatment of masochism without some mention of masochism in women, as different from that in men. The theoretical understanding of masochism in women obviously can affect their treatment. If, for instance, women are assumed to be normally masochistic, then a particular masochistic trait in a particular female patient might not be addressed in treatment. On the other hand, a particular behavior in a woman, not experienced as masochistic by the woman—for instance, devotion to a child—might be viewed as masochistic by a male therapist and treated as pathological.

Freud postulated a special feminine masochism, an expression of intrinsic feminine nature, linking passivity, submission, masochism, and femininity. This was supposedly based on drive endowment—a constitutional, basic female capacity to experience pleasure in pain and a tendency in women toward internalization of aggressions; on anatomical sex differences, the discovery of which turns the girl from active to passive and from mother to father, in order to achieve satisfaction by submission to father to get the penis-child; and on oedipal fantasies. This conceptualization was expanded on and supported by Helene Deutsch (1944), who felt that the truly feminine (erotic) woman was one who joyfully embraced the pain of defloration, penetration, menstruation, childbirth, and motherhood. Deutsch postulated masochism, passivity, and narcissism as the three basic feminine traits.

No evidence has been found that women have a greater endowment for deriving pleasure from pain, and the theories of feminine development based on defect have been largely discarded today (Blum, 1977). Any greater frequency of masochism in women, as evidenced by masochistic sexual fantasies and general masochistic behavior, has been attributed to other factors relating to early development, child rearing, and socialization, such as: ego ideal factors involving identification with a mother's masochistic self-representation; parental attitudes toward boys and girls, and internalization of a dependent, passive, childlike, or devalued female gender role model learned from mother or father; superego aspects involving greater prohibition against, and therefore greater guilt around, sexual activity in girls; and the realities of greater male power and privilege in our culture—all these leading to "seduction of the aggressor," masochism being the "weapon of the weak."

Actually it is my thesis that there is no more masochism among women than among men. Perhaps it surfaces in different areas because of the different value systems and content of the male and female superego and ego ideal. But I am not even sure of that. Some behavior that is seen as masochistic in women may be seen as such only by men but not experienced as such by women. Maternal devotion, for example, or faithful support of a loved one's achievement, is likely to be the pleasurable gratification of a loving feeling and should not be confused with masochistic renunciation or enslavement or guilt over aggression. Of course, some masochistic women do choose the arena of maternal or marital relations to express their masochism. In the case discussed earlier, the presenting problem was a masochistic relationship with a man.

Is this picture of masochistic interpersonal relationships then what we see predominantly in masochistic women, as differentiated from masochistic men? Hardly—literature is rich with examples of men whose behavior repetitively provokes painful rejection or deprivation from women, the very thing they presumably do not want, and men who masochistically tie themselves to ungiving, abusive, or exploitative women—one need think only of Somerset Maugham's *Of Human Bondage* for an example. Our clinical experience is also rich with such examples. Nor are early developmental issues of narcissistic repair for lost omnipotence or of separation and self-delineation functions of masochism found less frequently in men than women. What may be the case is that these issues of men's masochistic relationships to women often emerge only later in the analysis of men—after some regression has taken place, after some of the more obvious self-defeating, success-fearing, guilt-ridden patterns in relation to work and career have been worked through, such issues as painful overwork, repetitive professional failure, and being "wrecked by success." In the analysis of men, issues about relationships to women, to start with, sometimes seem to be presented in terms of lack of intimacy, distance, or potency disturbances rather than pain-dependent attachment. This is perhaps still a reflection of the difference in male and female ego ideal content; lack of relatedness may still be more acceptable than submission as part of the male gender role.

This raises an interesting question: How does analyst gender influence the clinical process? Can it be that certain masochistic patterns in both men and women are more prevalent or apparent in treatment with a female therapist, experienced transferentially as the preoedipal mother (or, of course, with a male therapist who is aware of and permits a preoedipal maternal transference to develop)? For instance, masochism, when equated with passivity, might be more admittable in front of mother; or analysis with a woman may be more easily equated with submission to the preoedipal mother and thus reveal early masochistic defenses. Regression to "seduction of the aggressor" as a mechanism may emerge more readily in the transference to the preoedipal mother, as a way of dealing with aggression and avoidance of punishment as well as a plea for love. The need for separateness to protect against the wish for and fear or remerger with mother during the reworking of the rapprochement phase of separation-individuation may be in sharper relief in the transference to a female therapist, and thus the issue of pain and guilt in relation to self definition and self-object differentiation might be more evident.

In my experience (Meyers, 1986), analyst gender may influence the sequence of certain transference reactions, their intensity and inescapability, and their temporary displacement to extratransference objects, but the work of the analysis of the multiple dimensions of masochism remains.

REFERENCES

Bergler, E. (1961), *Curable and Incurable Neurotics*, New York: Liveright.
Berliner, B. (1958), The role of object relations in moral masochism. *Psychoanal. Q.*, 27:38–56.
Blos, P. (1968), Character formation in adolescence. *The Psychoanalytic Study of the Child*, 23:245–263. New Haven: Yale University Press.
Blum, H. P. (1977), Masochism, the ego ideal, and psychology of women. *J. Amer. Psychoanal. Assn.*, Supplement, 24:157–191.
Deutsch, H. (1944), *Psychology of Women*, I: New York: Straton.
Eidelberg, L. (1959) Humiliation and masochism. *J. Amer. Psychoanal. Assn.*, 7:274–283.
Freud, S. (1924), The economic problem of masochism. *Standard Edition*, 19:159–170. London: Hogarth Press, 1961.
Kernberg, O. (1975), *Borderline Conditions and Pathological Narcissism*. New York: Aronson.
Loewald, H. (1960), On the therapeutic action of psychoanalysis. *Internat. J. Psycho-Anal.*, 41:16–33.
Loewenstein, R. M. (1957), A contribution to the psychoanalytic theory on masochism. *J. Amer. Psychoanal. Assn.*, 5:197–234.
Maleson, F. (1984), The multiple meanings of masochism in psychoanalytic discourse. *J. Amer. Psychoanal. Assn.*, 32:325–357.
Meyers, H. (1986), Analytic work by and with women: the complexity and the challenge. In: *Between Analyst and Patient: New Dimensions in Countertransference and Transference*, ed. H. Meyers. Hillsdale, NJ: The Analytic Press.
Rado, S. (1969), Development of conscience. In: *Adaptational Psychodynamics*. New York: Science House, pp. 128–137.
Reich, W. (1953), *Character Analysis*. New York: Orgone Institute Press.
Reik, T. (1941), *Masochism and Modern Man*. New York: Fauer and Strauss.
Smirnoff, V. M. (1969), The masochistic contract. *Internat. J. Psycho-Anal.*, 50:665–672.
Stolorow, R. D. (1975), The narcissistic function of masochism (and sadism). *Internat. J. Psycho-Anal.*, 56:441–448.

11 / The Precursors of Masochism:

Protomasochism

Eleanor Galenson

I can no longer understand how we can have overlooked the ubiquity of non-erotic aggressivity and destructiveness.—Freud (1930, p. 120)

THE TERM "MASOCHISM" has been variously used in the psychoanalytic literature to connote, among other states, a metapsychological construct, actions, attitudes and thoughts, defenses against and expressions of aggression, and defense against an unloving object. While the only feature common to these disparate states is the element of suffering or renunciation (Maleson, 1984), the clinical material derived from knowledge of adult patients with masochistic perversions, as described by Loewenstein (1955), shows striking similarities: the suffering is self-limited in intensity and form, a sexual partner participates in the sexual scene or fantasy—that is, it is a dyadic interplay—and the type of threat is always related to castration. Loewenstein postulated that masochistic perversions are modified repetitions of childhood situations in which attempts at sexual rapprochement with the mother were rebuffed either by actual or imaginary ridicule, threat or punishment, the perversion representing an undoing of the rebuff. However, the perversion itself does not appear before the oedipal period. Loewenstein also remarked that passivity is a prerequisite for masochism rather than a result of it, and he pointed out the pregenital features in the sexuality of the masochistic perversion, following along with Freud's insistence that fixation to pregenital, especially anal, erotism plays an essential role in the genesis of masochism.

Freud's conceptualizations concerning masochism changed with the development of his structural perspective; the role of the real object received less emphasis, while conflict was seen to derive in greater part from the pressure of id forces. However, although Freud recognized that the pressure of internal forces was a major source of the fear of castration, he never abandoned his view of the influence of the external object. Anna Freud (1936) continued this emphasis in her concept of "identification with the aggressor," a concept since elaborated by other authors as well.

In regard to the area of developing object relations, Loewenstein and others have related masochism to an early imbalance between libidinal and aggressive components of the infant's early ties to the mother. They hypothesized that the child's approaches to the mother are met with disapproval or rebuff together with actual or imaginary ridicule, threat, or punishment. The child then attempts to "seduce the aggressor," thereby averting the catastrophe of loss of love. Thus, libidinal attachment becomes intimately associated with aggression, leading toward a special type of sexuality. As a result of various types of excessive stimulation or other unpleasure induced by the mother, the parent has become the "aggressor" and the child the "protomasochist" in this interchange, and the child's potential for investing normal aggression in the parent has been modified. Does this shift lay the basis for the development of masochism, providing a means of survival against the danger of parental aggression? This protodefense may prevail in all infants but would be exaggerated where the aggression or anxiety in relation to the mother is more intense than usual.

Other experiences of early childhood, such as separations and serious physical traumata, have been described (Spitz, 1953; Bernstein, 1983; Glenn, 1984) as setting the stage for masochistic responses through a very early predefense similar to identification with the aggressor. In this view, such children connect the mother with pain, thereby erotizing suffering and fostering a desire for a repetition of the early painful experiences.

Implicit in Freud's views concerning masochistic development, as well as those expressed by later authors, is the role of aggression in both child and parent in the development of masochism. Confusion in this area stems in part from the difficulty in finding agreement about both the source and manifestations of aggression in the young child. As Compton (1983) has noted, the theoretical dilemma of aggression may be related to a feature that he believes distinguishes libidinal from aggressive development. Compton reminds us that the early somatic referents for aggression, unlike those for libidinally related behavior, consist to a much greater extent of responses to environmental stimuli, such as frustration, rather than arising from within the infant. Anna Freud's (1936) concept of "identification with the aggressor" provides a potent theoretical construct for understanding the process whereby the quality of the parental object may arouse anxiety or other unpleasurable as well as pleasurable states in the child, particularly in its initial stages. Subsequently both members of the dyad contribute to the development and maldevelopment of aggression in an interactive manner, as is true of all early development.

In the first systematic attempt to present a genetic picture of the aggressive drive, Spitz (1953) suggested that aggressive manifestations begin at about two months, when pleasure and unpleasure, particularly in the form of rage, suggest the onset of drive differentiation. When goal-directed action begins, by about three months, angry screaming results when the human partner withdraws; it is a time when food withdrawal produces the same behavior. Spitz views this period as the beginning of specific resentment discharged via the general musculature, but not through specific acts as such. By about six months, aggressive manifestations become specific. Hitting, biting, scratching, pulling, and kicking are used to manipulate things, both animate and inanimate, acts that serve for mastery and to establish relations between the infant and the "thing," including the libidinal object.

Spitz maintained that the collaboration of the aggressive with the libidinal drive is *prerequisite* for the formation of object relations and that the nascent object is the target of simultaneous manifestations of both drives. The "I" is thereby gradually distinguished from the "non-I," the animate from the inanimate, and, finally, the friend from the stranger.

Spitz agreed with Hartmann, Kris, and Loewenstein (1949) that the infant's capacity to bear frustration (or as Freud (1920) said, to enforce the postponement of satisfaction) must be achieved before any perception of the object as such can emerge. Increasing frustration tolerance furthers perception and thought, initiating the discharge of both drives into aim-directed activities. In relation to aggression, a major aim-directed activity of the second half of the first year is grasping, and by eight months, aggression mobilizes the beginnings of the conquest of space, which eventuates in locomotion and the differentiation of things from humans—the inception of what Spitz considered to be full-fledged object relations.

The aspect of Spitz's contribution I wish to emphasize here is his formulation that aggressive drive development is released in its relation to *the love object* (the nursing infant who bites the nipple and grasps with his hands), both drives manifesting themselves simultaneously, concomitantly, or alternatively in response to the same object—the libidinal object. In Spitz's discussion of anaclitic depression, the results of the infant's deprivation of the libidinal object, he emphasizes that *both* drives are deprived of their target, and the infant then vents his aggression against the only available object, his own body, most often in the form of head banging. If the object returns after a limited period, while all functions expand, there is an excess of aggressive manifestations directed at others instead of himself. However, if the deprivation continues, aggression turned against the self may eventuate in death or, if the infant survives, in turning the aggression outward at everyone and everything in an "objectless destruction."

In a related but somewhat different approach to the development of aggression, Stone (1979) proposed an evolutionary view. He noted that oral cannibalistic fantasies, which begin at least with the onset of teething, are then deployed from the mouth and teeth to the hand, leaving the mouth free for the development of speech. According to Stone, the mother is the first object of these devouring 'fantasies' and impulses and of all other important strivings. He believes that aggression in its true sense does not appear until the child is aware of the impact of his actions upon the other. Further, Stone proposes that the prolonged nutritive dependence of the human infant is dynamically related to the intense cannibalistic fantasies and the subsequent incest complex characteristic of humans. The deployment of oral impulses to the use of the hands for a great variety of uses leaves the mouth free for the development of the uniquely human function of speech. Oral rage is replaced by the frustrations related to sphincter control, to be followed by other displacements as development proceeds. Stone believes that the anal sphere and its characteristic mode of functioning are the source of narcissistic mortification; the specifically human practice of toilet training adds a specific increment of object-directed anger, one that is particularly significant for structuralization since the struggle for impulse control is an *internal* one, unlike the feeding interaction.

In summary, Stone derives the development of object-related aggression from the original primacy of the oral sphere, despite the fact that behavioral manifestations of the infant might appear to indicate that self and object have not yet been differentiated. The oral patterning of aggression arises within the feeding situation and persists as one of the earliest and most powerful forces of the human unconscious.

While Spitz accepts the theoretical construct of a primary aggressive drive and Stone does not, both agree that the development of aggression begins during the early oral stage and becomes directed simultaneously with libidinal impulses toward the preobject (or object) and is subsequently deployed along other channels. Stone emphasizes the use of the hand and speech as early avenues of deployment of aggression, whereas Spitz emphasizes the use of the total musculature through which the infant discovers the object world.

In McDevitt's (1983) contribution to the development of aggression, he describes an increase in angry responses to frustrating outer experiences by about six months, shortly followed, as early as eight or nine months, by real anger against maternal restraints, although object-directed aggressive actions without anger, such as biting and pulling the mother's hair, also occur. The anger at the mother is then accompanied by efforts to overcome her restraints or frustrations and is particularly severe when the mother is highly stimulating, frustrating, or primitive, as Spitz had described earlier. McDevitt suggests that it is the attainment of sufficient *self-object differentiation* that is primarily responsible for the emergence of directed hostile behavior and that such hostile behavior does not occur spontaneously but only in response to frustration. Spitz and Stone postulate simultaneity and a close interrelatedness from the earliest months between the differentiation of libidinal and aggressive behavior, differentiation that complements and is complemented by ongoing self–object differentiation. In contrast, McDevitt distinguishes the hostile aggression that emerges in response to developing object relations from its "precursors," namely nonhostile aggression. This division tends to blur the continuity of aggressive development from its earliest forms through the multitude of later deployments, a continuity that I believe is essential for understanding the earliest roots of masochism.

McDevitt describes a normal developmental crisis at nine or ten months, when hostile behavior occurs in response to an immediate maternal frustration and then quickly disappears. This crisis is powerful enough to cause a variety of ego modifications, depending on the particular nature of the dyadic relationship. Our own direct observational data support this finding, and it is precisely at this point in development that the aggressive aspect of the infant's relationship to the mother appears to take a decisive turn. The more adaptive direction in the handling of aggression includes delay, control, mastery, and an admixture with affection toward the mother (such as teasing and playfully attacking her). We believe this adaptive mode is the natural outgrowth of the combined libido and aggression of the earlier part of the first year, when the infant first began to show recognition of the mother as a special person. However, if aggression was intensified by early traumata (Bernstein, 1983; Glenn, 1984), either physical or psychological in nature, or if the maternal response to the child's normal budding aggression is unduly restrictive and harsh, as in some of the syndromes we have described elsewhere (Galenson, 1986), more ominous tendencies appear: the normal ambitendency of the early second year becomes more heavily weighted with aggression of the hostile variety; intense negativism invades the earlier, more balanced investment of libido and aggression in the mother, and the mother–child relationship is seriously threatened. If the hostility becomes too great, the hostile aggression may then be turned inward against the self, resulting in such behavior as self-biting and self-hair-pulling, or there may be massive avoidance of the mother, along with serious regression.

The more adaptive pathway offered by most mothers leads to the usual channelling or modulation of aggressive impulses, and separation and individuation from the mother can then proceed, along with the beginning internalization of the mother's prohibitions and rules of conduct. Unduly intense maternal inner conflict concerning aggression interferes with both the modulation of aggression and the normal progression of the separation-individuation process.

As to the changing nature of the drives themselves, Shengold (1985) has characterized the anal period as a time of transformation of instincts and of complex psychic structuralization; he follows Abraham's (1921, 1924) suggested anal phase division into an earlier period, where the expelling aspect of the anal sphincter is experienced psychologically as a continuation of earlier oral devouring impulses, while the experience of anal contraction during the later anal period contributes to the formation of a sense of containment and body boundary formation. The second anal phase, which Shengold calls defensive anality, is crucial for the mastery of preponderantly aggressively charged anal (and urethral) drive influence and leads to the transformation of body sensation into thought.

Our direct observational data have provided rich material illustrating the complexity of normal anal phase development, both in regard to the behaviors and affects related to anal and urethral sphincter operation and the elaboration of the symbolic function (Galenson, 1984). Where anal phase development is distorted, our data derived from treatment of psychologically deviant infants have led us to understand the severe anal phase distortion involved in such syndromes as infant abuse, very early psychosis, and failure to thrive (in the absence of a known organic factor) (Galenson (1986).

Various types of psychopathology in the infant can be linked to maternal conflicts over aggression (conflicts stemming from her own early traumatic experiences). Extensive intolerance of her infant's normal hostile aggression may lead to excessive teasing, and a type of sadomasochistic mother–child interaction develops that often begins during the child's earliest months, emerging in full force during the second year. The mother appears to be experienced as the "aggressor" with whom the child identifies (A. Freud, 1936; Bernstein, 1983; Glenn, 1984). If the child's anger becomes too intense, the relationship with the mother is in jeopardy and the infant submits to her aggression more and more; eventually the infant becomes more and more passive, inhibited, and regressed. Girls become excessively clinging, anxious, and passive under such circumstances and fail to move ahead into the normal early erotic relationship with their father as part of the normal early genital phase (Galenson and Roiphe, 1971). The relationship with the father becomes excessively passive and eventually assumes a masochistic quality, presaging an oedipal relationship of a similar nature.

The sons of women who are in conflict over hostile aggression themselves tend to identify with the mother as the aggressor at first, but then retreat from the overaggressive maternal identification to a more passive position, thus seriously endangering the active aggressive strivings of normal anal phase development. This passivity and regression offers a far more serious threat to boys than to girls, with the advent of the genital phase (Galenson and Roiphe, 1971, 1980). The sense of sexual identity consequent to the discovery of the sexual difference is seriously threatened in those boys who have already adopted an excessively passive position during the early anal phase. The masochistic development that emerges during the oedipal phase is then inextricably bound to a basic instability in the sense of masculine identity.

These differing developmental lines in the early genital phases of the two sexes may account for the apparently far greater prevalence of masochism in women. While the retreat to a passive maternal relationship does not endanger the sense of sexual identity of girls, the more passive nature of their object relations leads toward a permanent masochistic distortion of their relationship to the father and later to all men. Boys who have retreated into a more passive early anal position are far more seriously compromised in that they sacrifice their basic sense of masculine sexual identity (Galenson, 1975) and develop a far more malignant type of masochism, which may include incipient perverse practices.

CLINICAL SYNDROMES ILLUSTRATING DISTURBANCES
IN THE DEVELOPMENT OF AGGRESSION:
PROTOMASOCHISM

The environmental stimuli of aggression may arise from a variety of
sources. Where the parents are the direct initiators, their own aggressive impulses may be consequent to many factors: their own past
experiences, current stresses in their lives, some particular characteristic of the infant that evokes an unfavorable parental response, and
so on. Other environmental causes of aggressive responses in the
infant include life-sustaining medical measures necessitated by pre-
maturity or illness in the infant, or environmental features, such as
excessive crowding or excessive noise and disorder, all of which
characterize the quality of life in the lower socioeconomic sectors of
our society. Not all of these stimuli are initiated by the primary
caretaker, of course; yet the very young infant can only experience
these stimuli as if they were connected in some manner with his most
intimate and meaningful caretaker, all good and bad experiences
ultimately appearing to derive from the same source, the primary
caretaker.

Although the following five psychopathological syndromes differ
markedly from one another in their manifestations, all the infants
suffering from these syndromes shared at least one psychological
feature: the infant's capacity for internalization of positive parental
attributes had been adversely affected in one way or another. In some
instances, there appeared to be little, if any, reciprocal affective
interchange of any depth between infant and primary caretaker. In
others, there was behavioral evidence of a considerable degree of
internalization of parental aggressive affect, to the exclusion of any
discernible positive affect. The developmental interferences that characterize all these psychopathological syndromes seem to be attributable, at least in part, to the manner in which the infant deals
psychologically with noxious external stimuli. Does the young infant
activate a barrier against a stimulus that arouses the discomfort of
aggressive drive arousal? Are there various degrees of effectiveness
with which this may be accomplished? Does the activation of this
hypothetical barrier preclude internalization of other varieties of
affective interchange as well, interfering with the infant's capacity to
internalize all types of experiences—affective, sensorimotor experiences, and the like? Does this interfere with and distort ongoing
formation of psychological structure at this highly vulnerable stage of
life?

The five psychopathological syndromes are (1) disorders in infants who have been physically abused, (2) psychosis in very young infants, (3) deviant patterns of early sexual development in female infants, (4) infants' failure to thrive in the absence of any known organic factor, and (5) infantile autism.

Disorders in Infants Who Have Been Physically Abused or Neglected

Spitz (1946) first called attention to the distortions in both libidinal and aggressive development in the institutionalized children he studied, findings later elaborated by others. More recently, Fraiberg (1980 offered a comprehensive and systematic description of five groups or types of behavior observed in the course of her work with abused or neglected infants during their first 18 months of life. Fraiberg thought that these might possibly lead later to specific defense mechanisms, although they could not yet be so defined at this early stage.

The babies described by Fraiberg had been alternately neglected by their mothers and subjected to outbursts of unpredictable maternal rage against them. The babies' negative reactions to their mother were divided into the following types: (a) avoidance of the mother in every sensory modality, reacting to her as if she were a definitely negative stimulus; (b) "freezing" behavior occurring as early as three months of age, characterized by complete immobilization, which was often followed by disorganized motility and screaming; (c) "fighting," seen mostly in toddlers who first avoided the mother, then demonstrated overt fearfulness of her, and finally erupted into a tantrum; (d) "transformation of affect," seen in babies between nine and sixteen months of age whose mothers had teased them from their earliest months; these babies soon began to participate in the teasing, becoming more and more pleasurably aroused and excited as the teasing continued; and (e) "reversal of aggression," behavior occurring as early as 13 months, consisting of the infant's attempts to hurt himself rather than the mother.

The last four types of "defensive" behavior share two features: the building up of tension as a response to the massive unpredictable aggression directed at them by the mother, and the discharge of the tension in some form of aggressive behavior, either directed outwards or towards the self. Furthermore, it is apparent that some type of communication of affect, albeit negative in character, takes place between infant and mother in the course of their interaction. In one form, to be discussed later, the mutual teasing eventually becomes a source of painful pleasure. However, in those infants who tend to avoid the mother, it may be assumed that little affective interchange takes place, and the introjective–projective mechanism ordinarily utilized by infants in the course of their earliest establishment of object relationships has at least temporarily ceased to operate.

In our study of a group of physically abused or neglected infants at the Mt. Sinai Hospital Infant Unit, which resembles Fraiberg's group, 65% of the babies demonstrated at least one of the types of behavior described by Fraiberg, and often several types were present in the same baby. Avoidance, freezing, and reversal of affect were particularly prominent in those infants whose mothers' rages were unpredictable and unrelated to any aspect of the infant's own behavior. Chronically depressed, shallow, infantile women, they are disorganized and erratic in their behavior and seem to lack a sense of both somatic and psychic self-regulation. Their outbursts of rage are not followed by relief and release but instead leave them feeling even more empty and lonely. Were their own infantile experiences precisely the type of aggressive maternal interaction they now have with their infants, a predominantly aggressive one in which unpleasure impinges on a vulnerable somatic and psychic infantile apparatus, interfering with sound psychological structuralization? Clinically, the prognosis for these infants is poor unless massive intervention is available.

A Clinical Case of Child Abuse

Fourteen-month-old Elaine and her mother serve as an example of this peculiar type of mother-infant relatedness. Frances, the mother, now 26 years old, had been an abused child who was taken from her home at the age of 13 years but returned repeatedly to rejoin her abusing mother, with whom she and Elaine still live. Elaine does not yet walk or talk, has been hospitalized many times for illnesses and injuries, some of which were suspected as possibly being the result of physical abuse. The mother has been involved in an endless series of provocative interchanges with hospital staff. As for her relationship with Elaine, Frances calls her "crazy and stupid," leaves her marooned in the center of our nursery, laughs at her fear, and then swoops down on her to turn her over with Elaine's head caught between her own knees, inspects her diaper, and then plunks her down in her stroller. Elaine remains largely impassive until her mother grabs her; then she obeys her mother's commands, doing whatever is asked of her.

These two are firmly bound together, as we get to know them, in a mutually provocative relationship that appears to offer both mother and daughter some degree of combined sexual and violent excite-

ment. And it is not an easy task to begin to separate them, little by
little, for each one lives not as a separate unit but through her
interchange with the other. Furthermore, as this separation proceeded under our therapeutic efforts, we found that we had precipitated the emergence of a massive depression in the mother, one
requiring hospitalization for several weeks. Elaine was hospitalized
with her for a short time as we attempted to preserve their attachment in spite of the mother's withdrawal. The outcome in this case is
problematic, although Elaine's ego development has spurted ahead;
now 2½ years old, she is at or near her age appropriate level in motor
and speech development and in her interaction with peers. However,
her semisymbolic play is sparse, and she can hardly be described as a
joyful child. Nor do we yet know what type of oedipal constellation
will emerge in this child who lives in a one-parent home, whose
mother's sexual experience with men has been characterized by much
violence, and whose mother speaks about men in only derogatory
terms.

We believe that cases like this represent the development of a
preoedipal, sadomasochistic type of object relationship deeply rooted
in the earliest days of the mother–infant relationship. Unfortunately,
since both sexuality and aggression appear to have suffered severe
distortion in their earliest development, only modest therapeutic
results can be expected.

In contrast to the physically abused group of infants are those in
our unit whose mothers do not physically attack them, but do so
psychologically in the form of teasing behavior. Often beginning with
their very early feedings, the mothers alternately offer and withdraw
the bottle until they evoke a crying protest. Only then is the baby
allowed to suck continuously. Gradually this becomes a mutually
exciting game for both mother and infant, and the baby's crying is
replaced by signs of pleasure and arousal. As the mutual teasing
extends, the infant's identification with the mother increases, coloring almost every aspect of their relationship. This gradually becomes
a prominent characteristic of the infant's relationship with his peers
during the early part of the second year; repeated and intense biting,
pinching and other forms of hostile aggression directed at peers are
followed by smiling and laughing, as these toddlers watch for and
appear to enjoy their infliction of pain on others. The few female
infants who have gone on to develop semisymbolic doll play treat
their dolls with the same hostile ambivalence and sadomasochistic
enjoyment.

As one would expect, the heterosexual relationships of these teasing mothers are characterized by the same sadomasochistic quality as their relationship with their infants. However, whereas the heterosexual relationships are transient, the mothers and infants are firmly attached to one another, each offering the other some essential emotional ingredient. When therapy succeeds in attenuating the sadomasochistic bond between mother and child, several of the mothers become severely depressed, and self-directed aggression appears in both members of the dyad.

PSYCHOSIS IN VERY YOUNG PSYCHOTIC INFANTS

Ten male infants, ranging in age from 15½ months to three years, all from lower middle class homes, were referred because of delayed language development. All demonstrated the gaze aversion and preference for the inanimate over the animate world that characterize the very young psychotic infant. The mothers all stated that they had experienced difficulty in establishing emotional contact with their infant from the earliest months. However, Massie's (1977) careful study of home movies of several of these infants revealed that while the infants themselves had attempted visual contact, the mothers gradually succeeded in disengaging the infants by avoiding visual contact with them. We learned over a period of months of therapeutic contact that six mothers had suffered from a severe depression during the infant's first year, while four others had experienced serious family losses during that time. It is possible that the mothers had unconsciously focused their anger on their infant, perhaps the male infant in particular, thus interfering with the mother–infant relationship. In any event, these infants all demonstrated deviant aggressive behavior. They had tantrums, hit out indiscriminately at others, and inflicted damage upon themselves by head-banging or other self-injury. However, the aggression was not focused upon the mother, neither was there evidence of a positive attachment to her; that is to say, there was a severe failure in attachment, of both a negative and a positive type, involving a distortion of both libidinal and aggressive drive development.

Deviant Patterns of Sexual Development in Female Infants

Eight female infants, all from the economically and socially disadvantaged sector, showed distorted sexual development during their second year. During their first year, the infants had related harmoniously to their mother; the mothers treated their babies tenderly and nurtured them effectively. However, as soon as autonomous strivings and independent ambulation appeared, the mothers abandoned their babies emotionally, cursing and striking them physically for being "bad and disobedient"; the infants would then hit back at their mothers and later at their dolls as well.

When the infants entered the early genital stage sometime between 16 and 19 months (Galenson and Roiphe, 1971; Roiphe and Galenson, 1981), the emergence of genital arousal and the subsequent aware-ness of the genital sexual difference was shortly followed by a combination of teasing and flirtatiousness with any adult men they encountered (their own fathers were usually unavailable to them). Unlike the usual pattern of sexual arousal, however, the strong admixture of aggression in these infants made it difficult to know whether they were loving or attacking these men. Furthermore, their attachment to the mother soon became overly aggressive, similar to the quality of the mother's relationships to men. It was at this time that many of the mothers, particularly the adolescent ones, aban-doned the baby to the care of the grandmother, and the baby's attachment then shifted to her. None of these girls went on to develop more than a shadowy, transient oedipal attachment.

Infants Who Fail to Thrive in the Absence of Any Known Organic Factor

Four infants satisfied the criteria for this syndrome: rejection of food offered by the mother, weight below the tenth percentile in their age group, a weight gain during hospitalization that is lost on returning home—symptoms for which no organic cause could be determined. In each instance, the mother had suffered from a serious disturbance in her relationship with her own mother during her own childhood, memories of which were revived as she struggled to feed her now unwilling infant. At times, the mother's food aversion was reflected behaviorally by her inappropriate positioning of the infant for feed-ing, and she was overtly angry at the baby's rejection of food.

Although it was not possible to establish whether the baby's initial food reaction was an unusual one, by the time we saw them, feeding had become the major battleground on which a conflict between mother and child was being acted out. Modification of the mothers' reactions to food was most difficult to effect; surrogate mothering along with therapeutic attempts to modify the infant's food aversion constituted the most effective therapeutic approach. Unfortunately, such severe oral aggressive drive disturbance seriously distorts devel-

opment as a whole, but particularly in regard to libidinal investment
of both the animate and inanimate world. Treatment of this condition
is prolonged and difficult.

Infantile Autism

The syndrome of infantile autism is now thought to consist of a
variety of psychopathological conditions due to a variety of factors.
However, occasionally a case so closely resembles Kanner's (1942–43)
original description that it argues for the existence of a special
subgroup within the larger variety of autistic disorders. A nine-
month-old girl was brought for consultation because she avoided all
eye contact, appeared to be deaf, and was content to remain passively
in her crib playing with her crib mobile. An unwanted pregnancy, she
was the youngest of four children of a young and overburdened
mother. She had been nursed from birth but began to avert her gaze
and attention from her mother and others by five or six months, as
her mother became ever more irritated and angry at the additional
responsibility of this infant.

Intensive conjoint treatment of mother and child was begun: when
the mother's anger could be expressed verbally to a greater extent,
and as others in the family came to the rescue, the mother began to
react to the infant more positively. However, the therapist's role as an
auxiliary ego for both mother and child was undoubtedly a key
element in treatment. By the time she was 13 months old, the infant's
attachment to the mother was of good quality, she was now walking
alone, and the inanimate world had receded to its appropriate position as an area for exploration and new experiences. At twenty
months, she continued to develop well in all areas.

CONCLUSION

Hostile wishes of a mother toward her infant are not accepted as
appropriate in our society, although infanticide has been present
since recorded human history and is currently practiced in almost
every culture—whether sanctioned by society or carried out secretly,
or in maternal fantasy. Parental aggression toward infants assumes
many different forms depending on social and economic class, tradi-
tion, individual history, and experience. No group of people is
immune to this problem. To this end, I have presented five forms of
psychopathology in infants where excessive aggression from the
environment impinges on the infant, appearing to endanger the

infant's earliest development and apparently laying the groundwork for sadomasochistic developments of many varieties.

Masochism, the capacity for experiencing pleasure in unpleasure or pain, is preceded by protomasochistic precursors in the latter part of the first year and particularly during the second year, when oral aggression is normally transformed into anal and urethral patterns of drive discharge and patterning. Internal or external influences that tend to unduly stimulate aggression give rise to an excessively hostile maternal relationship. The defenses of identification with the aggressor turn aggression against the self, and passivity and regression may ensue, leading to various forms of protomasochistic development at the time of emergence of the early genital phase. This protomasochistic development is more prevalent in girls, but it is less damaging to their developing sexual identity; whereas boys who become excessively passive during the early anal phase, in the face of intense hostile maternal conflicts, suffer a serious blow to their sense of masculine identity with the advent of the early genital phase; their object relationships assume a truly masochistic character with oedipal development, along with the emergence of true perversions.

REFERENCES

Abraham, K. (1921). Contributions to the theory of the anal character. In: *Selected Papers on Psycho-Analysis*. London: Hogarth Press, 1949.
———— (1924), A short study of the development of the libido viewed in the light of mental disorders. In: *Selected Papers on Psycho-Analysis*. London: Hogarth Press, 1949.
Bernstein, I. (1983), Masochistic pathology and feminine development. *J. Amer. Psychoanal. Assn.*, 31:467–486.
Compton, A. (1983), The current status of the psychoanalytic theory of instinctual drives, drive concept classification and development. *Psychoanal. Quart.*, 60:612–635.
Fraiberg, S. (1980), *Clinical Studies in Infant Mental Health*. New York: Basic Books.
Freud, A. (1936), *The Ego and the Mechanisms of Defense*. New York: International Universities Press, 1966.
Freud, S. (1919), A child is being beaten. *Standard Edition*, 17:177–204.
———— (1920), Beyond the pleasure principle. *Standard Edition*, 18:7–64. London: Hogarth Press, 1955.
Galenson, E. (1984), Influences on the development of the symbolic function. In: *Frontiers of Infant Psychiatry*, Vol. II, ed. J. D. Call, E. Galenson, & R. L. Tyson. New York: Basic Books.
Galenson, E. (1986), Some thoughts about infant psychopathology and aggressive development. *Internat. Rev. Psychoanal.*, 13:349–354.
Galenson, E., & Roiphe, H. (1971), The impact of early sexual discovery on mood, defensive organization, and symbolization. *The Psychoanalytic Study of the Child* 26:195–216. New Haven: Yale University Press.

Galenson, E., & Roiphe, H. (1980), The preoedipal development of the boy. *J. Amer. Psychoanal. Assn.*, 28:805–827.

Galenson, E., Vogel, S., Blau, S. & Roiphe, H. (1975), Disturbance in sexual identity beginning at 18 months of age. *Internat. J. Psycho-Anal.*, 2:390–397.

Glenn, J. (1984), A note on loss, pain, depression and masochism in children. *J. Amer. Psychoanal. Assn.*, 32:65–75.

Glenn, J. (1984), Psychic trauma and masochism. *J. Amer. Psychoanal. Assn.*, 32:357–380.

Hartmann, H., Kris, E., & Loewenstein, R. M. (1949), Notes on the theory of aggression. *The Psychoanalytic Study of the Child*, 3/4. New York: International Universities Press.

Kanner, L. (1942–43), Autistic disturbances of affective contact. *The Nervous Child*, 2:217–250.

Loewenstein, R. M. (1955). A contribution to the psychoanalytic theory of masochism. *J. Amer. Psychoanal. Assn.*, 5:197–234.

Maleson, F. G. (1984). The multiple meanings of masochism in psychoanalytic discourses. *J. Amer. Psychoanal. Assn.*, 32(2):325–356.

Massie, H. (1977), Patterns of mother-infant behavior and subsequent childhood psychoses. *Child Psychiat. & Human Dev.*, 7:211–230.

McDevitt, J. B. (1983). The emergence of hostile aggression and its defensive and adaptive modifications during the separation-individuation process. *J. Amer. Psychoanal. Assn.*, 31(Supp.):273–301.

Shengold, L. (1985). Defensive anality and anal narcissism. *Internat. J. Psycho-Anal.*, 66:47–73.

Spitz, R. A. (1946), Anaclitic depression: An inquiry into the genesis of psychiatric conditions in early childhood. *The Psychoanalytic Study of the Child*, 2:313–342. New York: International Universities Press.

Spitz, R. A. (1953). Aggression: Its role in the establishment of object relations. In: *Drives, Affects, Behavior*, ed. R. M. Loewenstein. New York: International Universities Press.

Stone, L. (1979). Remarks on certain unique conditions of human aggression (the Hand, Speech, and the Use of Fire). *J. Amer. Psychoanal. Assn.*, 27:27–33.

12 / Adolescent Masochism

Charles A. Sarnoff

THERE ARE FORMS OF MASOCHISM that are specific to each life phase. Forms found in the earlier phases provide the genetic complexes from which the forms of later stages are derived. Latency age masochistic fantasies persist into adolescence, acquiring manifest form dictated by progressions and regressions in object relations and cognition that are specific to the phase of adolescence. To understand the nature of the manifestations of masochism in adolescence, it is necessary that one understand the genetic complex in earlier childhood from which they have emerged. The manifestations of adolescent masochism are: masochistic bragadoccio, masochistic perversions, adolescent shyness, aspects of prepubescent schizophrenia, incipient masochistic character traits, and the misuse of free association during psychoanalytically oriented psychotherapy sessions.

THE LIFE PHASES OF MASOCHISM

Masochism (the passive experience of aggression accompanied by painful and excited affects) appears in all stages of human life and development. Its manifestations change with each age. Variations in intensity and modifications of the form of masochism result from phase-related alterations in object relations and cognition. Each developmental period contributes a unique step in the march of manifest masochism. A description of the steps follows.

This paper is an expanded version of one presented in December 1983 to the "Vulnerable Child" Study Group of the American Psychoanalytic Association Mid Winter Meeting. Reprinted from *Psychotherapeutic Strategies in Early Adolescence*, Copyright © 1987 by Charles A. Sarnoff. Reprinted by permission of the author and the publisher, Jason Aronson Inc.

Primary Masochism (the first months)

In the very earliest months of life, there is objectless, unbridled aggression. This takes the form of screaming, crying and thrashing about, which hurts only the crying child, who alone suffers whatever discomfort is to be felt and is exhausted in the end. Parents, as witnesses, may feel pain at the sight of the pained child, but their pain does not intrude upon the psychic reality of the child and does not take part in the interaction.

The masochism of this age is called "primary" (as in primary narcissism), for in his world of feebly perceived boundaries, there is no concept of an object and the child is limited to himself as persecutor. In later years, regression to this level of preobject relations colors those clinical states in which there is little relatedness to the therapist and in which symbols evoke moods rather than serving to communicate.

Protosymbols (the end of the first year)

The introduction of the parents as primitive persecutors awaits the development of *protosymbols*. These consist of bodily sensations (for example, affects) or organs of the child's body that symbolically represent other affects or organs; a piercing glance or a clenched fist can represent anger, or the hysteric's arm can have phallic significance. As cognition matures, they may be used to represent parts of the parents. Through such protosymbols, aggression aimed at the parent can be turned upon the self.

With the development of self–object differentiation, the fused libidinal and aggressive energies of the child can be perceived by the child as directed outward toward an object. Should the parent withdraw from contact or from view, the child can persist in contact with the parent through an internalized memory of the parent. This internalized image is called the introject. The aggression that had been directed toward the object accompanies the introject. It too is directed inward toward the self of the child. This produces a paradigm for the experience of self-directed aggression, called "secondary" masochism. This becomes the basis for the patterning of relationships in which masochism involves objects. Intensification of the secondary masochistic experience by actual aggression by the parents enhances the masochistic fantasies that will color the relationships of adult life. As a result, tolerance for such relationships heightens. This permits people to enter similar relationships without challenge, since that which would be extraordinary for the children of parents of ordinary demeanor becomes like home cooking for the children of cruel parents.

A protosymbol creates, in psychic representation, a syncretism of self and parent. The child's aggression directed toward the protosymbol is experienced as directed toward the self (that is, masochistically). Since the parent is the only reality object of which the child is aware, the parent is fantasied to be the source of the pain. Actual parental aggression, either spontaneous or stimulated by the child, can be adapted by the child as an actualization (appearance in reality) of these fantasies. In this way a real event can be recruited to serve as a fantasy derivative. This activity intensifies between 15 and 26 months, giving a provocative character to children's behavior. Hence the label, "the terrible twos." In adolescence, the child's response to the passivity that is felt when strivings for independence clash with parental power is often derivative of the experiences of this earlier phase.

Psychoanalytic Symbols (26 months)

Twenty-six months sees the development of repression and its concomitant in thought content, psychoanalytic symbols. There is some lessening of the actualization as a result of the use of fantasy to drain off some of the child's aggression. Sadomasochistic (anal-sadistic) fantasies persist (see Blanchard, 1953) but tend to be expressed with siblings and peers in place of parents. At this point, children begin to experience masochism as the sadism of symbolized whole objects that has been directed at the sufferer. This step in cognitive development produces changes during the prelatency period.

The Prelatency Period (26 months to 6 years)

The considerable use of symbols to interpret the environment causes the child's relation to reality to be primarily intuitive. Memory emphasizes affect and sensation, producing recall of totalities. External characteristics, rather than the abstract, intrinsic nature of things and situations, are used to recall the past and interpret the present. As a result, logic is not brought to bear to correct misapprehensions such as are produced by regressions to the cognitive world of primary masochism.

During this period, masochistic fantasy may undergo three vicissitudes:

(1) Real aggression and cruelty from parents, caretakers, or peers may reinforce the aggression that fuels it.

(2) Mastery through fantasy may dissipate it. Fantasies that use psychoanalytic symbols can effectively dissipate latent fantasy and drive. These symbols populate persecutory fantasies, animal pho-

bias, and the fears of amorphous attackers in the dark that are experienced when the child is going to sleep.

(3) Whether masochistic fantasy is reinforced or dissipated, it is subject to the modifying effects of the phallic phase. Progression through phallic phase interests (competition, object relatedness, penetrative urges, oedipal concerns) and parentally encouraged progress in cognitive development, which facilitates the neutralization of drive energies (i.e. acquisition of verbal-conceptual memory organizations), can modify the manifest strength of masochism. There can result a lessening of the anal-sadistic energy cathexes of the masochistic fantasies to the benefit of more mature functions.

Latency (six to twelve years)

As the child passes through the sixth year of life, the threatening nature of oedipal concerns calls regression into action as a defense, and anal sadistic drive energies are recathected.

Such recathexis of sadistic energies and fantasies does not result in manifest masochism. Ego mechanisms of restraint tend to mask overt sadism during this period, and provocative aggressive stimuli from the environment are buffered by the fantasizing function of the ego, which produces defensive play fantasies that discharge drive and master conflict on a symbolic level (see Sarnoff, 1976). As a result, the child appears to be calm, cooperative, and educable. These clinically observable traits dominate behavior from six to twelve years of age, a period referred to as the "latency period."

Play fantasies routinely provide the venue in which highly symbolized sadomasochistic content appears. Cops and robbers, war stories, kidnappings, cruel elements in fairy tales are some examples of this. The manifestation of masochism during this age period is primarily in the form of fantasy experienced internally or projected into an interpretation of relations with peers. The older the child, the more realistic is the source of the symbols called upon to represent the masochistic fantasy.

Sadomasochism lurks in wait until failure of the ego structures of latency permit the appearance of manifest derivatives of masochism. Foremost among these are playground teasing, night fears, and paranoid accusations of peers during periods of stress.

Adolescence (thirteen years of age to adulthood)

The onset of adolescence is heralded by an intensification of the anal sadistic drive organizations that have been blunted by the defenses of Latency. For the most part, the defense structures of latency hold masochistic fantasies and trends in check rather than processing them. Therefore, children enter adolescence with latent masochistic fantasy content little changed from what it was in the phallic phase. In early adolescence masochism is manifested in thinly masked derivatives that use reality elements rather than toys as symbolic representations.

One of the clinical characteristics of the psychological shift to adolescence is a loss of potency of toys and other play symbols to serve as substitute objects and tools for the discharge of drives and the mastery of conflict. As a result, there is an increased use of parts of the body and of people and peers to express, experience, and manifest masochistic fantasies. Manifest fantasy fails to serve this need. The world of reality and its parts are recruited to provide an arena in which masochistic fantasies can be lived out. In this way the masochistic fantasies that had fueled the play fantasies of latency are carried over to become the foundations for masochistic character formation.

One of the tasks of adolescence is disengagement of the drives from anal-sadistic discharge patterns and from character traits that are derived from them. This is done through either "removal" (see Katan, 1951) or the resolution of the oedipal conflicts, which, as we have noted, motivated the regressions that intensified masochistic drive activity during the latency years. This process of resolution can often be recognized in the masochistic derivatives seen in adolescence.

In early adolescence, the thinly masked *masochistic derivatives* can be seen for the most part in masochistic bragadoccio, masochistic perversions, and prepubescent schizophrenia. In later adolescence, the failure of resolution of masochistic trends can be followed through the clinical study of such derivatives of masochism as incipient masochistic character traits and through an explication of the way that masochism intrudes on the use of free association during psychoanalytic sessions.

MASOCHISTIC DERIVATIVES IN EARLY ADOLESCENCE

Masochistic Braggadocio (tales of borne pain,
proudly told)

Early in this century and late in the last, there existed at the University of Heidelberg in Germany highly regarded social organizations known as dueling clubs. Ostensibly they served those who wished to learn fencing. In the broader social context, they served to identify the elite. Since the end of a duel was reached with the inflicting of a wound that drew blood, members of these clubs could be easily identified through the permanent scars on their faces that proclaimed proudly to the world that they had been cut and had bled. Even in our own day, such a culturally adapted proclamation of borne pain is seen in fraternity pins, which identify those who have undergone hazing.

This late adolescent expression of masochism (a tendency to brag of suffering) finds a parallel in early adolescence. It is at this younger age that there is an attempt to process and master painful and traumatic experiences through re-evocation through words. In the verbal context, the person's suffering seems heroic; I call this behavior masochistic bragadoccio. There is a kind of Heidelberg-scar mentality to this stance. The image of manliness or courage is generated by this pseudostrength display:

> One child said, upon returning to analysis after the summer break, "In camp we really had it tough. We walked for miles without stopping. I got blisters so big that they bled." The affect was pride. He sought to evoke his own inner experience and to awe the listener. There was nothing here that would serve the search for insight. I wondered as he spoke if the child was complaining or bragging.

Looking more deeply into the psychology of that youngster, one could find a characterological context in which any form of pain or discomfort (experienced or remembered) was avoided rather than confronted. Bragging about experienced pain was a counterphobic means of mastering the fear of pain. Painful future activities were evoked prospectively. Placing himself in future danger was a form of advanced bragging rather than future planning.

> He once called an end to his treatment (with his father's consent) so that he could join the high school football team. Both he and his father agreed that participation in sports would affirm his masculinity and comfort doubts about his gender identity. He planned to miss many sessions and possibly to interrupt treatment. He missed but one session in the process. On the day of the second session to be missed, he arrived unannounced in my waiting room at his usual time. When I asked him what had happened, he told me that when the first few plays were run right through his position, he had realized that it hurt to be a football hero. He was interested in the gain but not the pain.

One of the elements that potentiate adolescent vulnerability to masochistic conflict resolutions is a failure in the development of the symbolizing function. There is a failure in negotiating the developmental shift from evocative to communicative symbols. There is normally a shift from the use of symbols that evoke moods to the use of symbols that communicate information in expressing drive manifestations (see Sarnoff, 1987b). The more primitive evocative symbols continue to evoke feelings and memory of trauma in the service of discharge without mastery. They are not used to communicate or for reparative mastery. They are not viewed from a therapeutic distance. For therapists who have worked with adult cases, such activity is familiar. It occurs in repetitive traumatic anxiety dreams.

In the late latency, early adolescent who repeats masochistic patterns endlessly, there is clinical failure of mastery through repetition. This failure is attributable to a regression to the objectless, "primary" masochism of the earliest days of childhood. This is syncretic with the fact that for these people the symbolizing function has not matured to the point where symbols can be used for communication.

A communicative level of symbol use supports the discharge of drives and the mastery of trauma in a corrective reality context. It also reinforces the guarantees of the autonomous functioning of the ego in relation to the id. Failure to achieve a communicative level in symbol formation results in symbols (evocative) that can only evoke inner moods and past events over and over again.

In adolescence, evocative mode symbols used during free association in psychotherapy attempt to draw sympathy from the therapist and evoke prior painful affect and ego states instead of serving psychotherapeutic goals. A form of repetition compulsion is produced. In the psychotherapy situation, the therapist is converted from a helper who aims his skills at adjustment into a witness to past pain, which the patient proudly shares. What does the patient derive from this situation? Narcissistic injury is overcome. The masochist's narcissism is served when he can present his pain as an experience without equal. Masochistic braggadoccio is the tendency to brag about pain and suffering. The pain of recent experience is mastered at the expense of the long-range goals of the therapy.

MASOCHISTIC PERVERSION

Developmental Changes in the Symbolizing Function

The following case (presented in Sarnoff, 1975; see also Sarnoff, 1987a) illustrates variations in masochism associated with developmental changes in the symbolizing function. There is a developmen-

tal march in the characteristics of the symbols that are protagonists in
the persecutory fantasies and their derivatives. The metamorphoses
implied by this march inform and color the nature of the shifting
symbolic form fantasies that accompany the transition through latency and adolescence. The steps in the march of symbols are: in early
latency—persecutory symbols experienced in fantasy; at the end of
latency—parts of the body used as symbols to express masochistic
fantasy; in early adolescence—enlistment of real people as symbols to
express masochistic fantasy; maturity—using symbols to communicate reality.

As the presentation unfolds, consider the effect on the psychopathology of the adult should the source of symbols, instead of
progressing, be fixed at one of the foregoing points in the developmental line.

> E. P. was 16½ years old when seen. He was the son of divorced
> parents. His mother had left the marriage when she learned that his
> father had teased, beaten, and tortured the child for no apparent
> reason, whenever he was left alone with the boy. The patient could
> recall these incidents as occurring when he was but two years old. The
> boy lived with his mother after the divorce.
>
> His latency period was characterized by unexceptional evening fears
> early on and a strong capacity to develop states of latency. (See Sarnoff,
> 1976). When the boy reached the age of 11, he had an erection every
> time he saw himself or another boy without a shirt on. He could
> produce an erection by standing nude before a mirror. He responded to
> these erections by making cuts into the skin of his back with a knife.
> The appearance and flow of blood was accompanied by a release of
> feelings similar to orgasm. When he had achieved physiological ejacu-
> lation and orgasm readiness, he found that it was possible for him to
> masturbate successfully with a fantasy about a girl. He reported no
> cruelty in this fantasy. When he began dating, at the age of 16, he
> sought to hide his relationships with the girls, whom he had chosen for
> their full and voluptuous figures. These characteristics, as he viewed
> them, demeaned him and caused him to feel embarrassed in public.

This pattern is not unusual and has been described elsewhere (see
Werner and Levine, 1967). The pattern starts with early exposure to a
sadistic parent. This reinforces anal-sadistic fantasies that are maintained in repression after six years of age by latency defenses. At age
11, as the latency defenses weaken, a masochistic masturbation
fantasy becomes consciously manifest. In it, masochistic submission
to the sadistic parent of infancy is actively and passively relived. The
fantasy is not confined to mental expression. The representations
chosen as symbols are not fantastic or distorted images. They are real,

of the same sex as the child, and acted out with real objects (knife and self). With the onset of ejaculation, the representations become sadistic, heterosexual objects.

In consonance with the developmental march of symbols, the manifestations of masochism change with growth, demonstrating for each stage its characteristics and varying degrees of visibility and implied degree of pathology. The developmental events of adolescence can uncover previously undetected fantasy structures such as those which produce masochistic behavior and can make structural weaknesses and aberrations in ego formation visible. These weaknesses and aberrations can, in turn, persist when adolescent development is blocked, or become less virulent when normal development causes their manifestations to be clothed in less distressing guises.

ADOLESCENT SHYNESS AND PREPUBESCENT SCHIZOPHRENIA

Pathological Relationships with Introjects

In both adolescent shyness and prepubescent schizophrenia adolescent masochism appears to be a manifestation of the persistence in memory of parental *introjects*.

Adolescent shyness is a common condition, occurring primarily in early adolescence, which is characterized by avoidance of contacts with peers or adults in authority because of false beliefs. The contents of these false beliefs are feelings of inferiority or defect, which the child feels would be known to or recognized by others and would result in the child's rejection.

Prepubescent schizophrenia is a rare condition with onset usually after 11 years of age. It is a manifestation of childhood schizophrenia of relatively late onset. The cardinal signs of this condition are delusional thinking involving pain and aggression directed toward self or others, poor peer relations, and an absent history of projected introjects (night fears or phobias) during early latency.

Introjects and Adolescent Masochism

The paradigmatic model of a masochistic relationship can be seen in the context of a punishing parent confronting and disciplining a defenseless child. The conduit that carries this context from early childhood through latency and then into adolescence and beyond is the introject. The introject refers to the product of the human tendency to respond to loss by re-evoking the memory of a departed loved one. Departure can refer to a brief parting or death. Loss can also be experienced when the sense of the presence of the object appears changed by cognitive maturation, which can change the nature of the way things are seen. Such a reorganization of perception can produce apparent changes and loss in the environment. For instance, the parent who has been seen to be a "pal" in fantasy may come to be seen as the distant person he is in reality.

The memory of the lost one becomes a source of replacement. If the lost one was primarily experienced in the context of a masochistic relationship, then duplicates of such a relationship may be sought as a means to recapture the lost one. Thus, remembrance of things past can be experienced in newly generated words and experiences. The persistence in memory of parental introjects in the context of early traumatic situations becomes the source of multiple actualizations (recruitment of elements from the real world to play out concepts patterned after the original). When these actualizations place the adolescent in the passive role of the child, the situation is called masochism.

When the child internalizes a relationship, the seed of an introject is produced. Such an introject can grow to become the raw material of fantasy. Thenceforth the youngster will have a pattern after which to fashion his relationships with later significant and sometimes loved objects.

The impact of such masochistic paradigms on later relationships is especially strong when there is exaggeration of parental aggression. This can occur when the child projects his own aggression into his interpretation of the parent's behavior. For instance, if the child in the early childhood situation projected his own anger onto the parent, the parent's aggression will be exaggerated in the child's memory. As a result, parental aggression in the model situation becomes more marked. At the least it will be remembered as such. Should the child then base his parental introject on this false image of the parent, he will acquire a distorted (e.g. fantasy) base to draw from when the need for re-evocation reshapes his world. This major factor intensifying adolescent masochism is called *projective identification* (identifying with parents whose anger is perceived to be stronger than it is as the result of the projection of the child's own aggression onto the parent).

Distortions in early parental introjects can lead to a distortion of self-image as well. When the introjected parent is seen as hostile or cruel, self-image declines. This is especially so when the child sees all the manifestations of thought or ideas within himself, even those derived solely from the image of the parent, as personal characteristics without origins external to himself. This psychic self-perception makes the child vulnerable to the occurrence of adolescent masochism especially in the form of adolescent shyness. In that condition, the avoidance that takes place is the product of a projection of a low opinion of oneself into the thinking of peers.

Other factors can create vulnerability to masochism in early adolescence. Among these is the presence of a cathexis of the fantasy inner life at the expense of reality. This leads to distortions of the perception of the world and impairs object relations.

Also present are ego impairments, such as dimmed ability to differentiate self-image from the hostile, internalized parental imago (see Mahler and Gosliner, 1955, p. 208). Such factors, which influence cathexis and content, strengthen the child's ability to intensify his experience of introjects colored by parental aggression. Should these memories become strong enough to influence the child's interpretation of reality, the masochistically colored introjects, so evoked can serve as a determinant of adolescent and adult behavior.

THE PHENOMENOLOGY OF ADOLESCENT MASOCHISM

In conducting a psychotherapy that deals with masochism in adolescence, it is important for the therapist to realize and to interpret to the patient that situations which are feared in advance or are repeatedly experienced subjectively as painful are *interpretations* of reality rather than reality itself. Though the people and the situations differ, the content of the fears and complaints of the patient are consistent and are marked by sameness. Latency fantasy, which takes its shape from internalization of a child's relationship to a hostile, punishing parent, becomes the model for masochistic relationships. In adolescence, when the discharge of drives shifts from manifest fantasy formation to actualization (Living out of fantasy), peers are recruited to serve as symbols of the punishing introject.

As symbols that are more human and real appearing come to be better tolerated, with the move into early adolescent cognition, real people can be recruited to serve as manifest symbol representations. Real interactions with others begin to take on the masochistic cast prescribed by the persistent child-introject relationships in latent fantasy content. Clinically, this may be seen in tolerance for painful experiences in the presence of potential comfort. The well-trod paths of masochism provide the security of familiar territory. The child tends not to tred far from the path. The devil that one knows feels safer than the angel who comes as a stranger. Should the pattern become fixed, the fantasy, now characterological, will influence the object relations patterns of adult life.

Adolescent masochism may be viewed as the living out of the relationship between the child and the hostile introject. What appears to be reality takes form from the ways of the introject (the parent remembered).

Adolescent Shyness Compared with Prepubescent Schizophrenia

In adolescent shyness, a masochistic confrontation is feared and avoided. In prepubescent schizophrenia, the masochistic fantasy is experienced with psychotic intensity; the sense of reality is strongly linked to fantasy at the same time that reality testing is suspended.

A third situation exists. (See below, "Incipient Masochistic Character Traits") In this situation, peers are interpreted to be or induced to be cruel. (This is masochistic characterological behavior.) In real situations there is less cathexis of inner fantasy, permitting a certain amount of cathexis of reality. Relationships develop with real objects. The relationships are colored by the same driven need to relive the past through interactions with new objects that occur in the peer relationships of prepubescent schizophrenics, who complain of being treated badly. Delusions are not present in the child with masochistic character traits. The impact of the model role of the introjected hostile parent who punishes in fantasy is the same. The pattern of behavior is lived out with real objects rather than experienced as fear fantasies. In this regard, among the cases that follow, J.P.D. contains elements of both and may be considered to a transitional case, whereas L.L.L. is dominated by an arena of activity that is confined to his inner world. On the other hand, in adolescent shyness there is fear of pain at the hands of real objects, and there is a near delusional fear of real people.

Adolescent Shyness

Adolescent shyness is marked by avoidance of others as a result of feelings of being inferior. The child fears that this inferiority would be recognized by others resulting in rejection. Though object relationship is avoided, real objects are recruited to serve in the child's fear fantasies. A shift to a real object in the outside world as the symbolic representation of the "persecutor" in the typical latency age persecutory fantasy occurs in early adolescence. This shift sets the stage for turning the manifest form taken by drive derivatives from persecutory fantasies to masochistic character activity. Adolescent shyness, as reflected in the following cases, is an early manifestation of this dynamic.

> L.V. went away to summer camp for the first time at the age of 12. She became quite depressed and frightened that people would not like her or would find her boring. She spoke of herself as boring. She had projected this opinion of herself to others. When younger, she had activated feelings of boredom when she needed to suppress memories of her mother's aggressive scolding. In effect, her view of herself as boring was a defense against an aggressive identification with her mother. An introject had been formed that she could not differentiate from herself. A sense of being boring was substituted for aggression. In this way, she defended against an activity that would have made her too much like her mother. Her attempt to individuate herself from her mother was furthered by her projection of her mother's aggression onto her peers, who were seen as aggressors.

> L. G., at the age of 11, clowned in school to hide his fears that he would be rejected by peers as he was repeatedly rejected by his psychotic mother, who had beaten him and yelled at him since he was a baby. He shouted down and belittled his teachers. Analysis revealed that this behavior mirrored his mother's. He identified with her as the aggressor and then had great difficulty differentiating himself from this internalized image of her. He then projected this image of himself, derived from the maternal introject, into the minds of teachers and peers and clowned to defend himself against their criticism, which in reality was his own. His provocations often enlisted his teachers and peers in hostile activity in the mode of his mother. His sufferings cast his early adolescence in a masochistic light.

These youngsters imputed to others their own vision of themselves. They confused their self-image with the early hostile mother imago. The hostile mother imago was intensified by introjection during teenage separations, making the situation worse. As a result of this dynamic, separations provoked crises. Thus was created a masochistic context to accompany the sullen mood of loneliness that is part of teenage separation experiences.

PREPUBESCENT SCHIZOPHRENIA

Perhaps the most striking clinical context for studying the relation of introjects to adolescent masochism is prepubescent schizophrenia, a late onset form of childhood schizophrenia. Poor peer relations, delusional thinking, and an absence of the normal neurosis of latency characterize this disorder. In contrast to normal children, who begin to project introjects by the age of four, prepubertal schizophrenics begin to project introjects at the age of 11 (Bender, 1947). Their auditory hallucinations are experienced as coming from within their bodies, as is typical of younger childhood schizophrenics. They experience internal persecutory fantasy objects, which are derived from introjects. However, the symptomatology is often blurred by the presence of masochistic object relations. These youngsters begin to get into scrapes with others since they are entering upon the age at which for them peers can first be used as symbols. In essence, at this age the memory of the introject can be evoked through the peer or other person in the environment whose characteristics will permit him or her to be used as the armature around which the masochistic fantasy can be shaped. This manner of dealing with objects character-izes masochistic object relations.

> Typical of the type of prepubescent schizophrenic who is persecuted from within and without was 12-year-old J.F.D. He suffered severe pain when he tried to walk because of an imagined iron bar that pierced both of his heels and impeded walking. If he suppressed this hallucina-tion, he suffered severe stomach cramps, which were attributed by his family to an allergy to macaroni. He also had fugue states in which he dissociated himself from his classroom and found himself in a cave 150 feet below the surface of the earth. There he sat before the devil and a crowd of accusers. The devil bore a strong resemblance to a girl in his class who picked on him on the school bus. His father rejected the "theory" that the boy's difficulties were emotional in origin and en-couraged his son to beat up the girl.

Note in this case the concurrent existence of painful, body-oriented hallucination, persecutory fantasy, and masochistic relationship with a peer.

A pattern formed of the latter two symptoms is sometimes also seen in latency age children when there has been a breakdown in the mechanisms of restraint.

> L.L.L. presents us with an example of a prepubescent schizophrenic child with a cruel, commanding internal fantasy object, which he cannot separate from himself, but which he tries to externalize. No external persecutors were created. L.L.L., age 12, was hospitalized in the children's unit in an hospital in Beijing, China, when seen. His head, face, and nose were covered with scabs, scars, and abrasions, all self-inflicted. A shy boy, with few friends and difficulty speaking because of a malformation of his palate, he had begun to show signs of

behavioral change at the time of the exams that decide one's life course in China. Antipsychotic drugs had been used to no avail. He was now heavily sedated. The current drug regimen was undertaken to keep him from injuring himself and those around him. He hit himself and others at the verbal command of "The Monkey King," who resided in his stomach. He repeatedly went to the toilet, where he attempted to expel the Monkey King. (The Monkey King is the main character in a Buddhist fairy tale, *Journey to the West* (Wu Cheng'en, 1575). He has prodigious skills and in an animated film version available to children in China *Havoc in Heaven*, is a successful challenger of authority and passivity.)

Note L.L.L.'s misinterpretation of his own anger. He could not differentiate his aggression from that of an introject and tried to expel it.

L.T.L. was 15. He experienced his flatus as offensive (contrary to the usual experience of sensing narcissistic extensions of oneself as above reproach). He felt that the odor hung about him, and he interpreted the movement of people away from him as a sign of their rejection of his emunctory odor. He needed see but a few people walk in a direction that took them away from him to confirm his negative image of himself.

L.T.L. presents us with an example of a transition step in the continuum of symptoms that starts with the internal persecutor of childhood and ends in the imagined external persecutor experienced in adolescent shyness. The internal persecutor is clearly delusional. In this transition step, a negative product of the rejected self is considered to be the object of a delusional rejection by the world. The symbol of self-degradation is bizarre and irrational. In this continuum, the masochistic experience of adolescent shyness can be seen as the healthier pole. In the latter situation, the person who does the hurting is identifiable as a someone known and the reason for rejection (e.g. "I'm boring." I'm not pretty enough". "I deserve it. I'm hateful and bad") is rationalized to the point that it can be understood and seems logical.

Causative Factors in Adolescent Masochism

Traumatic and painful experiences are common in early childhood. Early trauma and persistent masochistic fantasy make a child vulnerable to masochistic traits in adolescence and, later, in adulthood.

There are other determining factors in addition to early life trauma and masochistic fantasy—which, after all, are universal—that have clinical significance for manifest masochism. These other elements lead to specific forms of masochism and in some cases even decide whether masochistic elements will dominate one's life. Patients have tales to tell of pain at the hands of the parents. Parental behavior that is interpreted as cruel, however, does not account for those who are free of symptoms although they have the same parents as those who are afflicted. Among the additional determining factors that encourage manifest masochism during adolescence, developmental variants in the cognitive organization of the mind stand out.

The shift from evocative to communicative symbols may be inadequate; and in the developmental march of symbols, the choice of objects for representation, which shifts away from fantasy objects toward the self briefly before it goes on to enlist peers in the roles of persecutors and lovers, may remain fixated on the self as object. Projection undergoes marked and many vicissitudes, providing a multitude of variants in the defenses used to express aggression (Sarnoff, 1972). And there are remarkable variations in the characteristic way of dealing with introjects in early adolescence. These changes in the cognitive style of defense organizations contribute to the characteristic appearance of masochism in adolescence.

PLACEMENT OF THE INTROJECT ABOUT THE MARGINS OF THE PSYCHOLOGICAL BOUNDARIES OF THE SELF

These cases present in direct and exaggerated form the dynamics by which youngsters deal with introjects during early adolescence. Adolescent masochism can be interpreted to be a manifestation of the placement of the persecutory introject in the person of a peer outside the self in the *location continuum* of persecutors developed in the child's psychic reality. What are the primary locations on this continuum? The introject can exist within the psychological boundaries of the self; it can exist in the interface between self and the object world; it can be assigned to feared fantasy objects; it can be interpreted into the actions of well-known peers. The variations in location of objects used as sadists in adolescent masochism are derived from these placements.

Within the psychological boundary of the self, introject placement takes four forms. In the first, the introject remains within the boundary of the self and takes the form of the demanding contents of the superego. These contents serve to find fault with the self and provoke guilt.

In the second, the introject also remains within the boundary of the self. Despised portions of the self, which are experienced intensely in adolescence, generate low self-esteem. They can be recognized to be a misunderstood remnant of the hostile parental introject of early childhood. The part of the self that cannot be separated from the introject becomes the object of rejection. The remainder of the self rejects the introject.

In the third, the hostile introject can be placed within the boundary of the self in the form of an angry, delusional, internal fantasy object. Such an object can be experienced as the source of insulting command hallucinations from within.

In the fourth, the introject can serve as one of the hostile fantasy elements in the person's latent fantasy life. (When the fantasy is lived out through placement in a person recruited from beyond the boundary of the self, the early childhood relationship that contributed to the content of the introject becomes the basis for adolescent masochistic experiences involving peers.)

At the psychological boundary of the self, the introject can be represented in any body product that can leave the body. There are many examples of the use of body products as animistically endowed beings or part-beings, which can in turn be used in persecutory fantasies, fantasies of vulnerability, and fantasies of the extension of power. Hair trimmings, nail trimmings, excreta, flatus, "the soul," semen, and menstrual blood have all been used as vehicles to carry the power and the vulnerabilities of the self as shaped by parental introjects.

Beyond the psychological boundary of the self, the characteristics of introjects are invested in heard external voices, peers, persecutors, and lovers. When externalized, the voice of the conscience can become the voice heard in dreams and delusions as well as the voice of conscience and the sense of guilt felt by some when a policeman comes into view. Peers, persecutors, and lovers, when invested with the attributes of the hostile introject and when related to in the context of a primordial paradigmatic painful relationship to the person introjected, become the protagonists in the life of the masochistic character.

MASOCHISTIC DERIVATIVES IN LATER ADOLESCENCE

Incipient Masochistic Character Traits: Psychotherapeutic Considerations

The selection of cases for psychoanalytically oriented psychotherapy in adolescence requires the existence of an internalized conflict, coupled with a capacity for object relations. Thus, the best candidates for such treatment are those who involve some real objects in the masochistic experiences they report. Children with adolescent shyness have a better prognosis than have prepubescent schizophrenic children, who maintain their introjects within or on the borders of the self. Where outside figures are recruited to play out the masochistic fantasy, transference neuroses can be expected to develop and therapeutic gain expected. To the extent that outside figures are involved, the patient can be said to have incipient masochistic character traits. Strategies must be devised to involve objects in the world in activities of the patient and in the patient's associations. It is necessary to encourage free associations that pursue insight to replace the misuse of free association through a self-oriented constant retelling of ominously similar masochistic adventures.

ADOLESCENT MISUSES OF FREE ASSOCIATION

Psychoanalysis and psychoanalytic psychotherapy will progress if free association can take place. A problem arises if the patient uses free association (an opportunity for unlimited communication with the analyst) to serve purposes other than the search for insight. Often the patient seeks to relieve tension by communication aimed at the evocation and immediate mastery of a recent traumatic situation. Typical of this is a recounting of an accident or a recent fight. At times, the past is searched and recalled memories are used to justify rather than modify current behavior. Typical of this is the patient who says "I have a right to be mean. Look how mean people were to me." Such patients are primarily interested in drawing sympathy from the analyst or creating a sad mood through memories that will serve as a comforting evocation of a lost, albeit painful, relationship. The analyst may be turned into a witness to pain bravely borne rather than the person engaged to help the patient to understand and resolve the problem of masochism. The use of evocative symbols in free association is a manifestation of a predisposition to repetition compulsion. Such behavior is a "more grown up" form of masochistic bragadoccio. Its clinical manifestation is the domination of session after session with repeated tales of discomfort and apparent complaints. All this is achieved at the expense of the pursuit of insight and long-range therapeutic gains. Therapeutic intervention requires a strategy that interprets this characterological "acting in" of repetition-compulsion based behavior.

CONCLUSIONS

Not all children exposed to cruelty while young or occupied with sadistic fantasies in early childhood are at risk for masochism during adolescence. There are a multitude of factors that determine this outcome. Foremost among these are evidence of pathological placement and psychic representation of introjects; failures in progression along the developmental march of symbols; repetition compulsion; and narcissistic hypercathexis of the sensation of reality at the expense of reality testing. Psychotherapeutic interventions must be aimed at the correction of these factors. The presence of these influences makes a person vulnerable to penetrations of the anal-sadistic phase memories that intrude upon and shape the relationships of late adolescent and adult life.

Masochistic fantasies themselves can be transmuted during the transition from latency to adolescence. These transmutations occur as the result of cognitive reorganizations that distort the memories of childhood. Such alterations of latent fantasy content affect the life experiences that are shaped in part or whole by fantasy.

The styles of recall of the memory of the actual infantile experiences and the infantile fantasies of the child are modified with the transition to adolescence. For instance, the various placements of the introject provide a variety of possible protagonists and plots for remembering the sadomasochistic past through the realities and experiences of the present. If there is a cognitive impairment of the ability to differentiate self from introject or a limitation of the ability to assign the introject to a placement in the world beyond the self, the recall of the infantile experiences will take place with more emphasis on delusion and less on the creatures of the object world.

In latency, the capacity to reshape fantasy in the service of the discharge of drives was limited to the use of symbols as the organ for discharge. Within this limited mental activity, the child could create symbols to be used to represent the primary objects of fantasies. A remnant of the cathexis of symbols as the organ for the discharge of drives persists into adolescence. The sweep of objects available to be used as symbols is markedly enhanced. In those who can achieve normal object cathexes and can place introjects beyond the boundaries of self, the symbolizing function turns more toward the world. It increases the available representations that can be used as symbols. Peers, loved ones, and reality objects such as houses, jewels, and money, which can be controlled and manipulated into scenarios, are enlisted in the service of the need of the fantasizing function of the ego to hide and distort original memories. To the extent that these elements are compliant, the fantasies in which they participate hew closely to their original sources. Less flexible symbols cause shifts from passivity to activity or from object to subject for the protagonist. Thus, a fantasy of being bullied may be lived out as a fantasy of bullying if the available objects are weak.

Weighing heavily in the balance of those elements which produce vulnerability is the inability to turn attention cathexes from memory and fantasy, diminishing the child's ability to invest reality with the right to call the tune. These sources of vulnerability to masochism in adolescence must be pursued, understood, and analysed if progress is to be made in psychotherapy.

REFERENCES

Bender, L. (1948), Childhood schizophrenia. *J. Acad. Orthopsychiat.*, 70:40–56.

Blanchard, P. (1953), Masturbation fantasies of children and adolescents. *Bull. Phila. Assn. Psychoanal.*, 3:25–38.

Katan, A. (1951), The role of "displacement" in agoraphobia. *Internat. J. Psycho-Anal.*, 32:41–50.

Mahler, M., & Gosliner, B. J. (1955), On symbiotic child psychosis. *The Psychoanalytic Study of the Child*, 10:195–214. New York: International Universities Press.

Sarnoff, C. A. (1972), The vicissitudes of projection during the analysis of a girl in late latency-early adolescence. *Internat. J. Psycho-Anal.* IV.

—— (1975), Narcissism, adolescent masturbation fantasies, and the search for reality. In: *Masturbation from Infancy to Senescence*, ed. L. Marcus & J. Francis. New York: International Universities Press.

—— (1976), *Latency* New York: Aronson.

—— (1987a), *Psychotherapeutic Strategies—Latency*. Northvale, NJ: Aronson.

—— (1987b), *Psychotherapeutic Strategies—Early Adolescence*. Northvale, NJ: Aronson.

Werner, H., & Levin, S. (1967), Masturbation fantasies—their changes with growth and development. *The Psychoanalytic Study of the Child*, 22:315–328. New York: International Universities Press.

Wu Cheng'en (1575), *Journey to the West*. Beijing: Foreign Languages Press, 1982.

Author Index

Subject Index

A

Acceptance, overdependency on, 63–64
Acting out, 31
Active role, 96
Adaptation
  defense and, 44
  of infant, 127–28
Adolescent masochism, 205–24
  causative factors in, 219–20
  character formation and, 36
  derivatives, 209–11, 221
  introjects and, 213–15
  masochistic perversion, 211–13
  phenomenology of, 215–17
  prepubescent schizophrenia and, 213–20
  shyness, 213–17
Affect, transformation of, 197, 198
Aggression, 18
  channeling or modulation of, 194
  development of, 191–94
    clinical syndromes illustrating disturbances in, 196
  difficulties in the expression of, 63, 64
  distribution of, 125–26
  environmental stimuli of, 196–200
  erotic masochism, 73–74
  libidinal drive and, 191
  maternal conflicts and, 195
  oral patterning of, 192
  preoedipal, 180–81
  pseudo-, 122–23

reversal of, 197
sadistic, 9–10
self-, 11
sexualization of hostile, 45
theoretical dilemma of, 190–91
See also Self-destructiveness
Aggressivization of object relations, 47
Aggressor
  identification with, 190–91
  seduction of, 12–13, 180–81, 190
Ambitions, childhood, 143
Anal character, 29–31
Anal period, 194
  narcissistic mortification and, 192
Anal sadistic drive organizations, intensification of, 208–9
"Analysis Terminable and Interminable" (Freud), 120
Analyst
  envy of, 76
  gender of, 187–88
  negative therapeutic reaction of, 111
Anxiety
  castration, 53–54, 70, 90
  depressive, 167
Asphyxia, autoerotic, 97
Association, adolescent misuses of free, 222
Autism, 161–63
  infantile, 202
Autoerotic asphyxia, 97
Autonomy
  secondary, 34
  through self-mutilation, 124, 125